IMAGES of Rail

BOSTON & MAINE TRAINS AND SERVICES

IMAGES
of Rail

BOSTON & MAINE TRAINS AND SERVICES

Bruce D. Heald, Ph.D.

ARCADIA
PUBLISHING

ISBN 978-0-7385-3875-4

Published by Arcadia Publishing
Charleston, South Carolina

Printed in the United States of America

Library of Congress Catalog Card Number: 2005926752

For all general information contact Arcadia Publishing at:
Telephone 843-853-2070
Fax 843-853-0044
E-mail sales@arcadiapublishing.com
For customer service and orders:
Toll-Free 1-888-313-2665

Visit us on the Internet at www.arcadiapublishing.com

Contents

ACKNOWLEDGMENTS

I would like to thank the following people and organizations for their assistance: Ted Anderson, Jack Armstrong, Alfred S. Arnold, Laurence Beake, Bert Boice, the Boston & Maine Railroad Historical Society, Henry Bowan, Charles A. Brown, Joseph Bush Sr., Carl Byron, Norton D. Clark, H. Bentley Crouch, Chuck Crouse, Dawn Dever, Peter Eddy, Arthur J. Egan, Ed Felten, Tim Gilbert, Ralph Hansen. Philip R. Hastings, Roger Hinman, Donald F. Hodge, David Johnson, Alan C. LaRue Jr., Ron LeBlond, E. J. Livermore, E. B. Luce collection, the Meredith Historical Society, Brent S. Michiels, Kenneth Milender, Russell Munroe, William Monypeny, Jim Nigzus, Rick Nowell, Thomas Pearson, Joseph N. Shaw, Lester H. Stephenson, Stanley Y. Whitney, and Lawrence Williams.

Introduction

The independent history of the Boston and Maine Railroad (B&M) stretches from 1833, when the Erie Canal was completed but eight years, to 1983, when the digital revolution was at hand. The B&M's influence across northern New England as its largest corporate entity, employer, and in many cases provider of the community's sole contact with the outside world is incomprehensible to the New England public of today.

The Boston and Maine Railroad was a potent financial, political, and engineering force between the mid-19th and mid-20th centuries. However, most New Englanders' dealings with the B&M revolved around the local depot. There, they bought their tickets and boarded the cars for Boston, New York, Chicago, Montreal, or other innumerable locations. At or nearby the depot were the freight and express offices, where packages of all types were sent and received. Less-than-carload (LCL) freight was also handled at the depot, where one also sent or received Western Union telegrams. The depot was the center of life in most New England communities for over a century.

Carloads of all kinds of material were set off at the local yard for distribution by the switcher to industries with individual sidings; the reverse was done with outbound goods. Each yard also contained a team track. The box, flat, or gondola car containing a company's shipment was placed there so the crew could unload it into its horse-drawn wagon—hence the "team" reference. By the mid-1920s, the wagon had been replaced with a truck, but the expression lingered on.

All those decades of service allowed for many types of cars, from the Civil War era's 25-foot wooden flatcar and the *c.* 1900 wooden, kerosene-lamp-equipped caboose, to the 1960s 89-foot auto rack car. Likewise for the rail diesel car (RDC); all were necessary members of the B&M's car fleet required to serve Northern New England's industry and people.

From the earliest years, all railroad cars were built entirely of wood. Even major components of truck frames—the structure under each end of a car holding a set of two or possibly three axles—were built of hardwoods such as oak or chestnut and held together by iron fittings. The use of iron and steel was limited because of their relatively high cost in the mid- and late 19th century.

Longer and heavier cars, by the early 1900s, brought the introduction of all-steel trucks and freight cars built on steel underframes. Horrific accidents worsened by the crushing, telescoping, and burning of wooden passenger cars led to the requirement that all wooden cars be rebuilt with steel underframes, and brought the introduction of all-steel cars about 1905.

Electric trolley lines began springing up in New England cities and towns in the 1890s and expanded quickly in the first decade of the 20th century. The electric cars provided faster, cleaner, and more frequent service than steam-powered locals, so the B&M responded by leasing or purchasing several of the larger operations, such as those in Manchester and Portsmouth, New Hampshire.

By World War I, the 15- or 20-ton, 40- or 50-foot wooden passenger car had changed into a 160,000-pound, 80- or 85-foot steel vehicle. Numerous versions were available, including baggage, Railway Post Office (RPO), dining, lounge, and observation to name a few. Common combinations of these cars included baggage and coach, baggage and RPO, coach or diner and lounge, and lounge or sleeper-lounge and observation.

In the early 1920s, the B&M was desperate to replace the foundering local service of a steam locomotive and several cars. The combination of a steel coach or coach-baggage car—not dissimilar to a steel trolley car, but with a gasoline engine for self-propulsion, rather than overhead wire—was a huge step forward. Mechanical transmissions did not work, but connecting the engine to an electric generator feeding power to motors located in the trucks did. By the late 1920s, many B&M branch passenger services had been supplied by the sputtering cars, sometimes hauling a trailer or boxcar behind.

Beginning in the mid-1930s, passenger car construction changed dramatically, with the introduction of cars fabricated from aluminum, lightweight, high-tensile-strength steel, or stainless steel. B&M's first example, delivered in February 1935, was the stainless-steel diesel-electric-powered three-car articulated streamliner *Flying Yankee*. The confluence of diesel-electric power, streamlining, and art deco design made travel by train the "in" thing for the decades of the 1930s and 1940s.

The post–World War II Boston and Maine presented a kaleidoscope of passenger car contrasts. Hundreds of steel-framed wooden passenger cars remained in local commuter service, many built in the last years of the 19th century. All-steel cars handled most of the local and intercity services, while limited stainless-steel streamliner service was available, mostly between Boston and Portland. The incongruity of new streamlined cars and diesel-electric locomotives, separated by the 50-plus-year-old decrepit steel-framed wooden baggage or baggage-express cars, was jarring to the artistic eye, to say the least, and the aged gas-electric cars only added to the eclectic mix. By 1960, the combination of the auto and jetliner swept all but the stainless-steel Budd RDC cars from North Station. Budd *Highliners* provided B&M commuter service to Boston's north and northwest suburbs until the Massachusetts Bay Transportation Authority absorbed the operation in 1986.

Freight car development roughly paralleled that of the passenger car. All-wood cars of the post–Civil War era reached 30 to 40 feet in the combination wood-and-steel-framed boxcars of the 1920s, which had expanded to become the 50-foot all-steel cars by the mid–20th century. Similar expansions in size, weight, and carrying capacity occurred in hopper, tank, and gondola cars as well. By the 1970s, car capacities were generally between 70 and 100 tons, with a total maximum weight of 125 tons. The caboose likewise metamorphosed from all wood, to wood on steel frame, to all-steel construction between 1900 and the post–World War II era.

As customer need and technological development increased across northern New England, the B&M responded with newer, larger, heavier, and in the passenger fleet, safer cars. Conversely, this hastened the branches' demise and concentrated traffic on the main lines.

It is time to join Dr. Heald on a journey back through time and space via the images on the following pages. From the High Iron to the branch lines, and from the Iron Men and wooden cars to the 125-ton behemoths of the 1980s, these photographs create for us a fleeting image of the Boston and Maine of yesterday.

All aboard! The cars await.

—Carl R. Byron

One

Passenger, Post Office, and Milk Trains

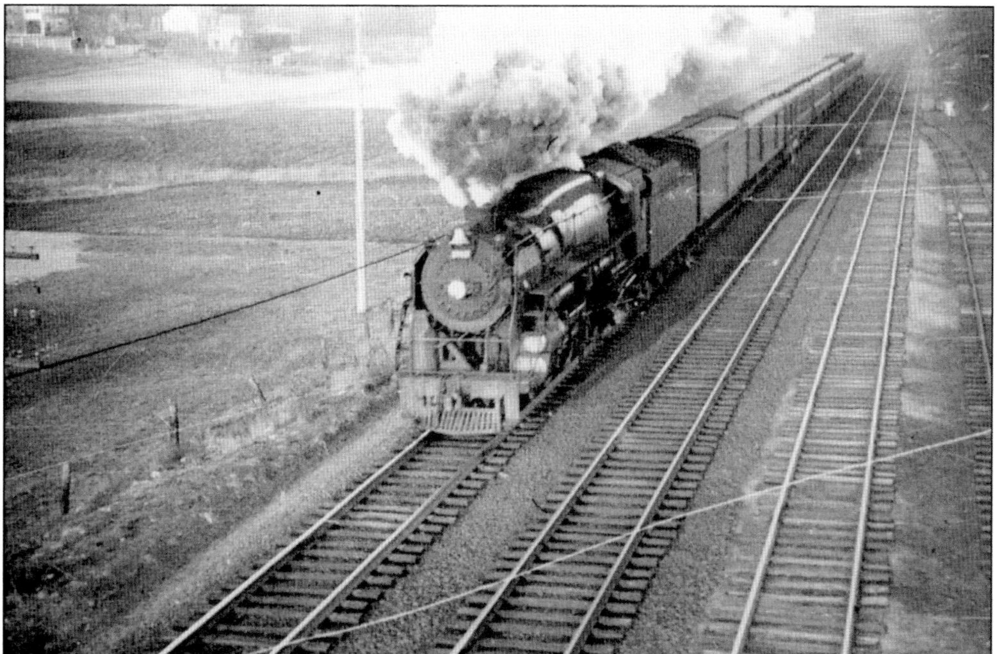

The B&M *Minute Man* is seen in Waltham, Massachusetts, in the 1940s. This was a common sight, as daily the train connected the city of Troy, New York, with Boston.

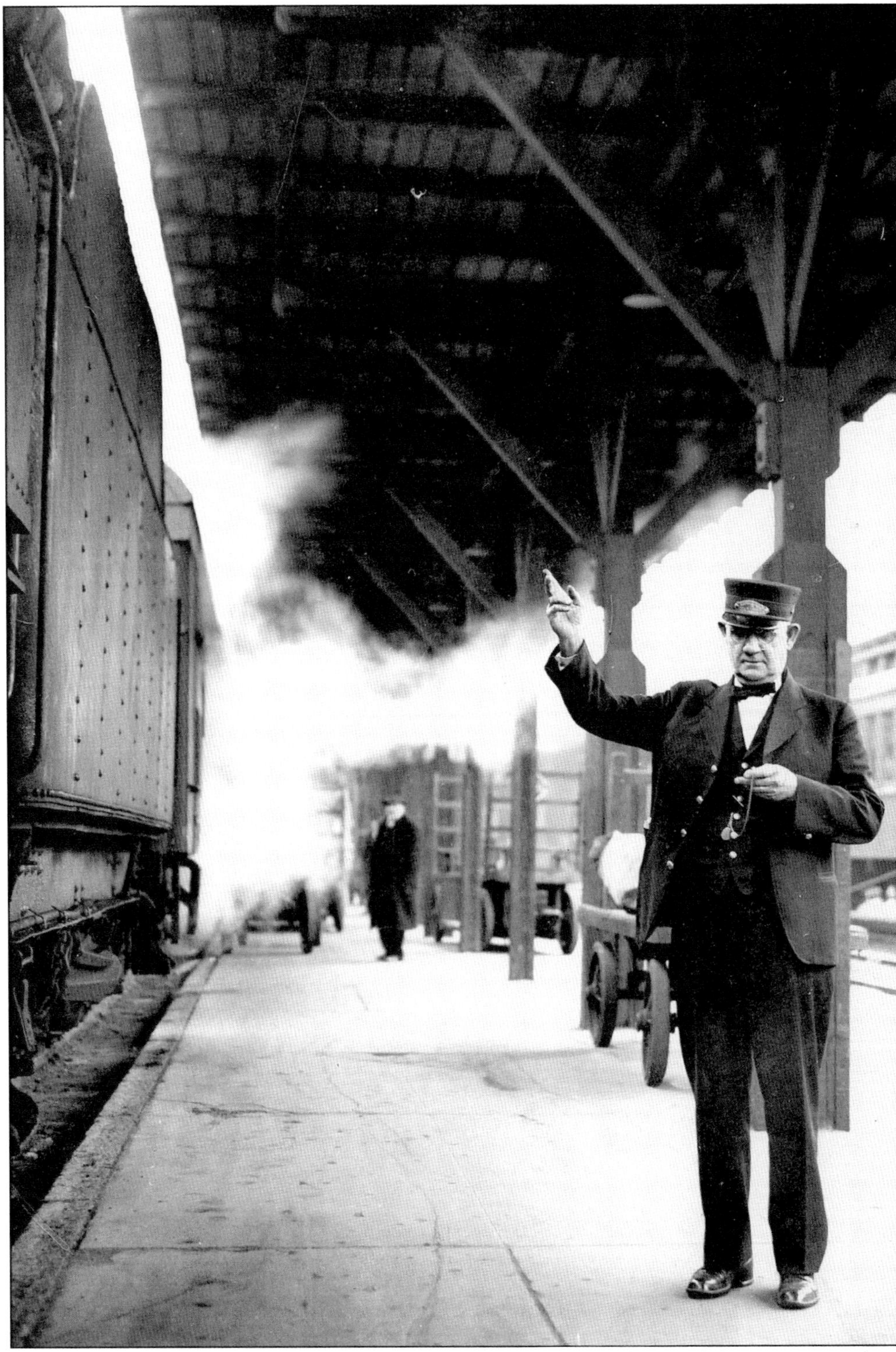

"All aboard!" is the announcement made by George Strout, conductor of the B&M's Portland Division, at North Station in the 1940s.

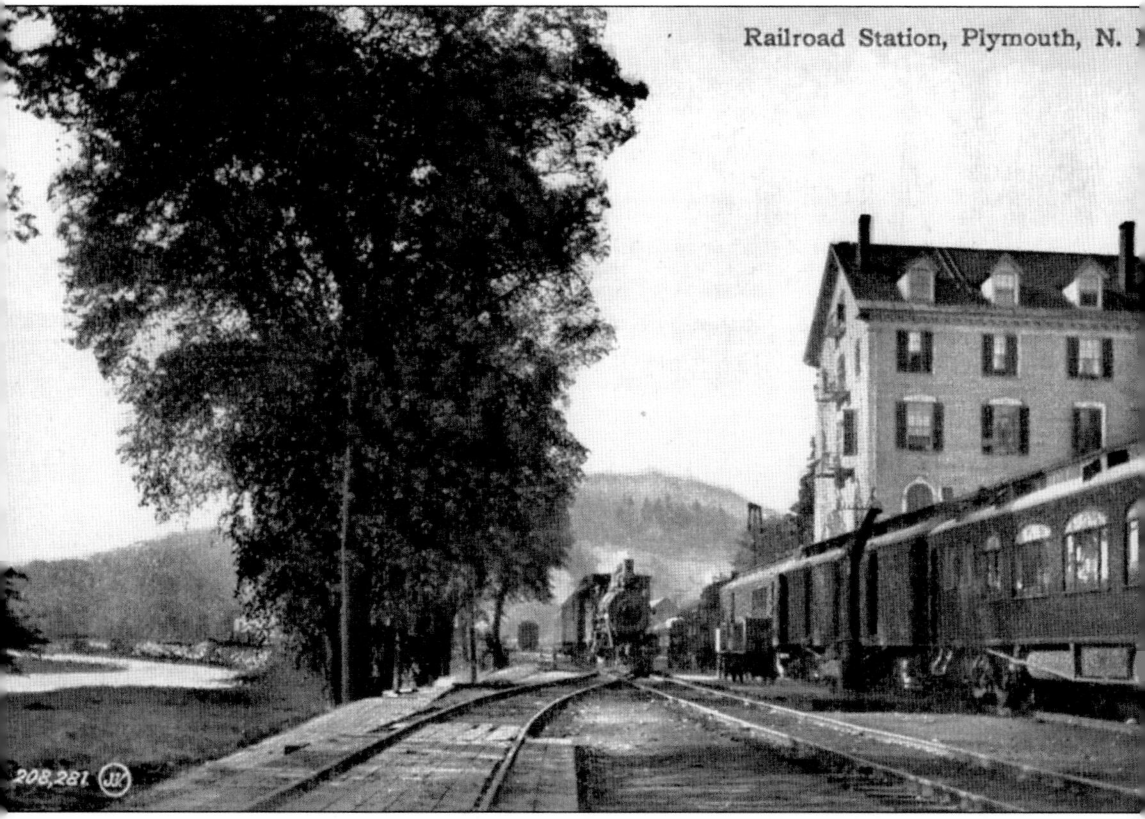

The Pemigewasset House and the Boston and Maine Railroad station in Plymouth, New Hampshire, are shown in the 1900s. Beginning in the late 1800s, the railroads made Plymouth a major tourist stop. There are numerous gateways to the White Mountains, but none more attractive than the "Winding Water among the Mountain Pines," the interpretation of the Native American name for the Pemigewasset Valley. In 1850, the Boston, Concord, and Montreal Railroad (BC&M) completed the road to Plymouth from Concord. In 1859, the BC&M leased the White Mountain Railroad, thus continuing the road from Plymouth to Littleton, and in 1872, the track from Wing Road toward the base of Mount Washington was begun. Tourist travel was boosted when Sylvester Marsh received a charter to build a steam railroad to the top of the mountain from a point near Fabyan's. The Railway to the Moon opened in 1869.

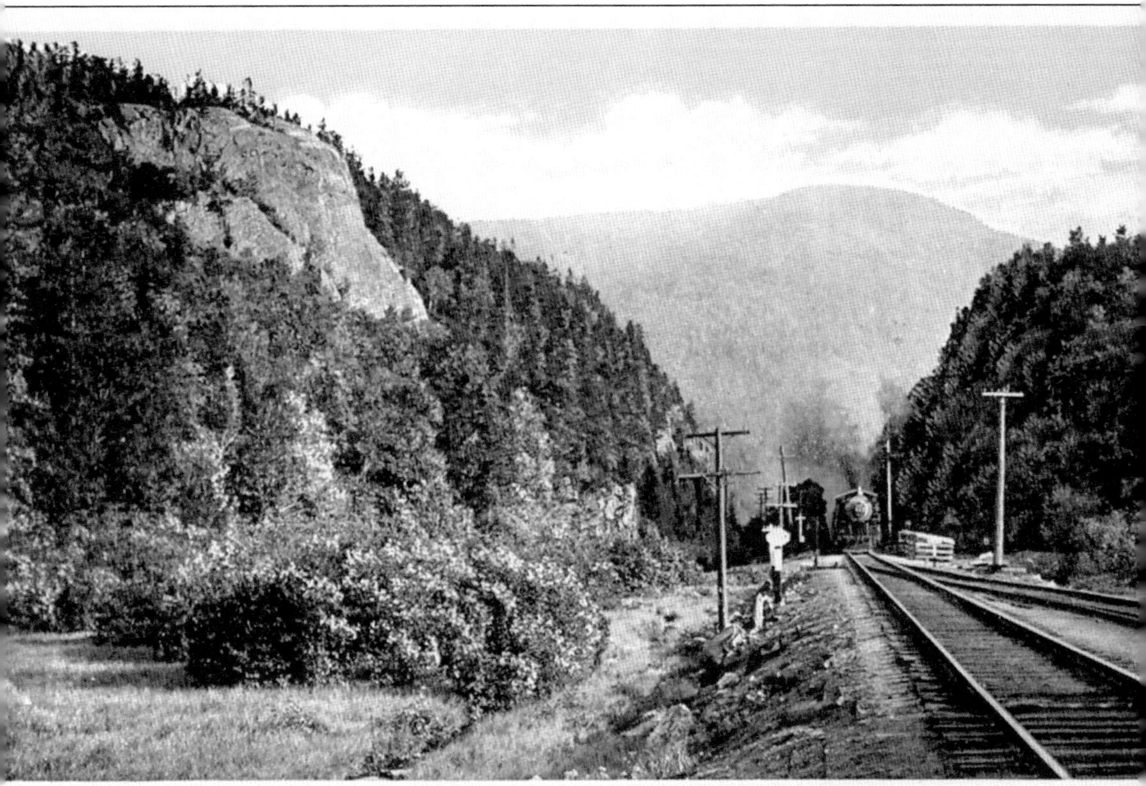

ELEPHANT'S HEAD AND GATE TO CRAWFORD NOTCH

The gateway to Crawford Notch appears in the 1880s. When Capt. Eleazer Rosebrook and his son-in-law built the first inns to accommodate travelers using the new turnpike through the White Mountains Notch (Crawford Notch) in the early 19th century, they could scarcely have envisioned the trend they were establishing. The first railroad to serve this growing vacation area was the White Mountains Railroad, which reached Littleton, New Hampshire, in 1853.

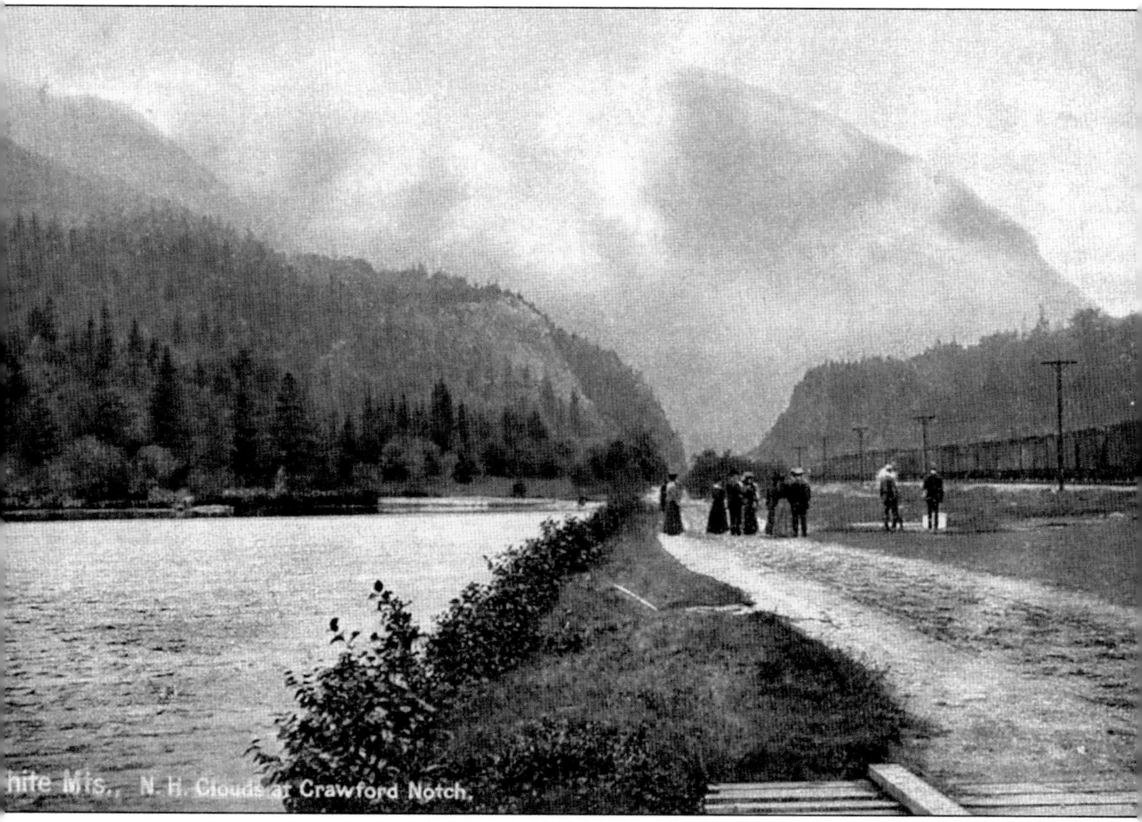

Guests from the city arrive at Crawford Notch via the Boston and Maine during the late 1800s. This area of the White Mountains and the grand hotels became popular for wealthy travelers during the summer months. After the Civil War, the railroads began to cater to the needs of a growing tourist trade. In order to attract this trade to New Hampshire, the railroads invested in hotels, particularly on the Seacoast and in the White Mountains.

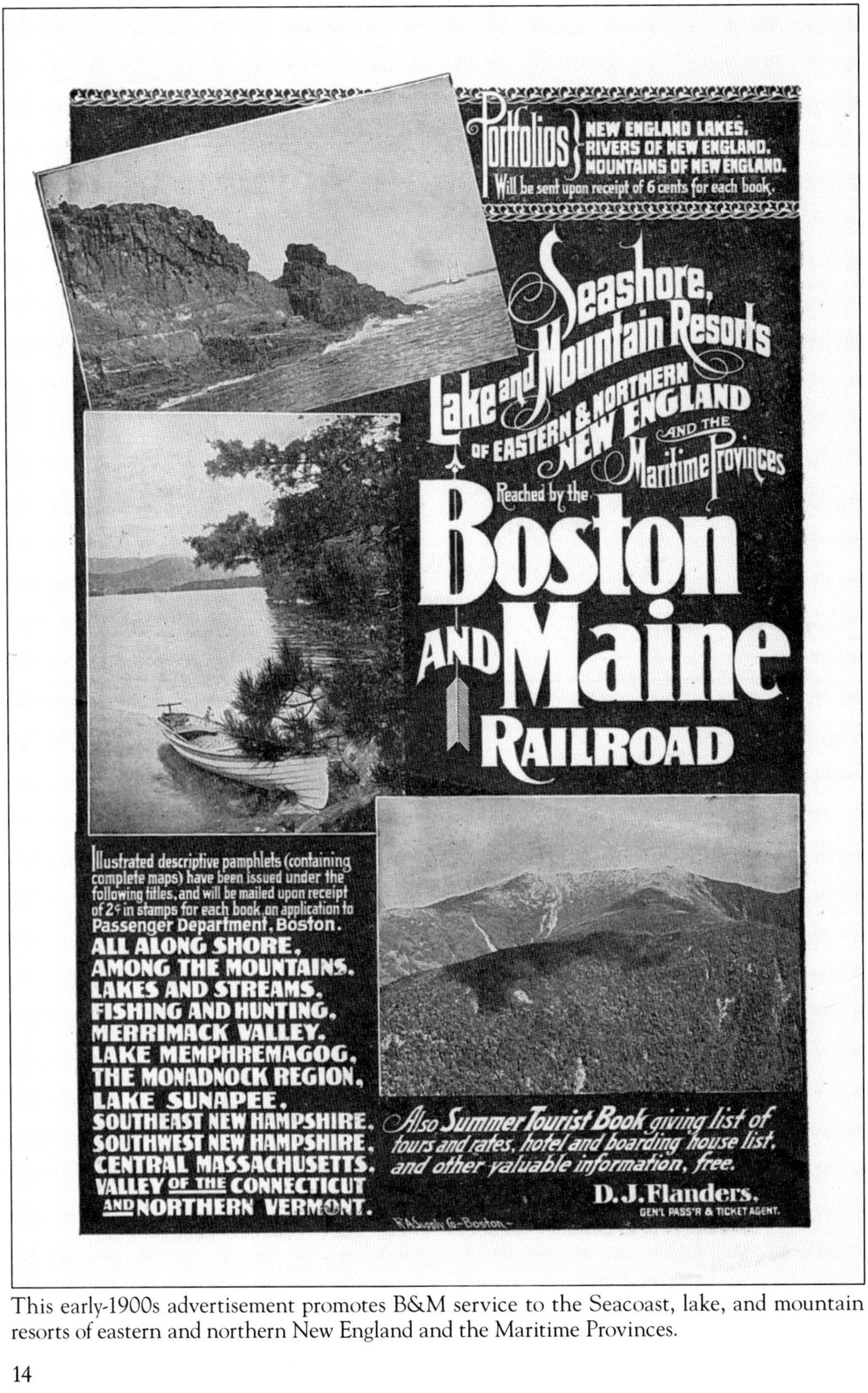

This early-1900s advertisement promotes B&M service to the Seacoast, lake, and mountain resorts of eastern and northern New England and the Maritime Provinces.

The Maine Central Railroad (MEC), shown in this early-1900s advertisement, later came under the control of the B&M.

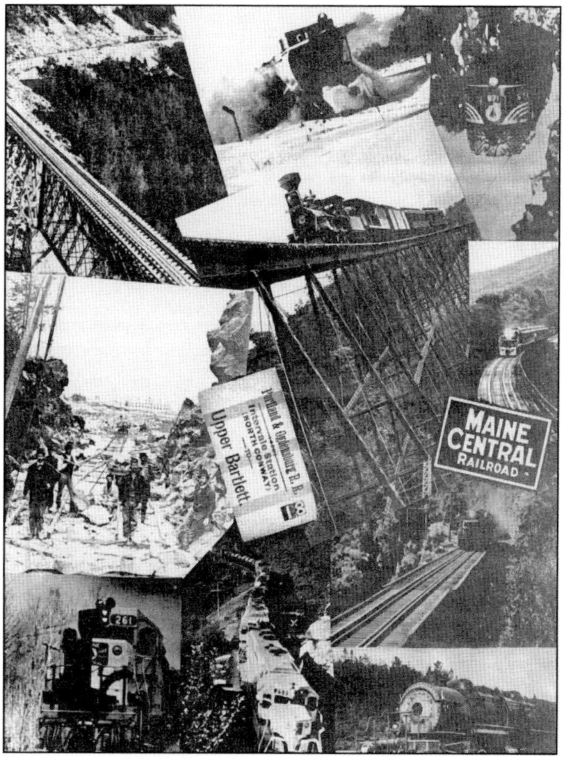

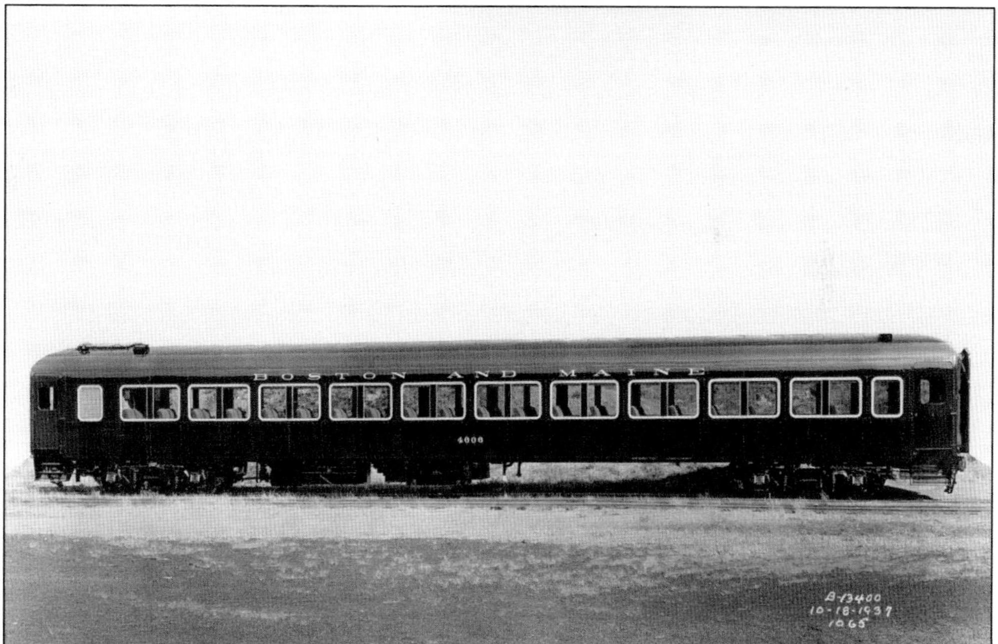

The B&M *American Flyer*, coach No. 4606, is new at the Pullman Company's Worcester, Massachusetts, plant on October 18, 1937. These coaches were to be found on all the B&M's tracks. For example, the morning train from Boston to North Conway, New Hampshire, regularly included one of these cars.

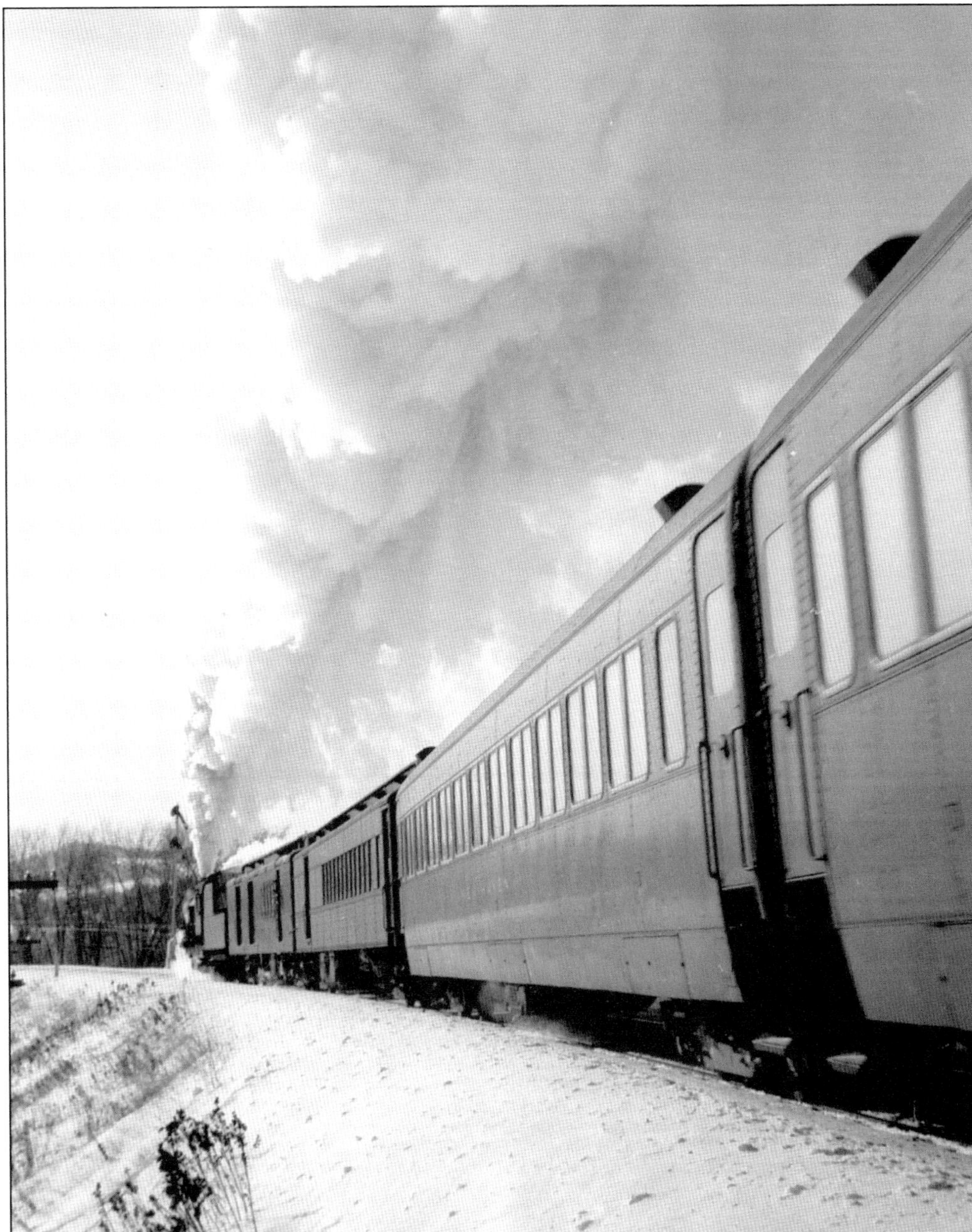

B&M passenger train No. 72, seen in Bradford, Vermont, in 1942, was known as the *Day White Mountains Express*. The locomotive was type 4-6-2. The B&M operated its first Sunday winter sports train on January 11, 1931, to Warner, New Hampshire, with 196 passengers.

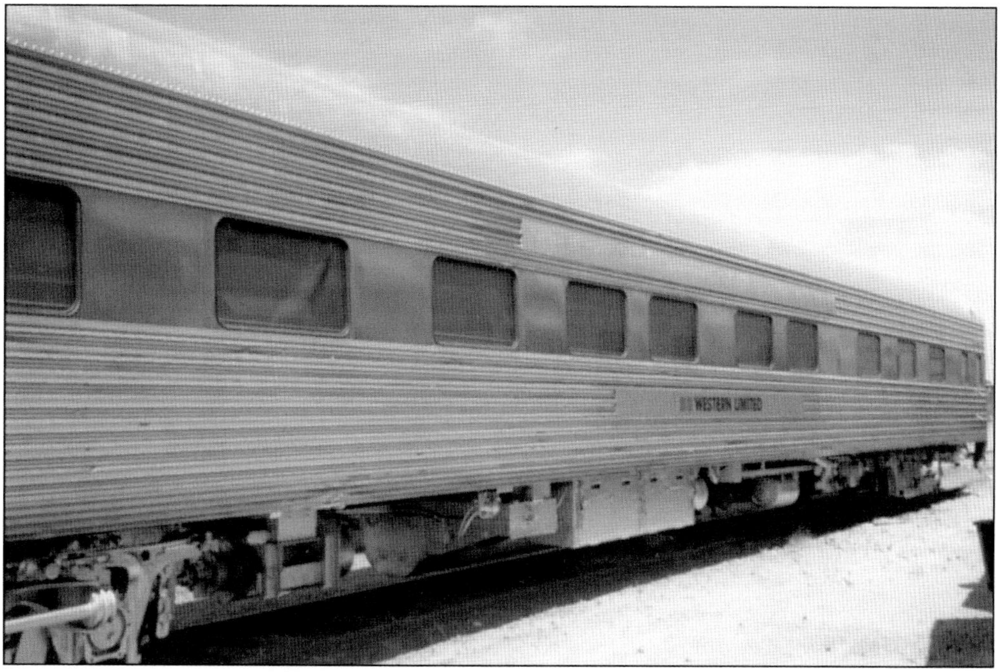

The B&M sleeping car *Salisbury Beach* was purchased and restored by Thomas C. Pearson. It is seen here, specifically painted and lettered for filming of the MGM movie *Species* in La Mirada, California, on August 17, 1994.

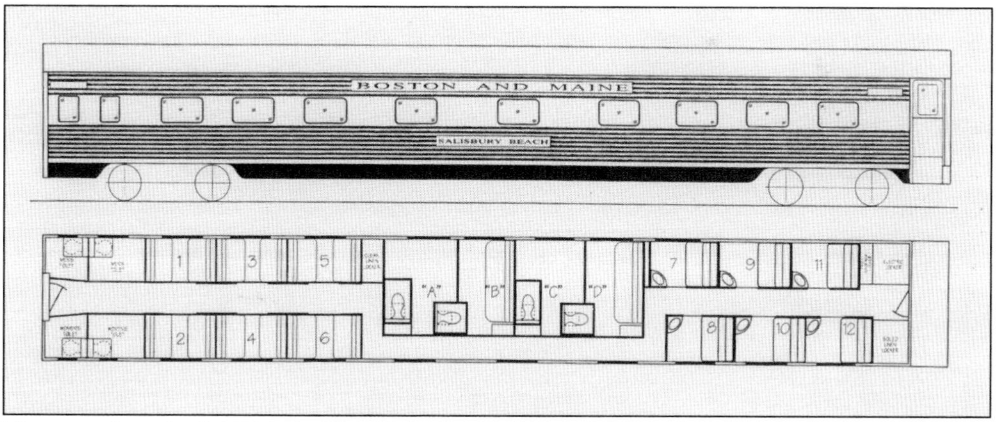

This is a plan of a B&M streamlined sleeping car. Prior to entering service in December 1954, the railroad operated a special exhibit train that toured the terminals in the Portland and New Hampshire Divisions. This drawing (not to scale) illustrates the six-section, four-bedroom, six-roomette arrangement found in the car. The interior configuration utilized advanced designs developed by Pullman-Standard for the roomettes and bedrooms. Roomettes featured cutaway beds and permanent sinks. Sections were of the classic design with no fundamental changes.

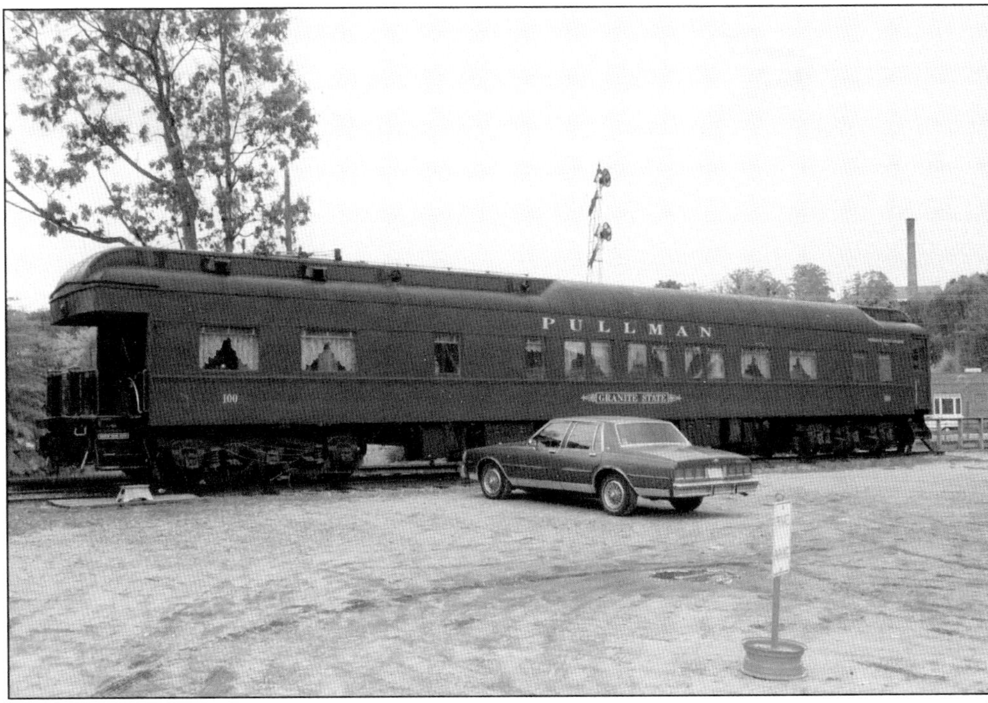

An executive's Pullman is parked at the headquarters of the State of New Hampshire Railroad. The car, just recently restored, is absolutely immaculate, not weathered at all. Note the working semaphores behind the car.

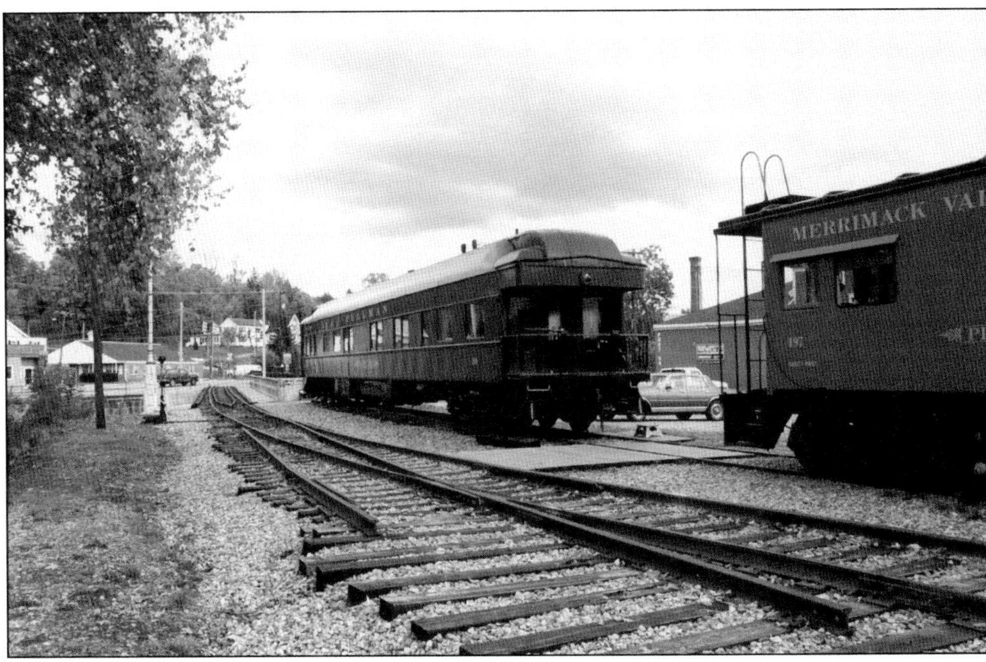

Shown here is an end view of the executive's Pullman car. The main line of the State of New Hampshire Railroad rises off to the right, and the tracks for a siding are being constructed; the ties and ballast look new.

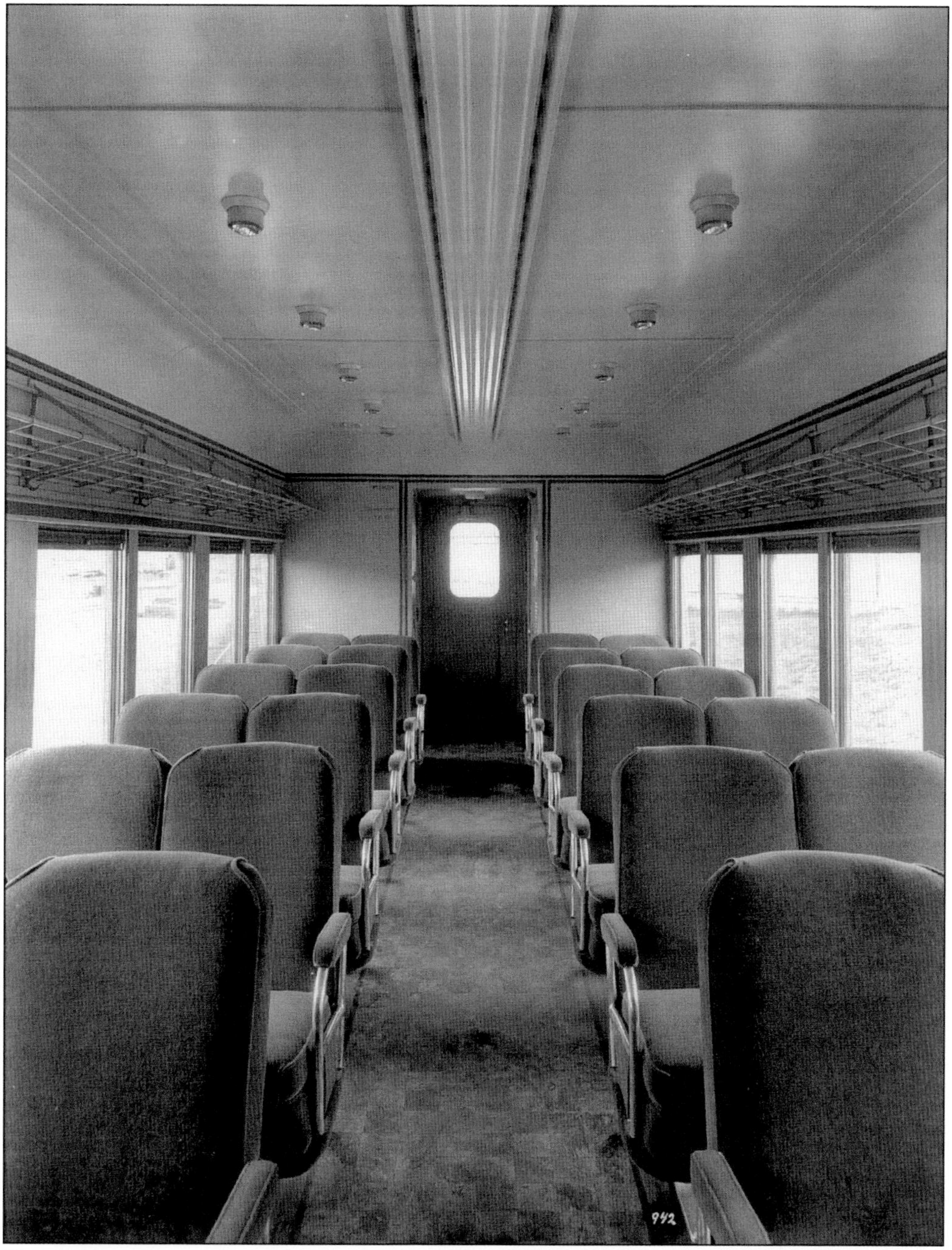

This lightweight coach car, known as the W942 Pullman/Worcester lot CO-12510, includes a typical interior for a Pullman commuter train: comfortable seats and clean windows.

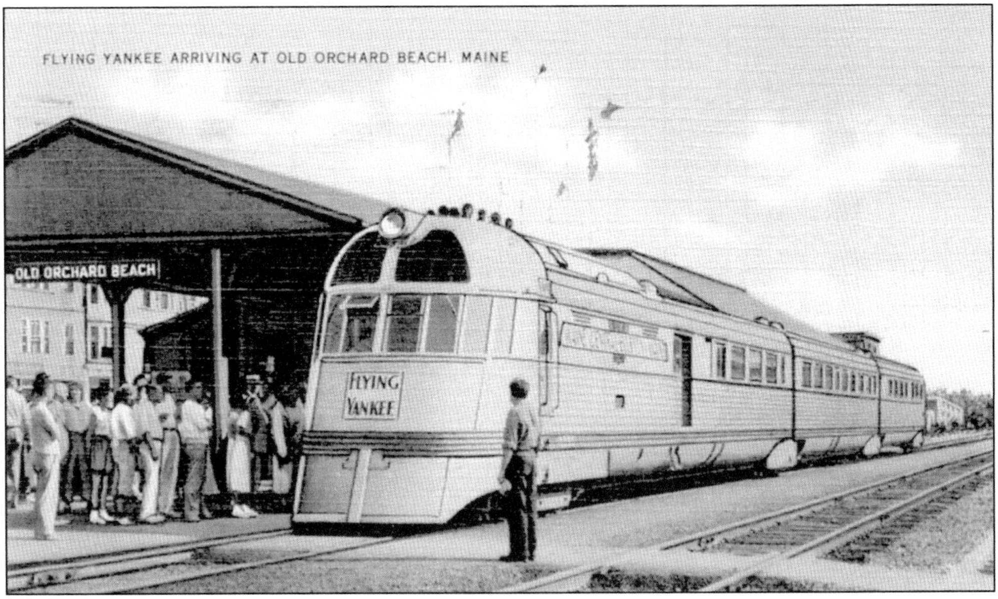

The B&M *Flying Yankee* arrives at Maine's Old Orchard Beach station in August 1935. The Boston and Maine began operations of the first lightweight streamlined diesel-powered train in the East. Starting on April 4, 1935, the *Flying Yankee*, called the *Mountaineer* in the 1940s, started a grueling Portland–Boston, Boston–Bangor, and Boston–Portland schedule of 733 miles per day. By 1937, B&M No. 6000 had its first overhaul at the Concord, New Hampshire, shops with 431,000 miles on the odometer. This duty continued nonstop until early 1941, when its seating capacity on the Boston–Portland–Bangor service became inadequate.

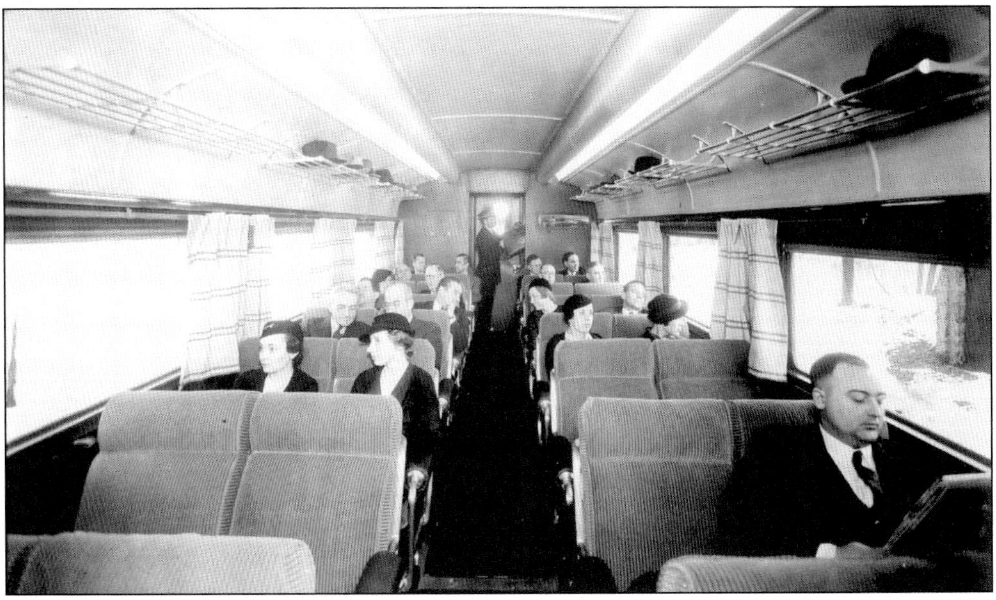

The passenger compartment in the new *Flying Yankee* is seen here. The finest moment in B&M passenger service—and its public relations department—was the February 9, 1935, arrival of the articulated streamliner. When the B&M ordered the *Flying Yankee* from Budd—with electrical gear subcontracted to General Electric—only the Burlington route had a diesel-powered, articulated streamliner on the rails.

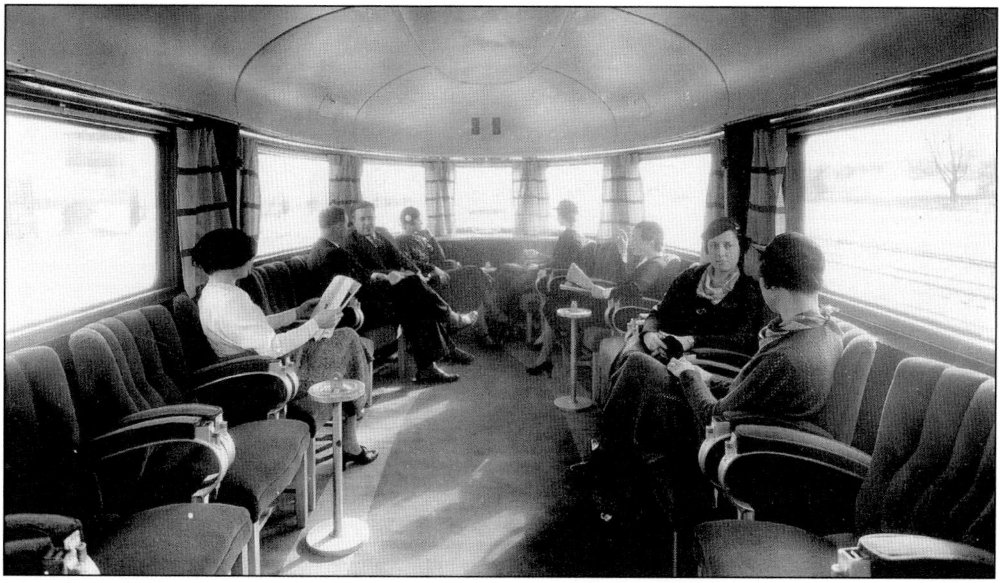

The *Flying Yankee* observation lounge car is shown around the 1940s. Industrial design came into play for the first time with early streamliners like the *Flying Yankee*. Noted designer Paul Cret, dean of the Philadelphia School of Architecture, designed the interiors for the train.

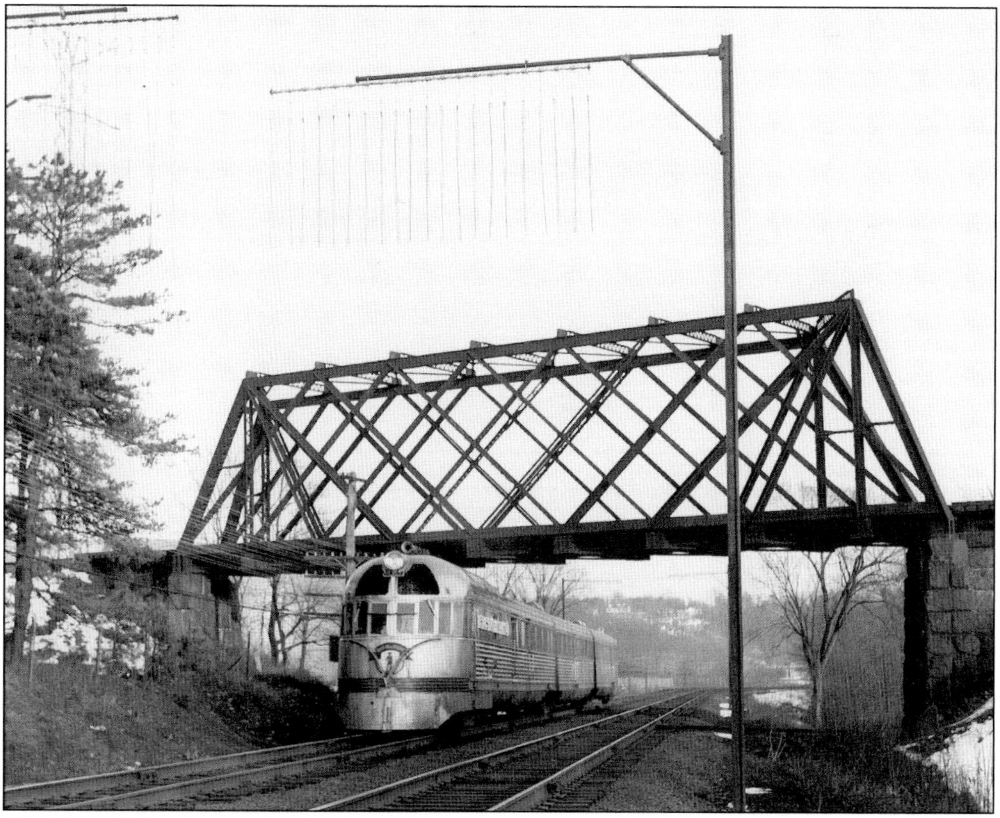

The No. 6000 passes under the Central Massachusetts trestle east of Kendal Green, with train No. 59, on April 11, 1956.

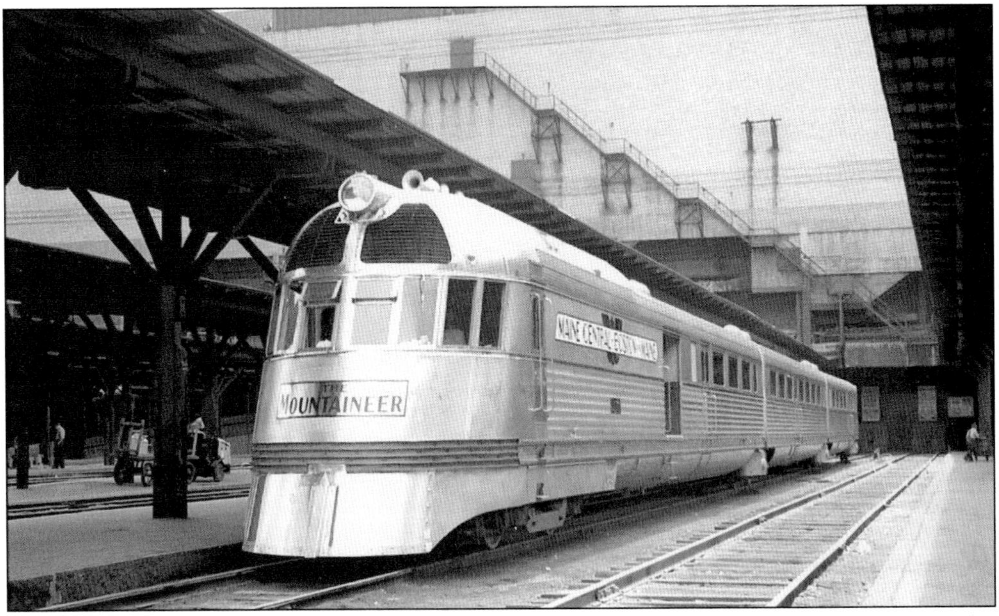

The B&M No. 6000 runs as the *Mountaineer* at North Station in Boston, likely during the summer of 1942. The train ran between Boston and Littleton, New Hampshire, via the B&M's Conway branch and the Maine Central's Mountain Division through Crawford Notch during most of World War II. A late-1944 reassignment placed the aging streamliner in Boston–Bellows Falls–White River Junction service as the *Cheshire*.

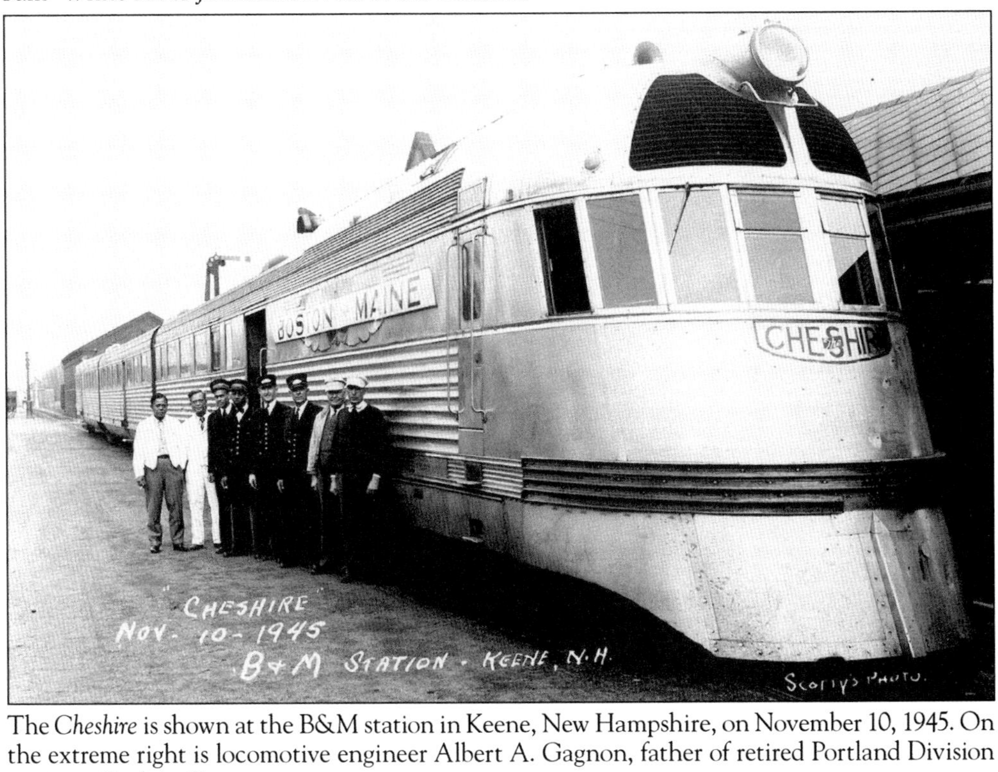

The *Cheshire* is shown at the B&M station in Keene, New Hampshire, on November 10, 1945. On the extreme right is locomotive engineer Albert A. Gagnon, father of retired Portland Division engineer Paul A. Gagnon.

The *Cheshire* leaves the station on the diamond at Bellows Falls in the 1940s.

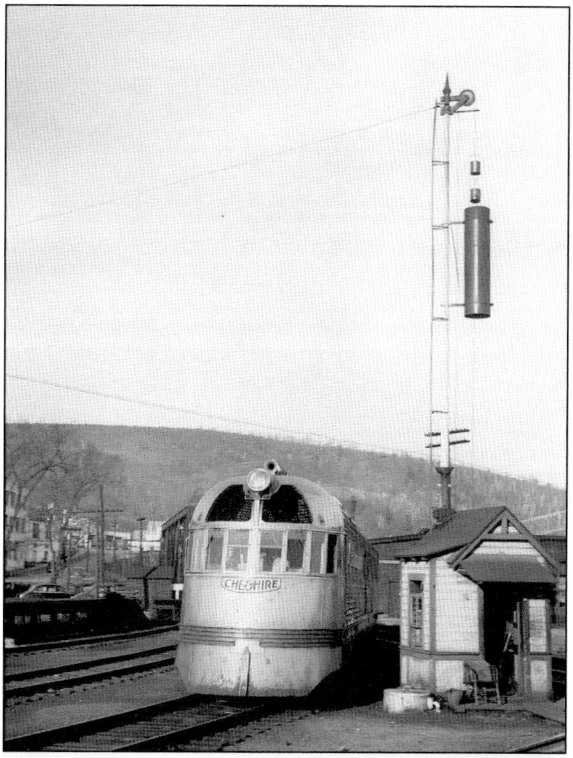

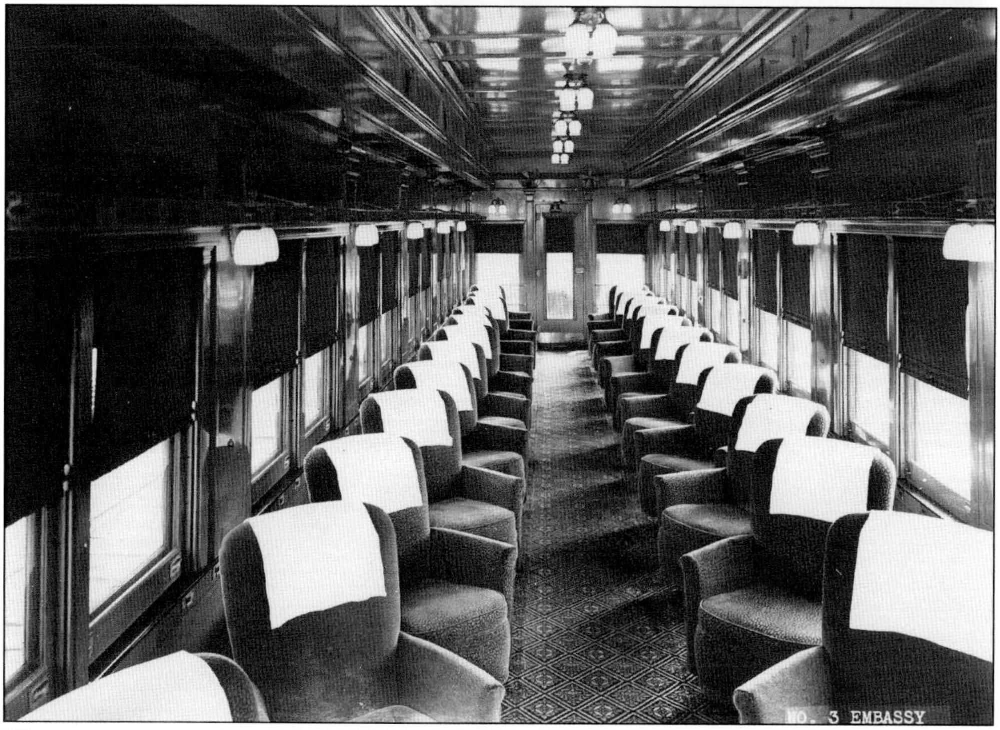

This is an interior view of the B&M *Ambassador*, Embassy parlor car No. 3, around the 1940s. Note the elegance of the car as the white head linen is place on each seat.

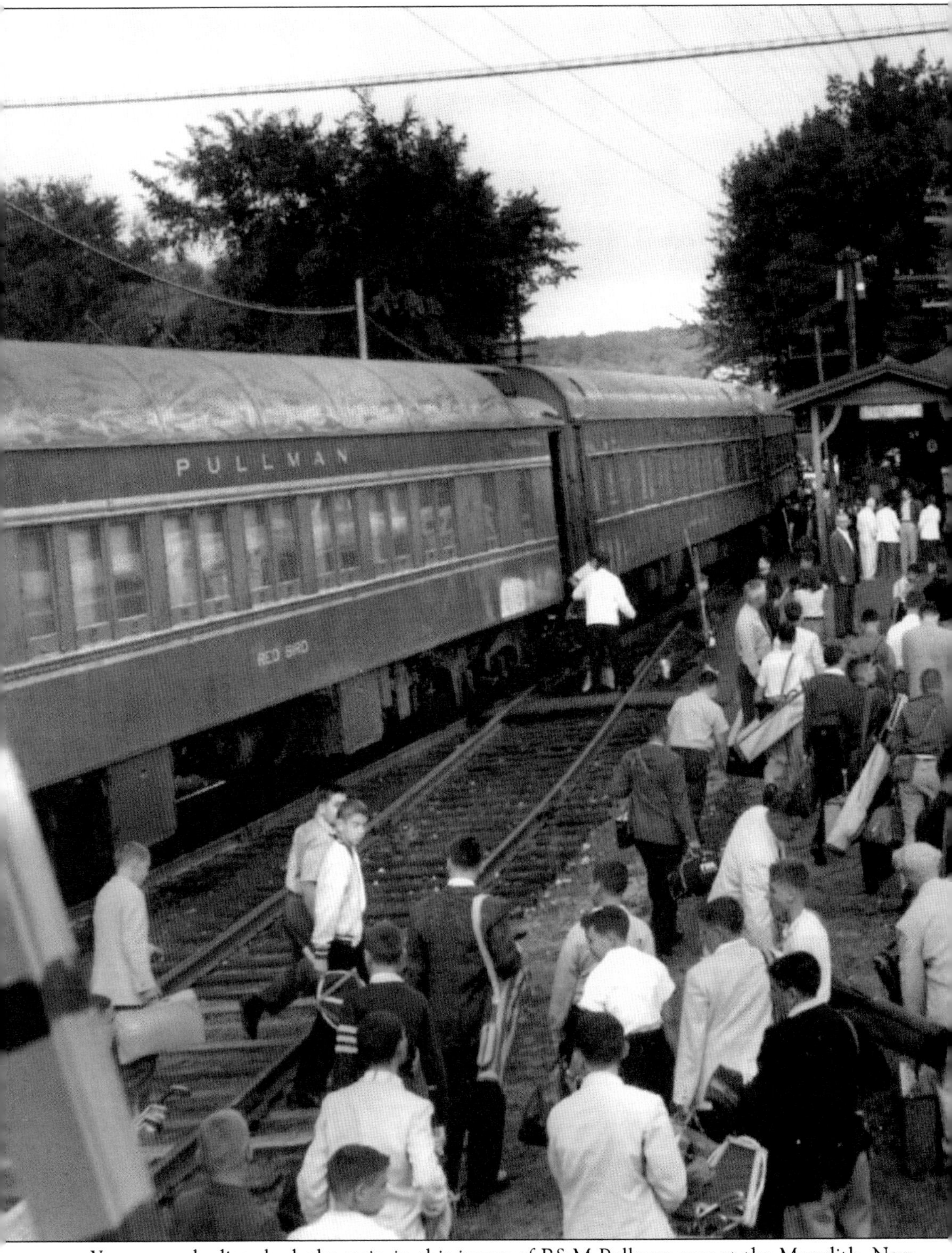

Young people disembark the train in this image of B&M Pullman cars at the Meredith, New Hampshire, station in the 1950s. A fleet of Sprague's buses waits to take them to summer camps

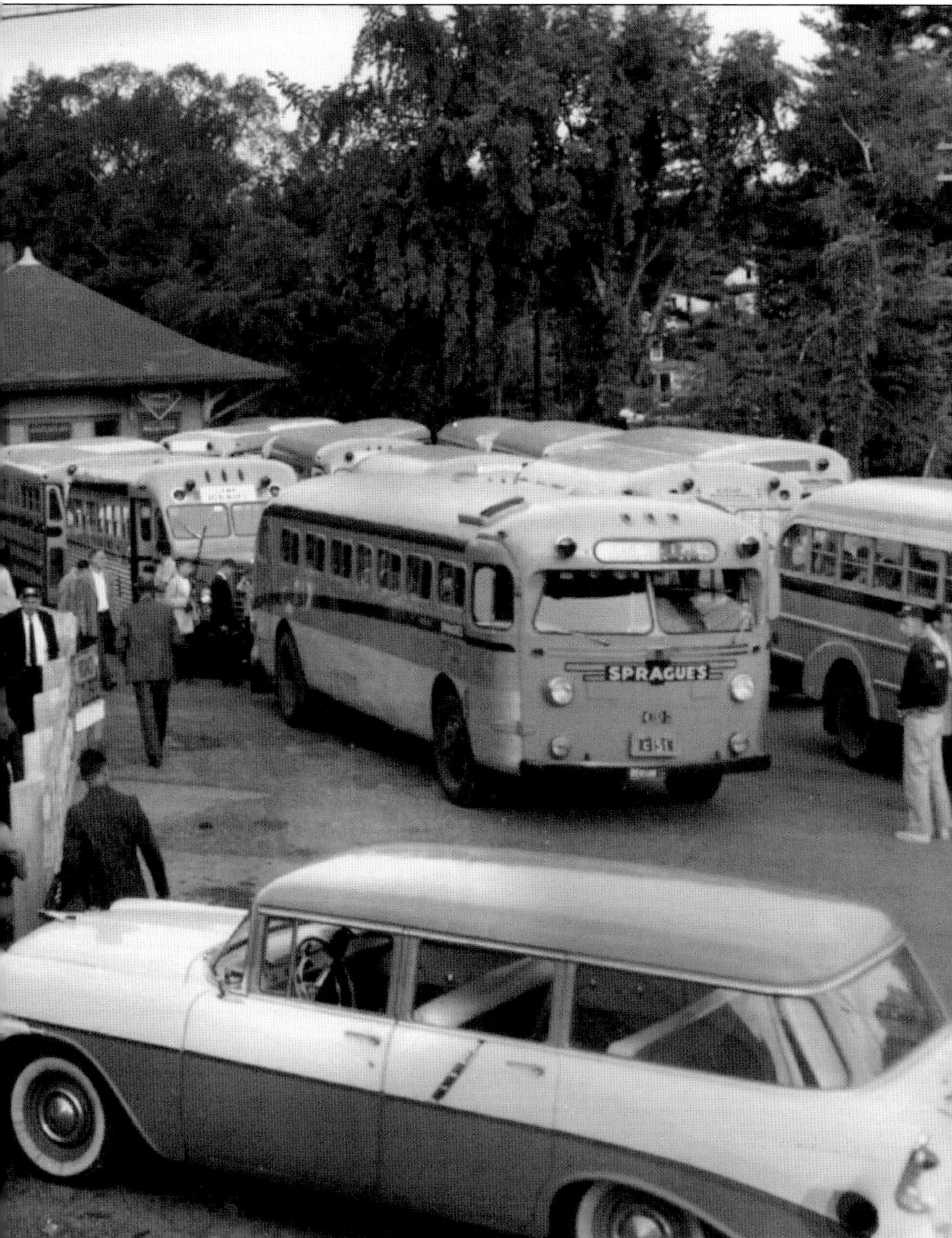

in the Lakes Region.

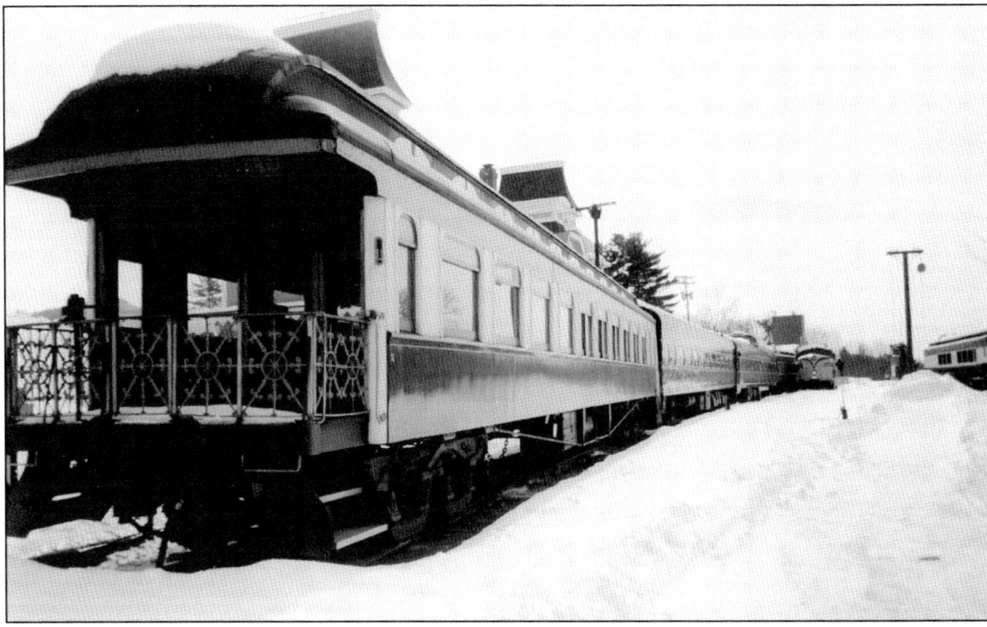

The *Gertrude Emma* was built by the Pullman Palace Car Company of Pullman, Illinois, in 1898 as a sleeper-parlor-observation car. The first Pullman sleeping car, constructed by George Pullman, was put into operation about 1865. Today, this car is located in North Conway, New Hampshire.

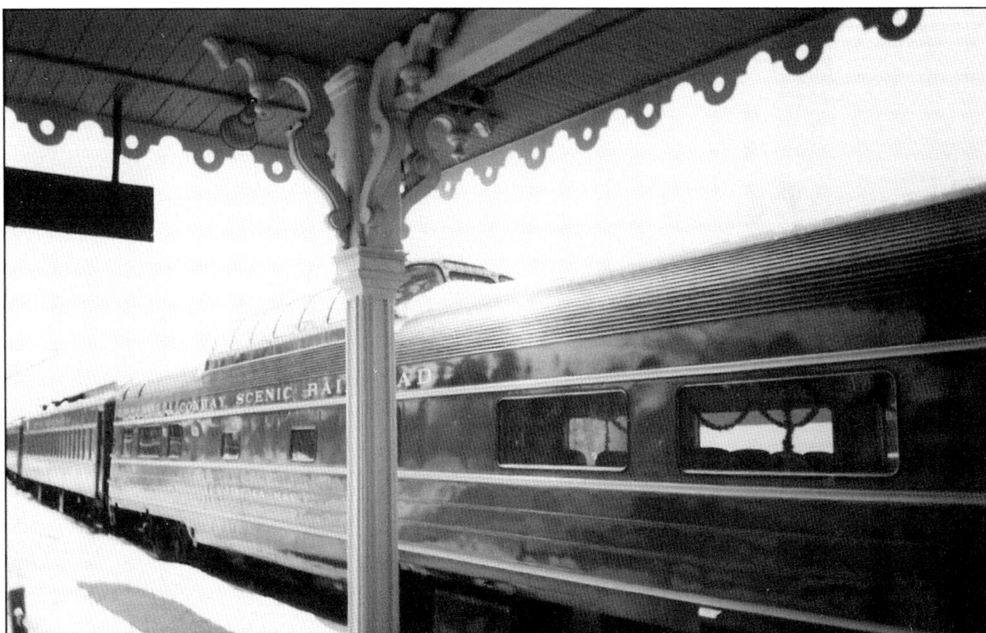

Dome coach No. 1329, the *Dorthea Mae*, was built by the Budd Company in 1955 for service on the *Empire Builder* and worked the Alaska and the Cape Cod Scenic Railroads. The car was purchased by the Conway Scenic Railroad Company in December 1997 for use on the Crawford Notch line.

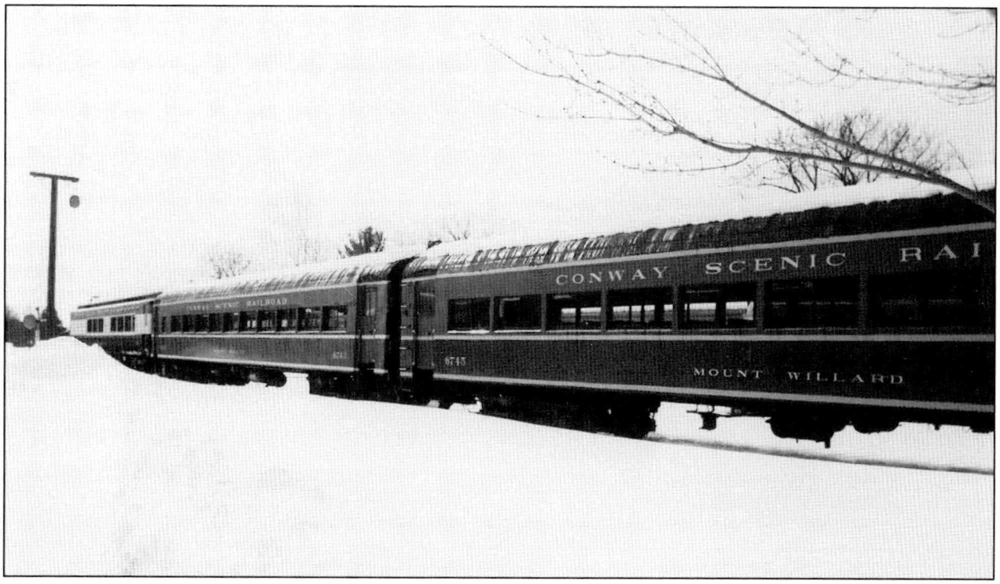

Passenger coach No. 6745, the *Mount Willard*, was built by the Canadian Car and Foundry in 1952 and was retired to the Conway Scenic Railroad in mid-1995 for removal of control cabs and conversion coaches. It is now used in Crawford Notch line service.

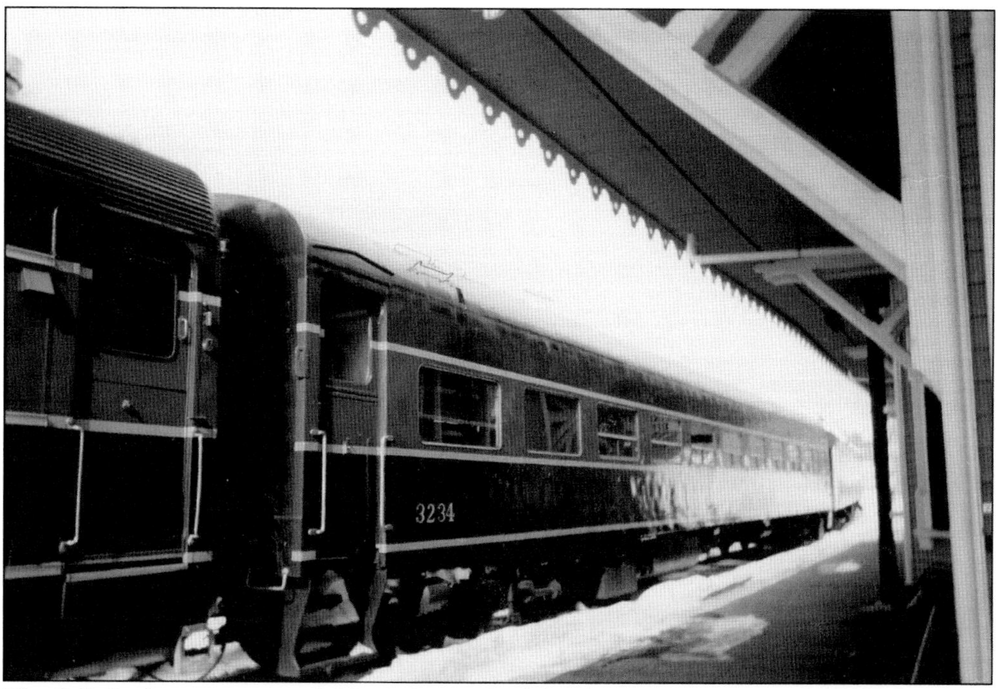

The *C.P. Reed*, passenger coach No. 3234, was built by the Canadian Car and Foundry in 1954. Today it is located in North Conway, New Hampshire.

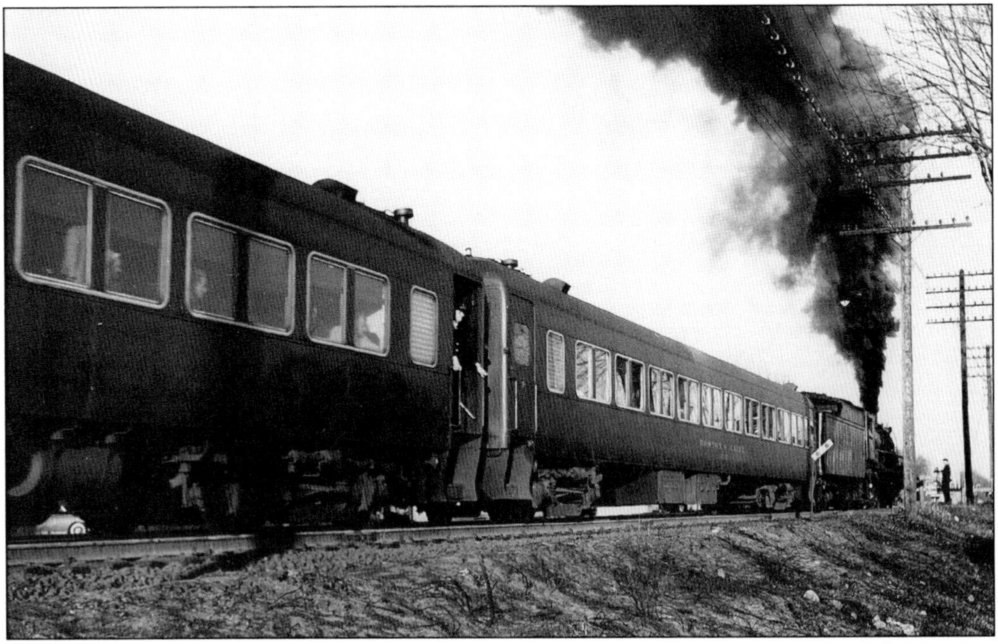

B&M commuter trains were very popular during the 1940s and 1950s. A common sight on most city-bound tracks were the commuter trains making daily runs between the suburbs and the city.

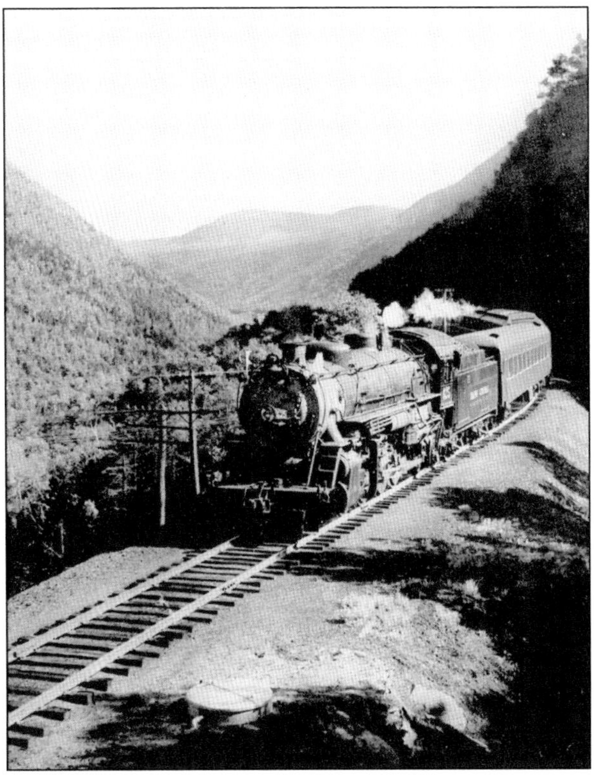

This postcard is entitled "On the Mountain Route of the Maine Central Railroad." One of the most picturesque rides in the East is this trip through the famous Crawford Notch in the White Mountains of New Hampshire. The locomotive, No. 625, is a Maine Central Mikado, Type 2-8-2, Class S.

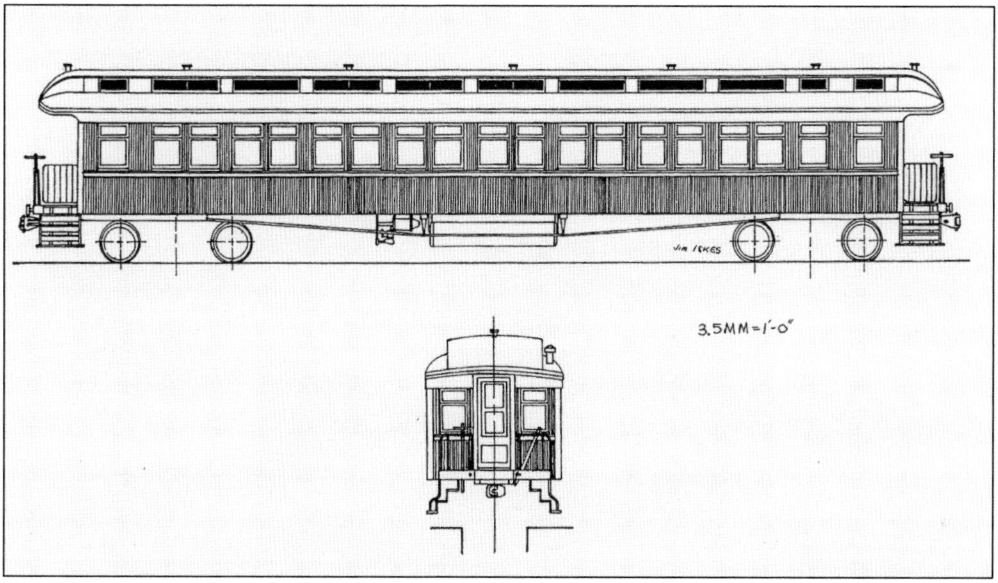

This is a plan of a wooden passenger car. Although wooden passenger equipment was taken out of revenue service on the Boston and Maine Railroad in the early 1950s, several former B&M wooden coaches and combines perform active tourist-train service to this day. The Guilford Railroad still has several pieces of vintage B&M wooden rolling stock left in work-train service, but the number is dwindling year by year. Many are on the Strasburg Railroad in Pennsylvania.

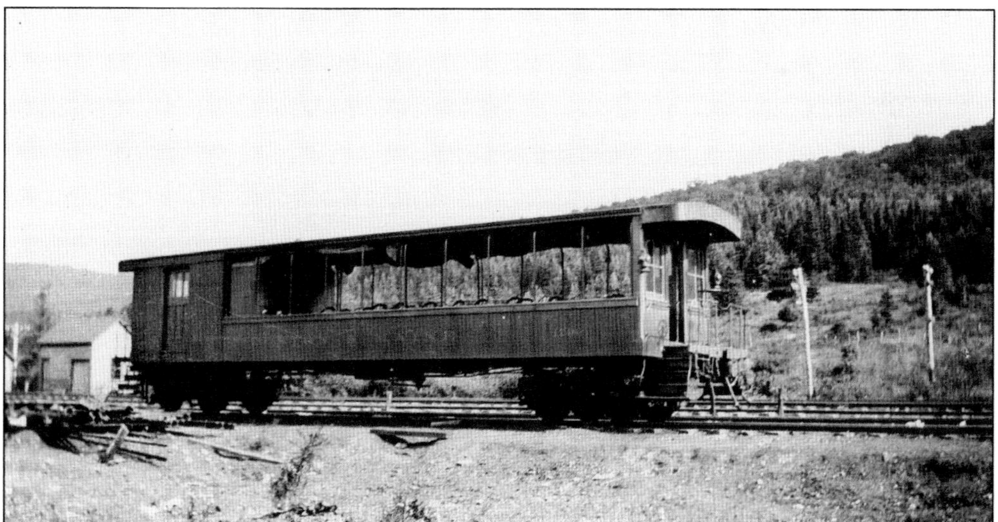

The B&M open-air observation passenger car was used on the Washington branch between Fabyan's and the Mount Washington Base Station, as seen here on September 5, 1928. Fabyan's was a popular station and hotel in the White Mountains.

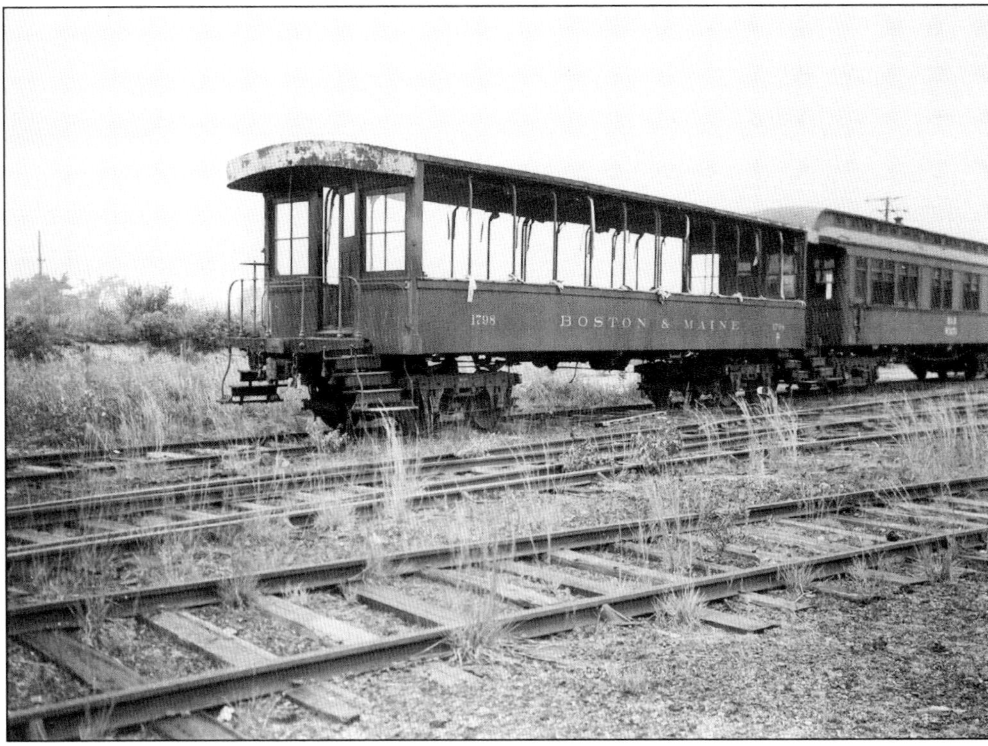

Open-air passenger car No. 1798 appears at North Billerica, Massachusetts, on August 19, 1939.

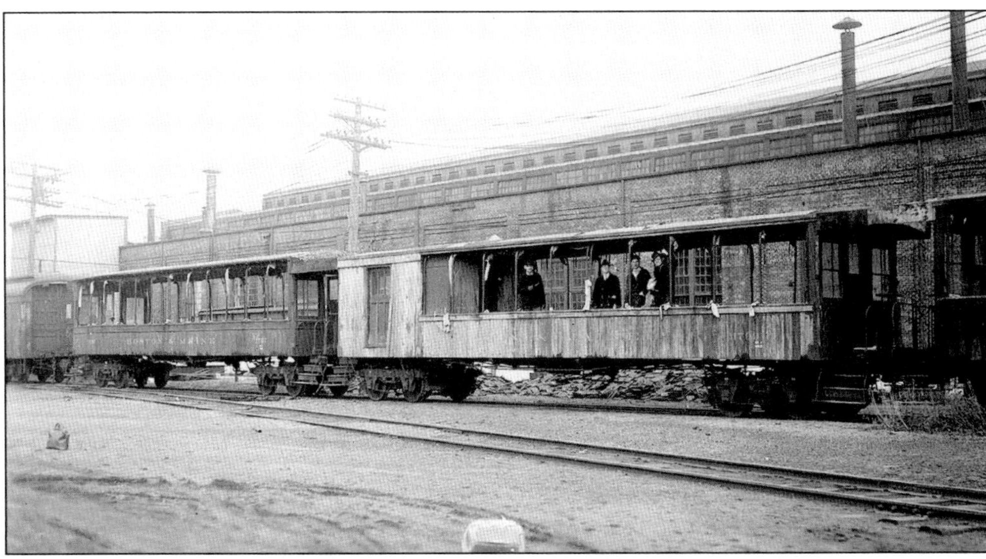
A B&M open-air passenger car is seen at Billerica, Massachusetts, in 1938.

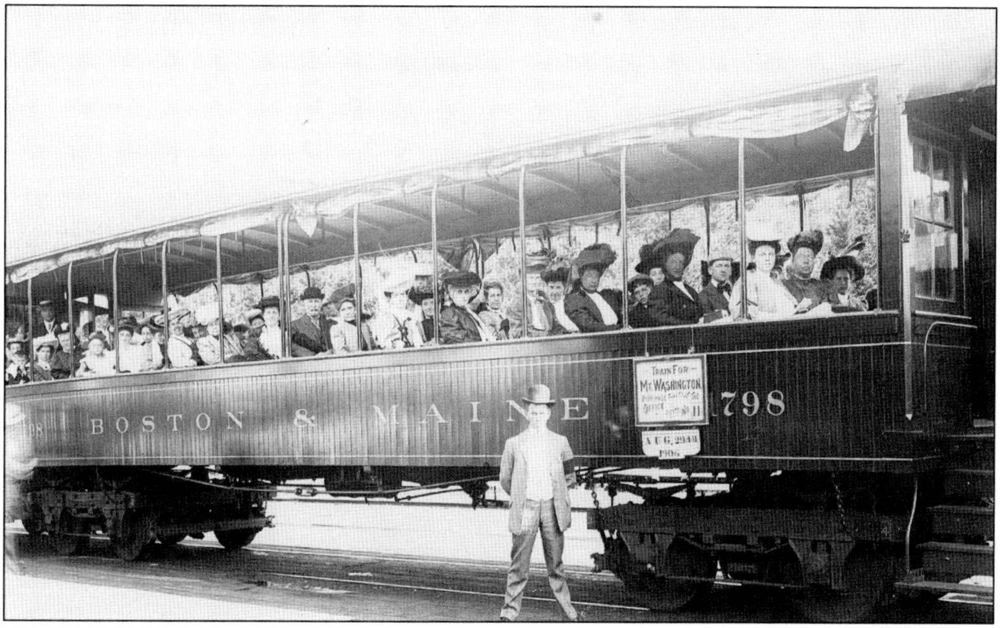

A B&M open-air observation passenger car travels between Fabyan's and the Mount Washington Base Station on August 29, 1906. It was in 1876 that Fabyan's and the Base Station of the Cog Railway were connected by rail.

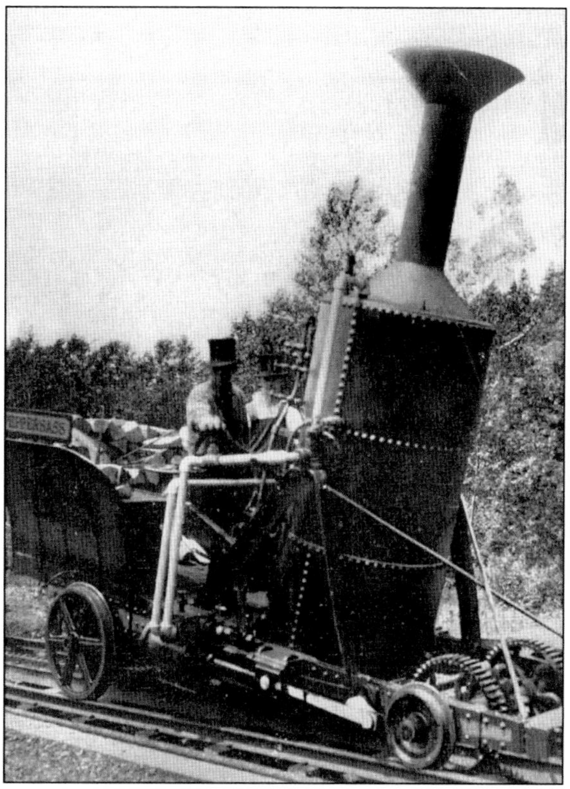
"Old Peppersass," built in 1866, was the first Cog Railway engine. At first, it was christened "the Hero." In this view, the engine, controlled by E. C. "Jack" Frost, climbs Mount Washington on July 20, 1929.

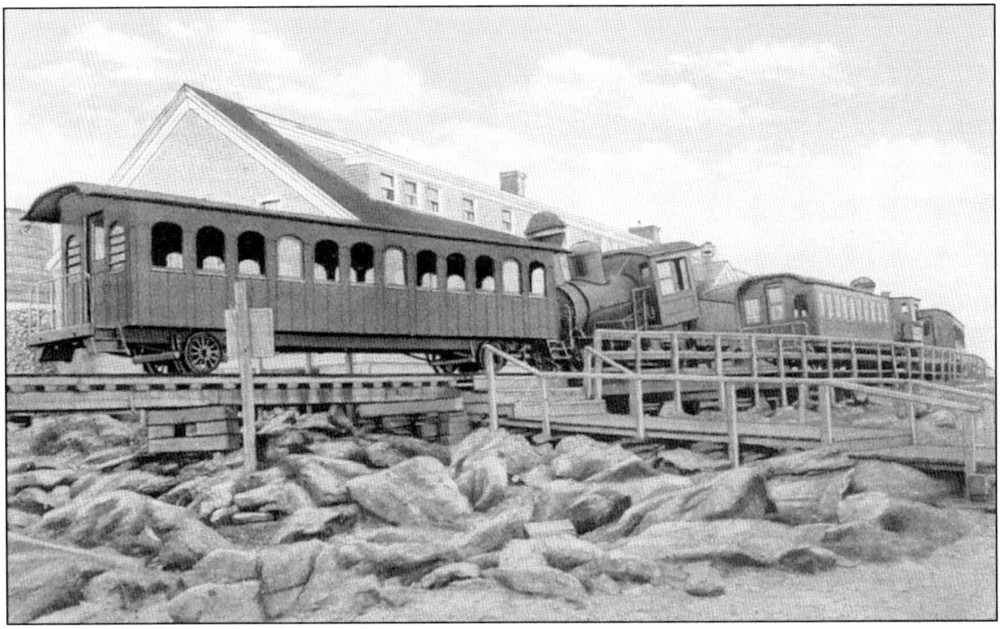

The Mount Washington Cog Railway has been in operation since 1869, carrying thousands of passengers, none ever injured. In 1895, the Boston and Maine leased this line connecting the Base Station with Fabyan's Station. The man posing is Aden L. Fuller, a B&M engineer who resided in Bellows Falls, Vermont.

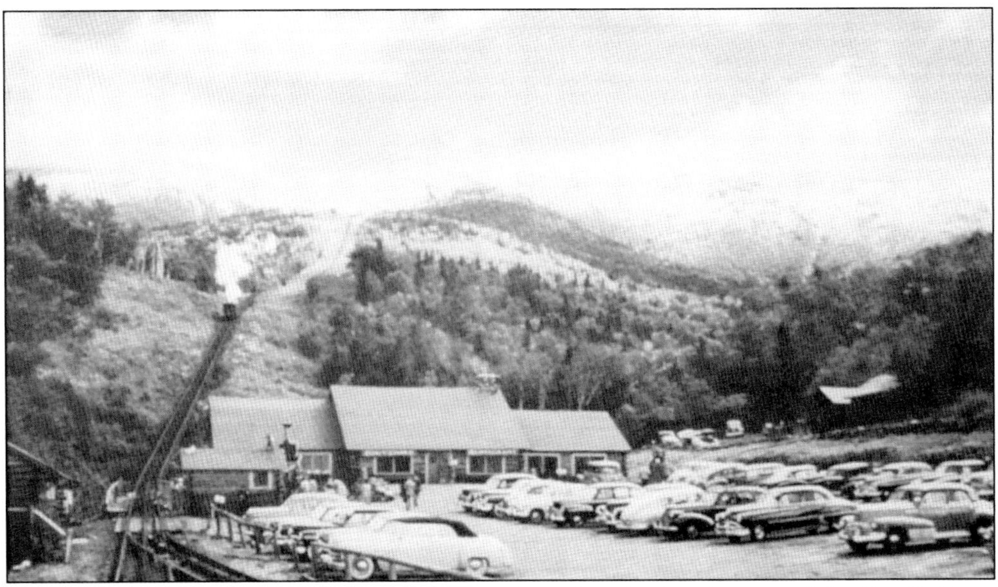

The Marshfield House, seen here in the 1950s, is located at the Base Station of the Cog Railway. In 1858, Sylvester Marsh of Littleton, New Hampshire, had the idea to build a mountain-climbing railroad. That year, he exhibited a model of his engine and the Cog Railway to the New Hampshire legislature; he was granted a charter to build up Mounts Washington and Lafayette. His first job was to build a turnpike to the location known as the Base Station, some distance below where passengers now take the train. This terminal is now at Marshfield, the name commemorating Sylvester Marsh and his partner, Darby Field.

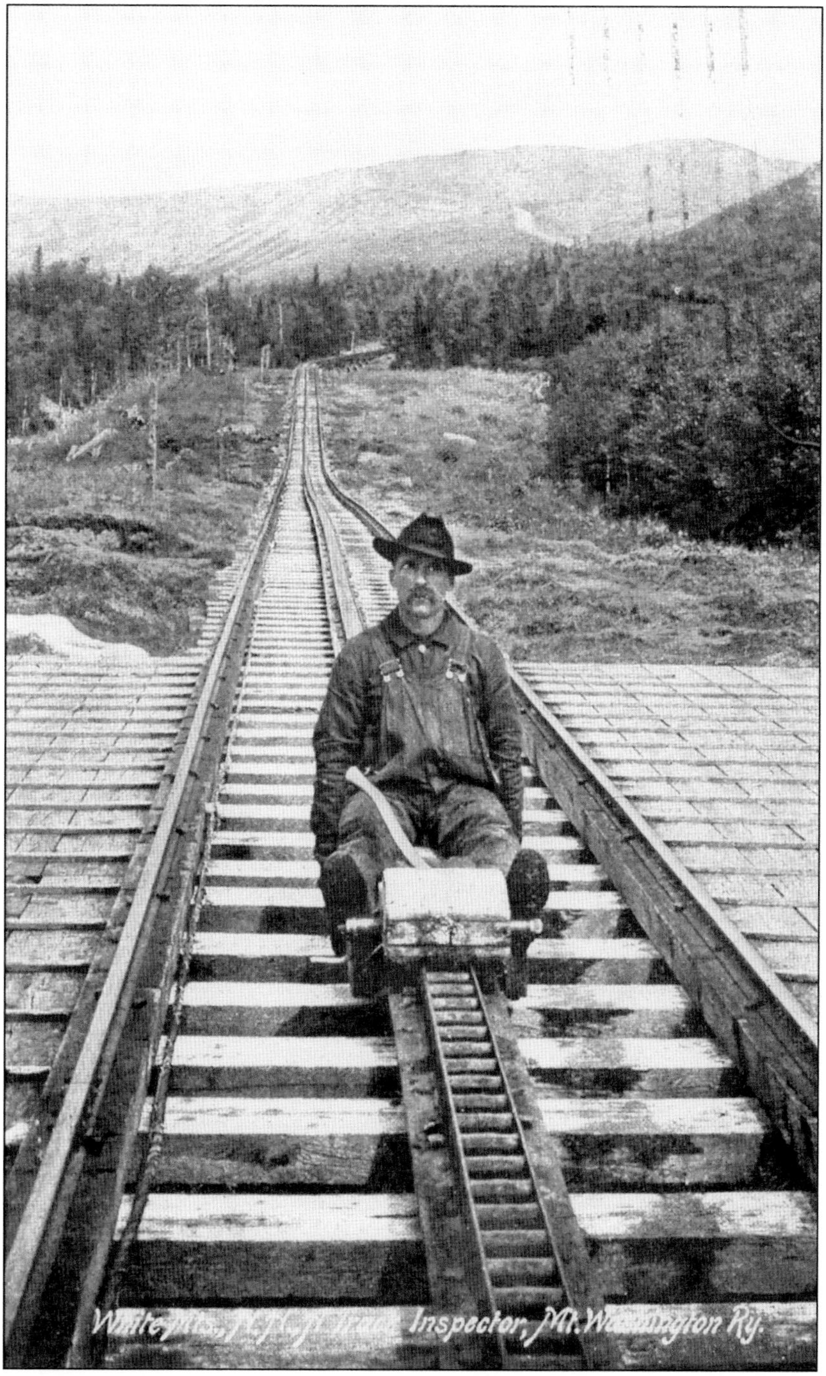

A track inspector watches over the Cog Railway in January 1929. The essential feature of this railway is its driving mechanism. On the track, in addition to the outside rails, there is a central cog rail consisting of two pieces of wrought angle iron, placed parallel and connected by iron pins four inches apart. Teeth on the driving wheel of the engine mesh with the cog rail and draw the whole train up the mountain. This mechanism has been copied for mountain railroads elsewhere in the world, including one on Mount Rigi in Switzerland.

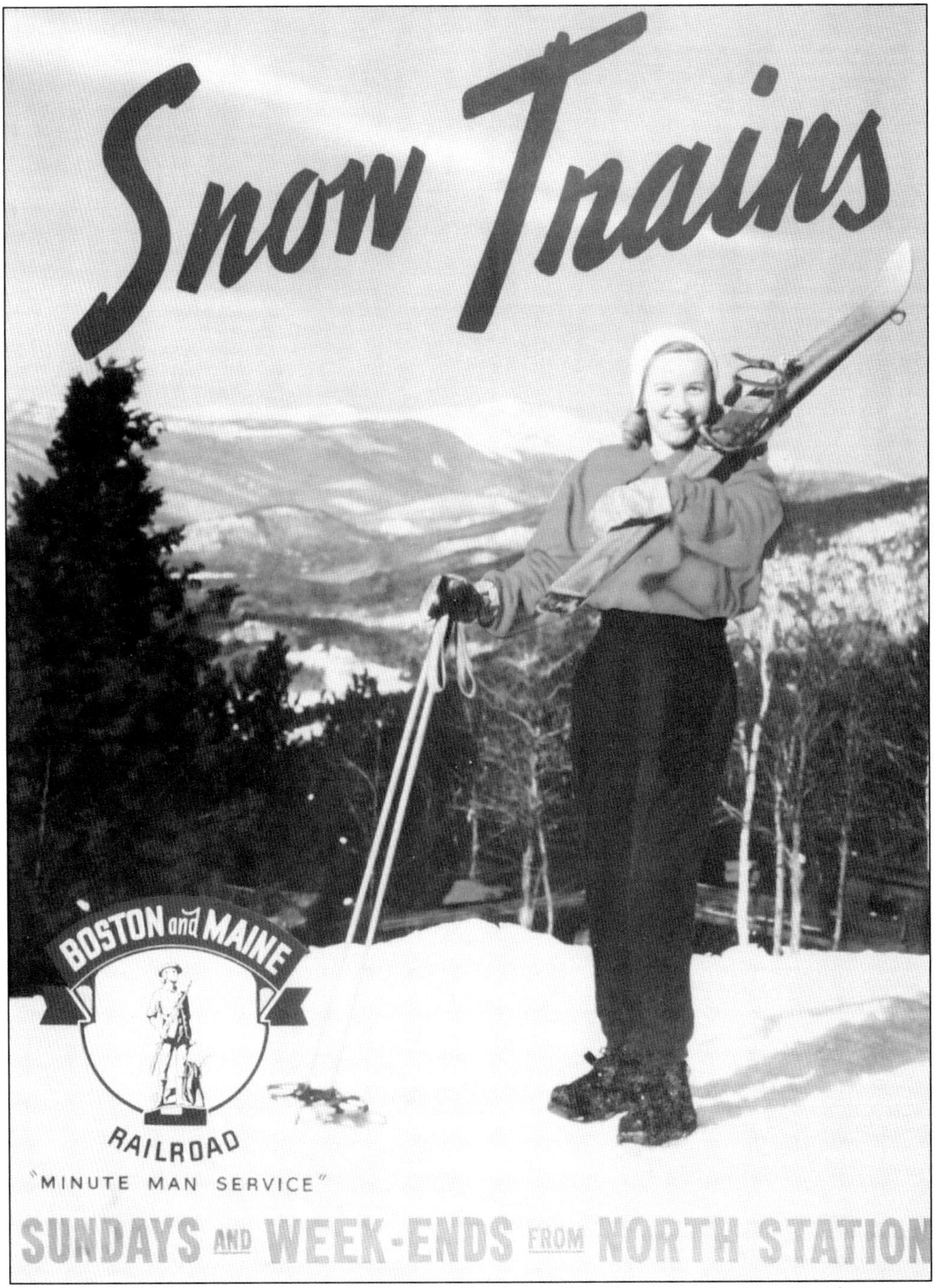

A late-1940s B&M snow train poster advertises Sunday and weekend service from North Station. In 1931, the railroad responded to the local effort to develop downhill skiing as a winter tourist attraction by running the first of its "snow" trains. Much preparation went into the snow train operation. It left North Station in Boston on Friday for North Conway (Mount Cranmore) and returned to Boston on Sunday, allowing for a two-day skiing retreat.

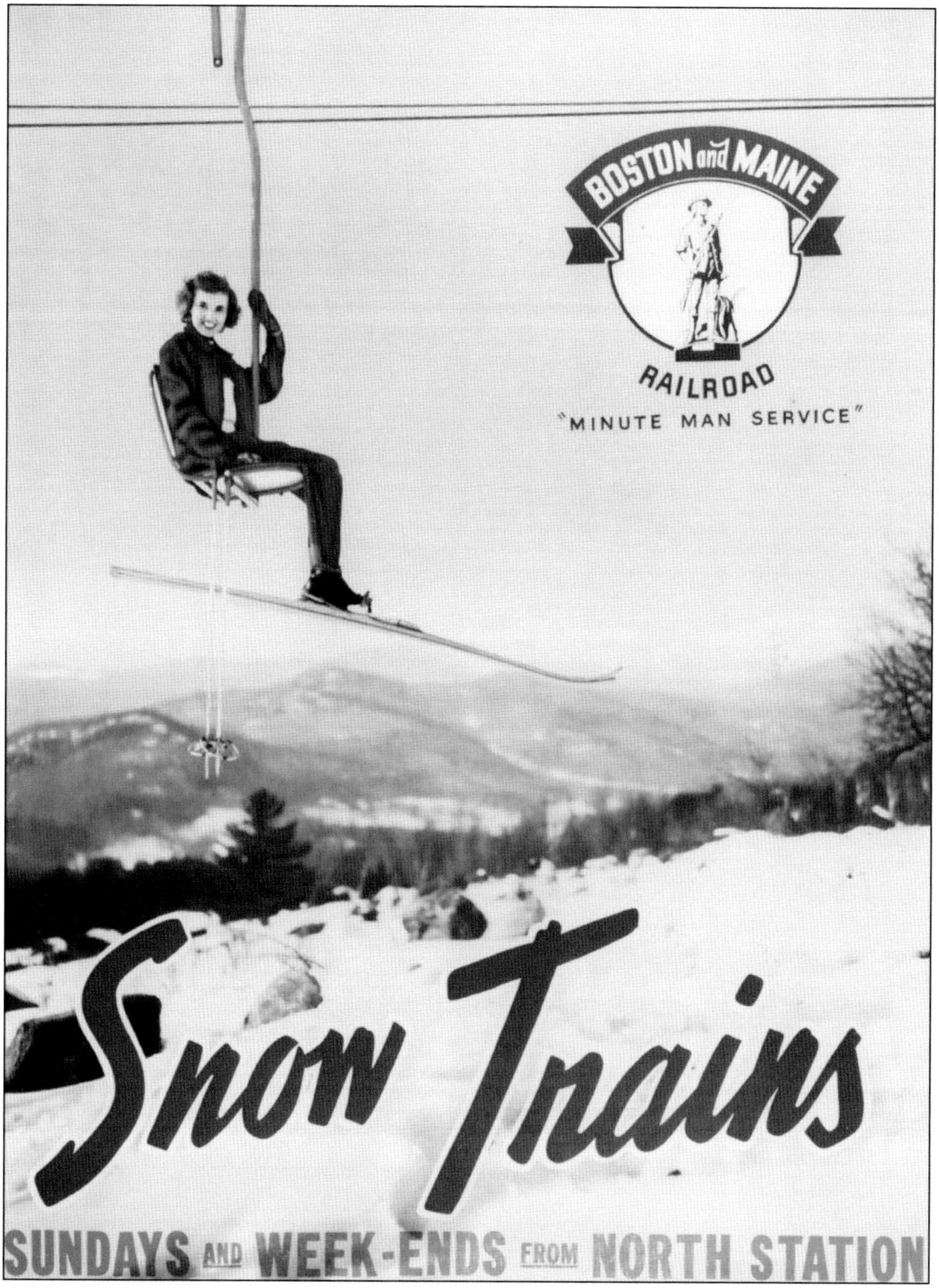

A B&M snow train poster promotes "Minute Man Service" from North Station in the late 1940s. A special snow train trip was made to Fabyan's, New Hampshire, on a February day of real wintry weather, which made the trip up Crawford Notch on the Maine Central line truly superb.

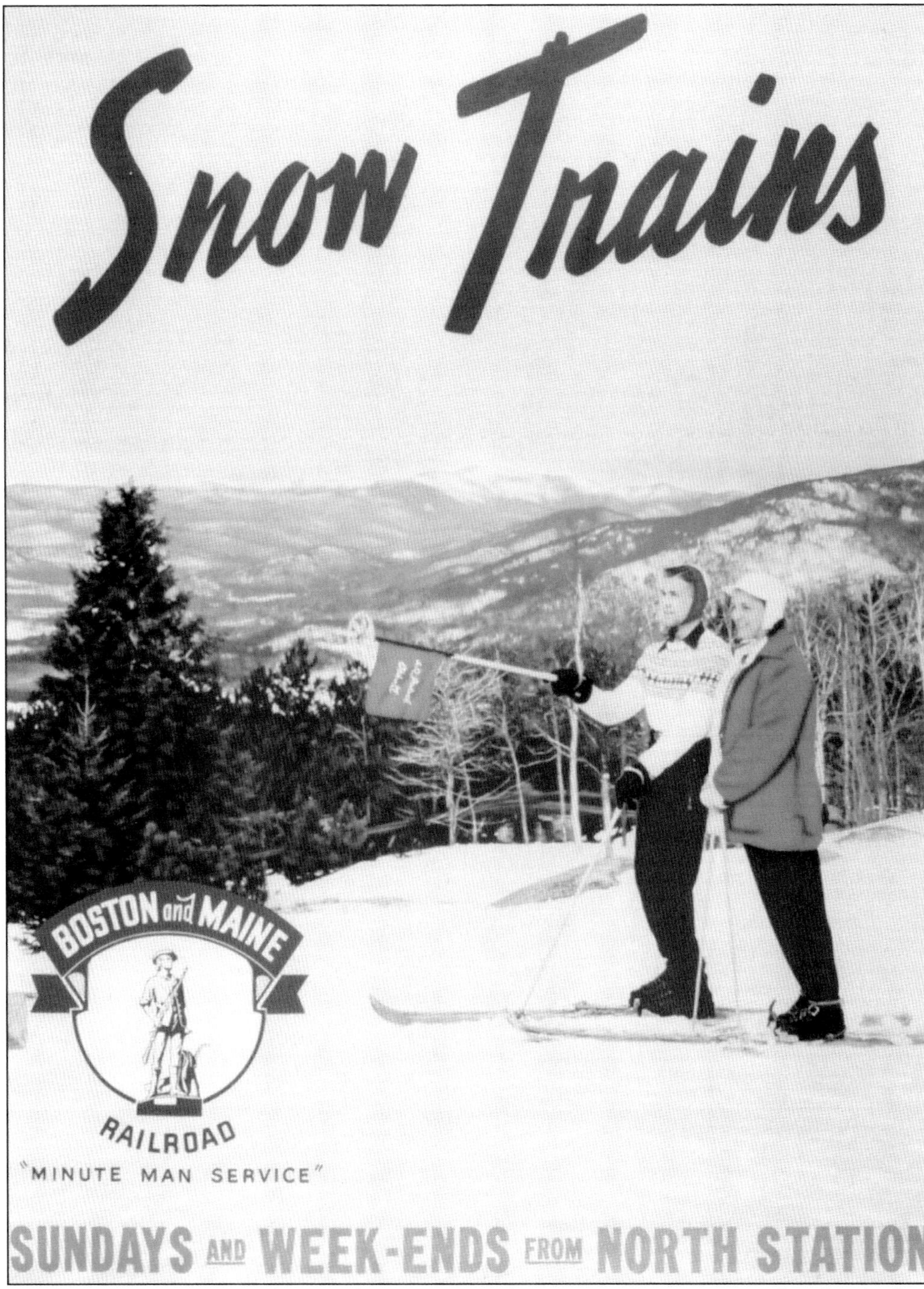

The last snow train operated to North Conway on February 26, 1972—40 years after the idea had first been realized by the B&M. Over 300 passengers traveled on the Budd car that day, about 30 of which may have been skiers.

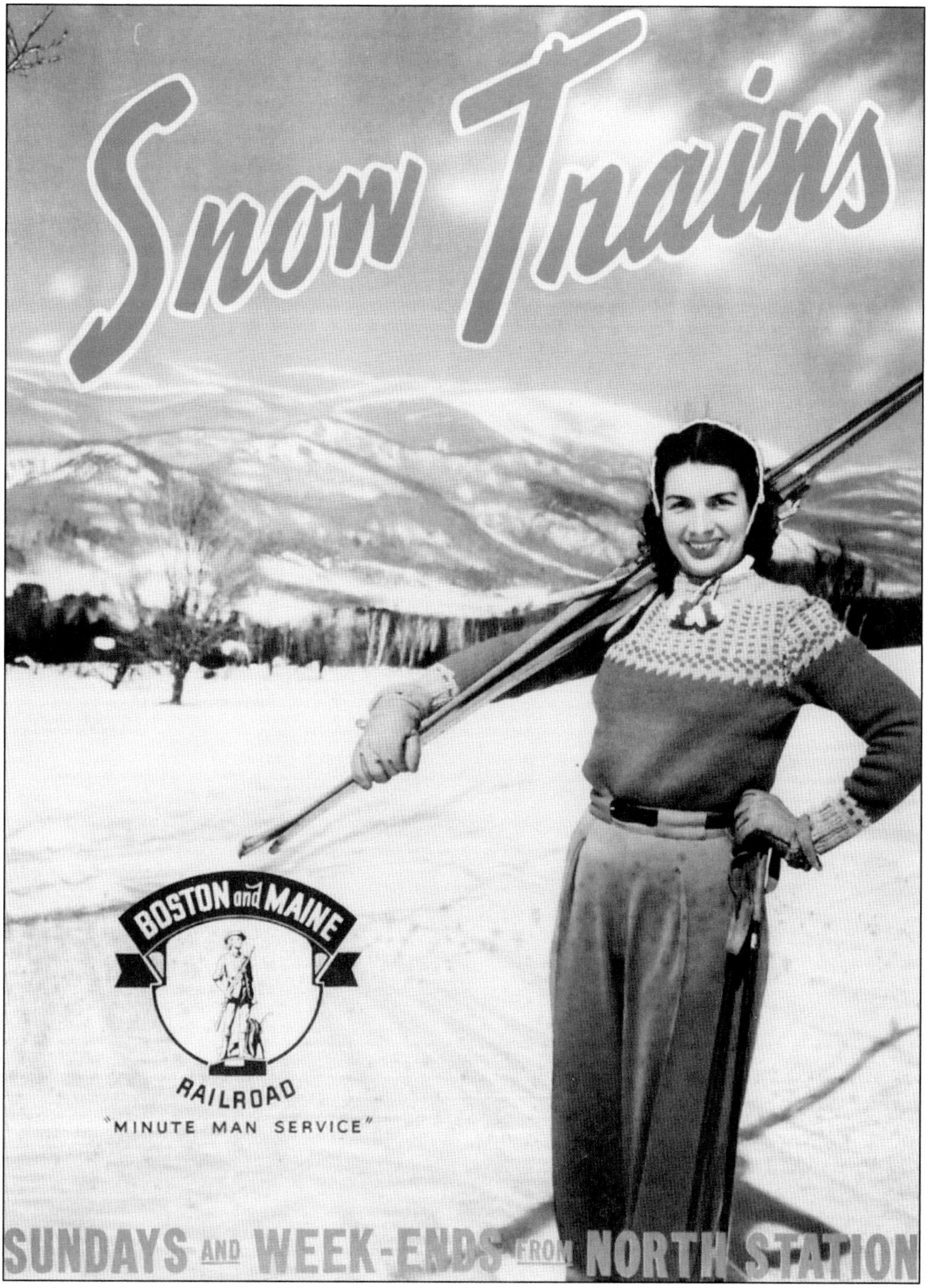

Pictured here is a B&M snow train poster from the late 1940s. The snow trains to the White Mountains became known as weekend party trains. The final one made it return trip to Boston from North Conway, New Hampshire, on February 26, 1972.

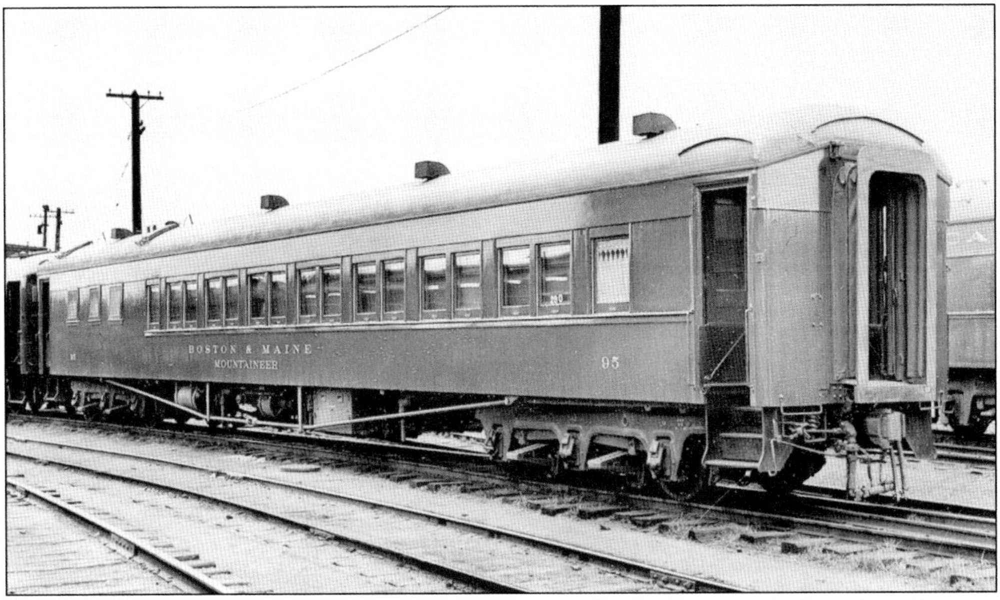

B&M wooden diner No. 95, the *Mountaineer*, is shown in Yard 4, East Cambridge, Massachusetts. The early dining cars usually had tables accommodating 36 people, as well as a full kitchen, complete with wood-fired range, iceboxes, hot and cold running water, and even a charcoal broiler.

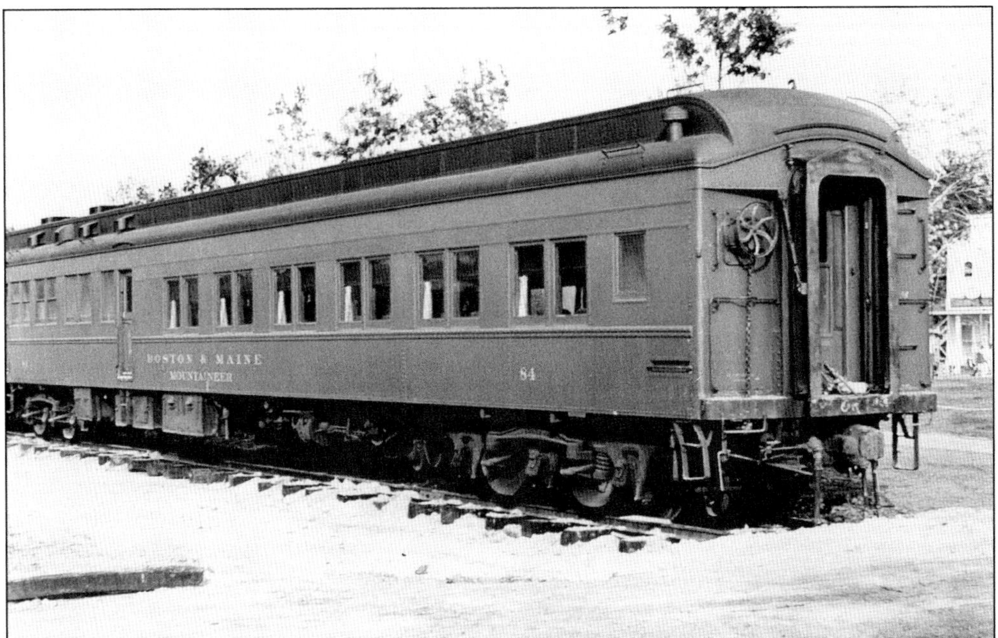

B&M dining car No. 84, the *Mountaineer*, was known to railroaders simply as a "36-seater." This car, and hundreds like it, represented the standard on American railroads from the 1880s until the late 1940s, and with some later modernizations, a number remained in service through the 1960s.

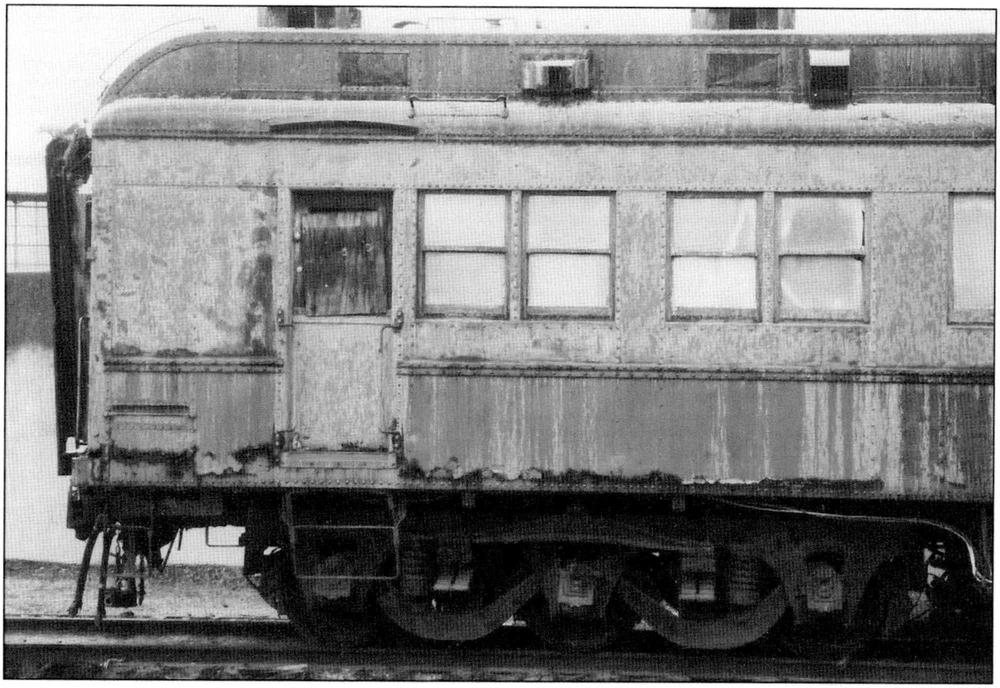

This is a side view of the B&M heavyweight diner *Maine*, later renamed the *Mountaineer.* This photograph was taken at Steamtown in Scranton, Pennsylvania, on May 26, 2003.

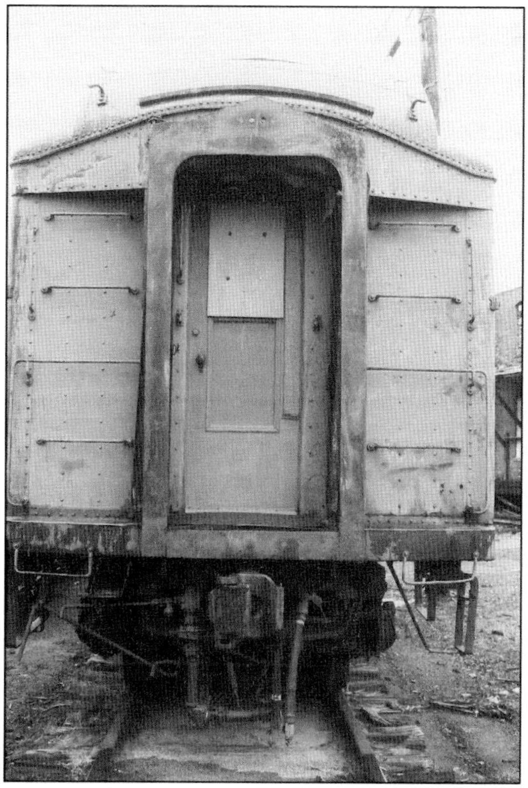

This is an end view of the B&M heavyweight diner *Maine*. The photograph was taken at Steamtown in Scranton, Pennsylvania, on May 26, 2003.

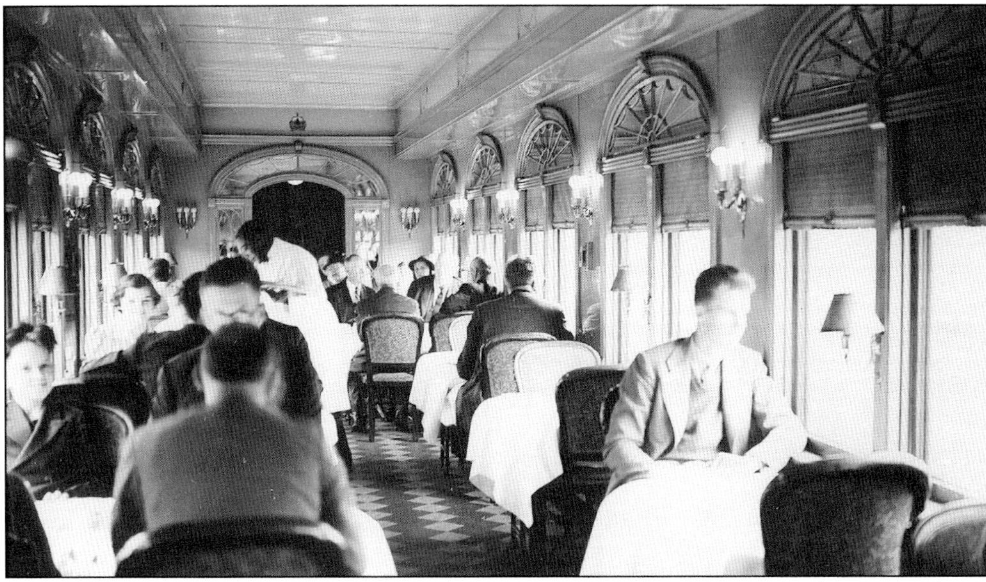

The interior of B&M dining car No. 86, the *Vermont*, is revealed here in 1930. Elegance in dining "first-class" was the byword of the railroad. A 36-seater normally carried an 11-person crew: a steward, six waiters, a chef, and three cooks.

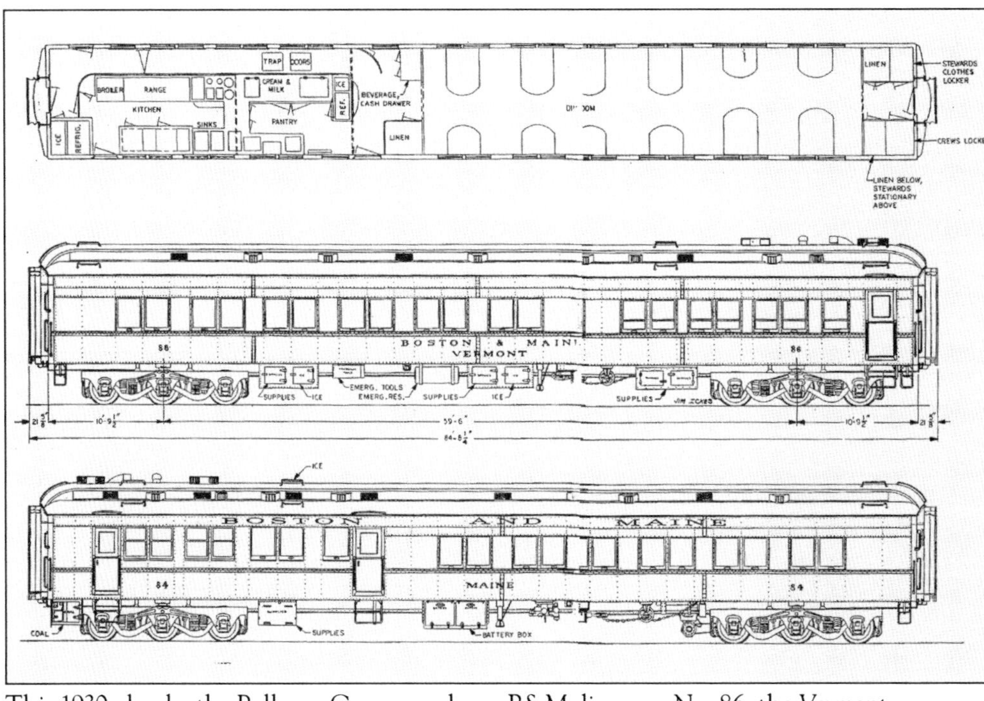

This 1930 plan by the Pullman Company shows B&M diner car No. 86, the *Vermont*.

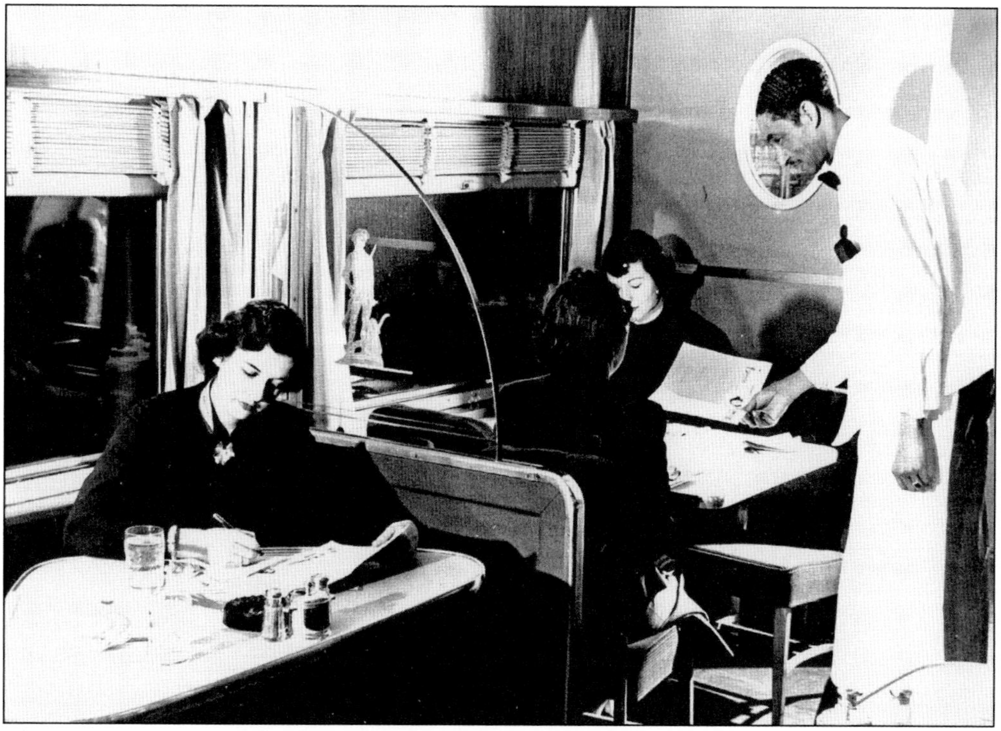

This c. 1950 photograph offers an interior view of the B&M streamlined restaurant-lounge car 70–71 series. Up until the late 1940s, a particular dining car always carried the same crew; it was their car. The steward was responsible for seating the customers, tallying checks, collecting payment, and otherwise seeing to the comfort and needs of the passengers.

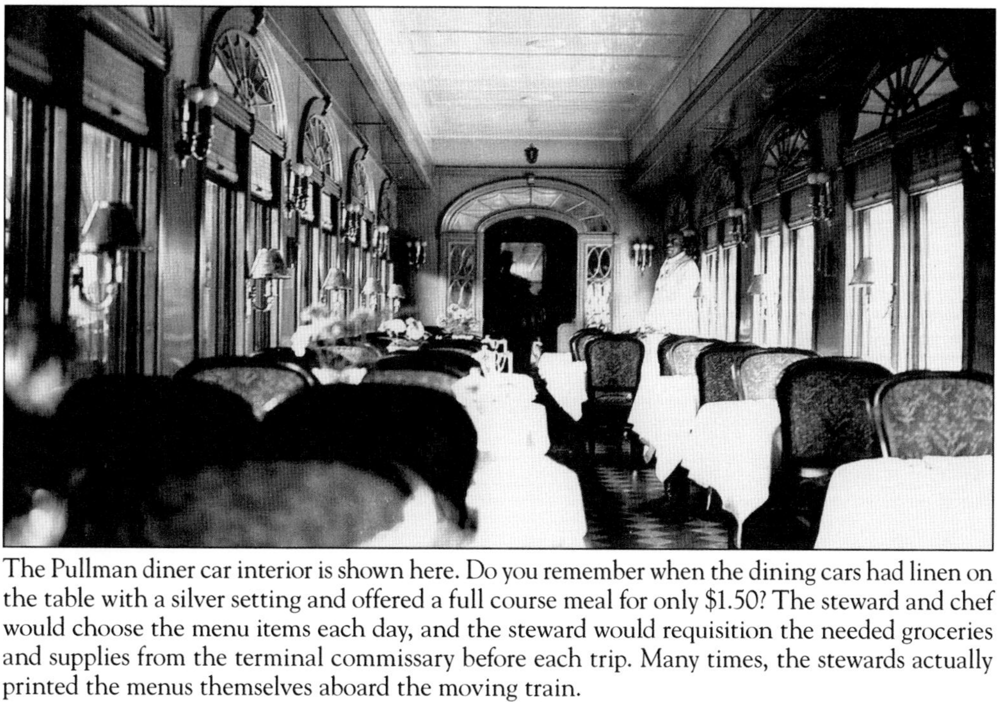

The Pullman diner car interior is shown here. Do you remember when the dining cars had linen on the table with a silver setting and offered a full course meal for only $1.50? The steward and chef would choose the menu items each day, and the steward would requisition the needed groceries and supplies from the terminal commissary before each trip. Many times, the stewards actually printed the menus themselves aboard the moving train.

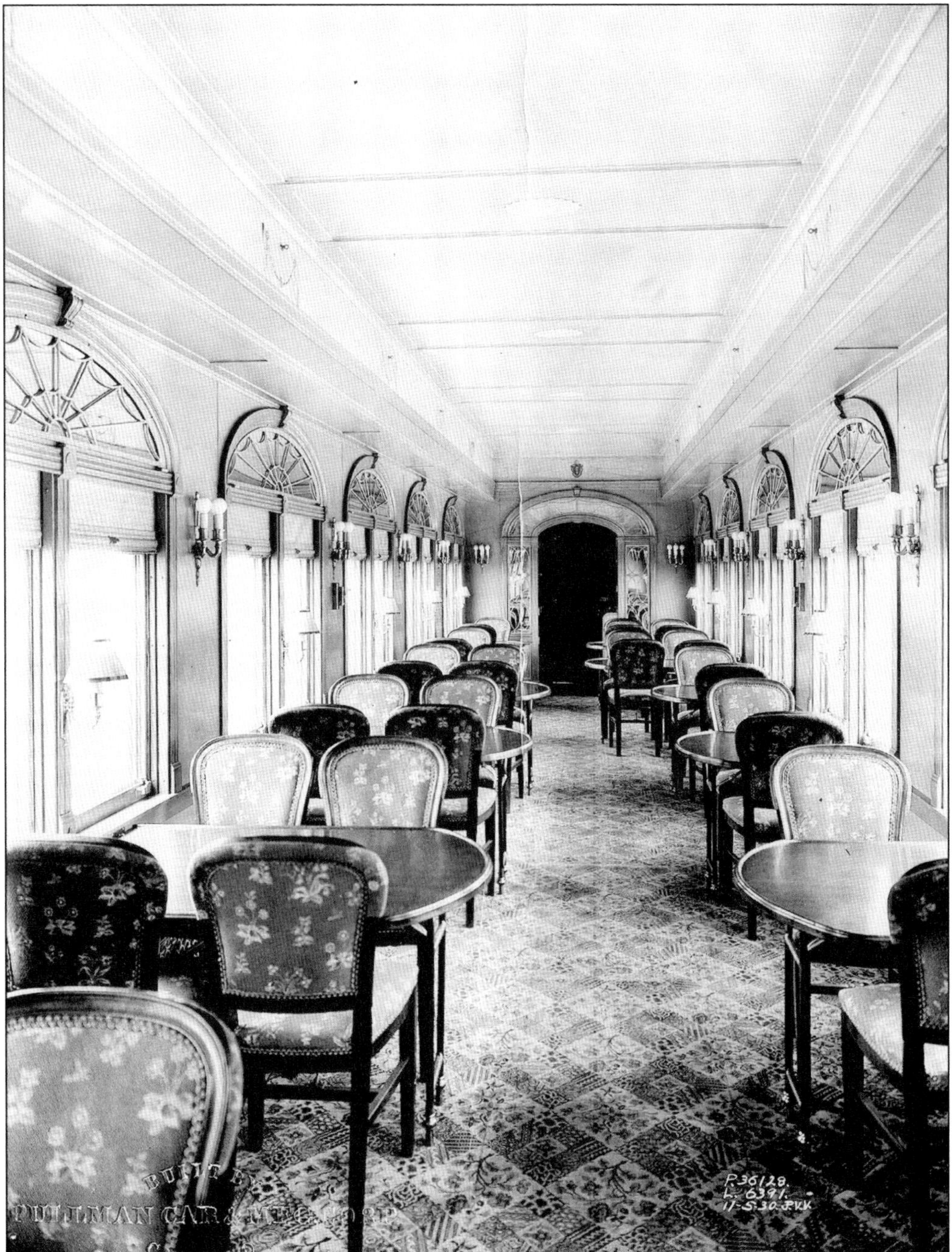

Pullman dining car No. 87, the *Massachusetts*, was built in 1930. Note the elegance of the fine furniture, wood panels, and beautiful wall-to-wall carpeting throughout the car.

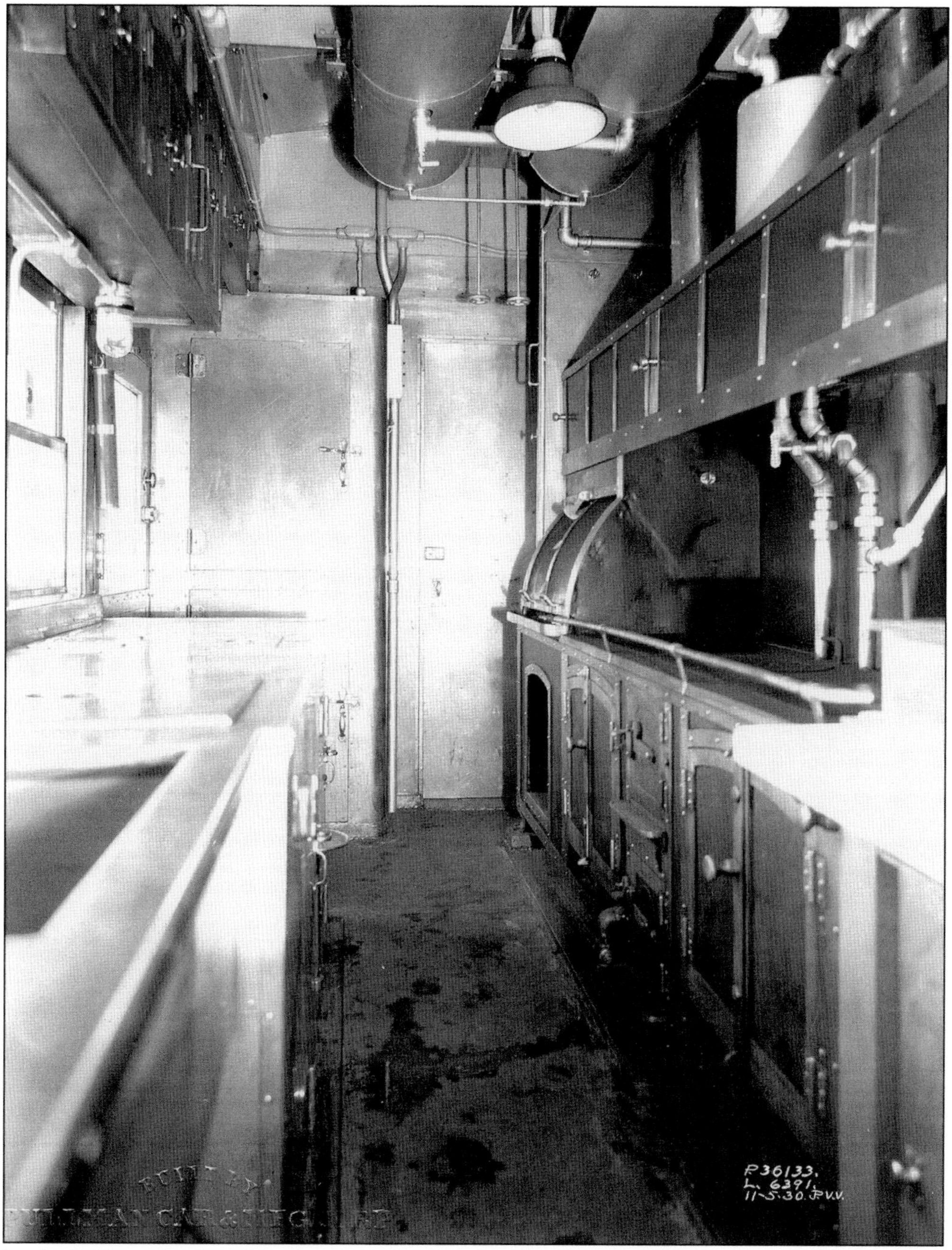

In the Pullman kitchen (which was cramped and hot), the chef and his assistant cooks prepared nearly 300 meals a day—and these were on par with any fine restaurant. Virtually everything was prepared on board. Meats were roasted. Soups and sauces were cooked. Even the pies were baked completely from scratch.

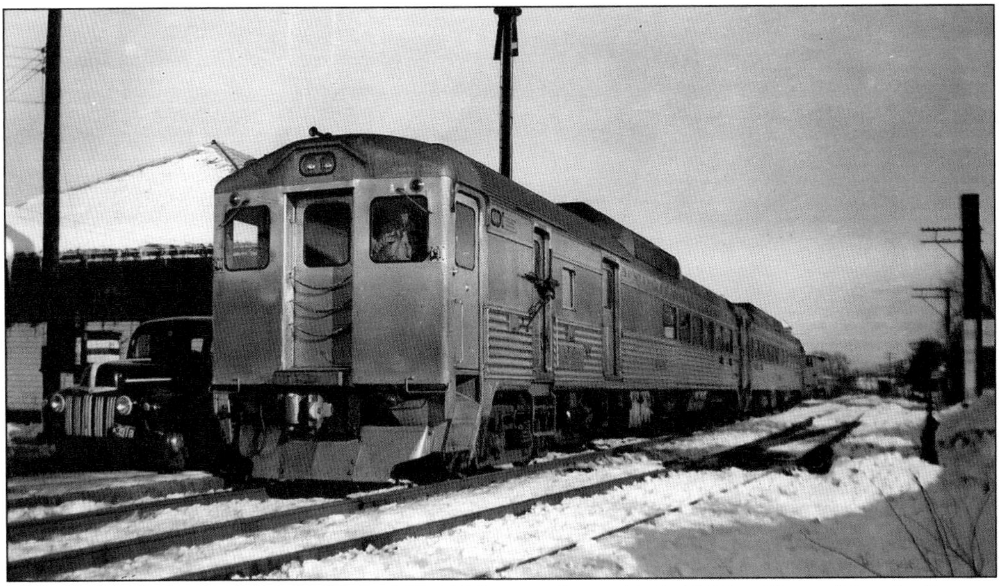

The first Boston and Maine Budd car, No. 6300 series, leaves Enfield, New Hampshire, for Boston in 1950. The B&M was not the first company to purchase the rail diesel car (RDC) but bought 109 of the Budd Company's 1949 innovation and was still operating most of them in 1986.

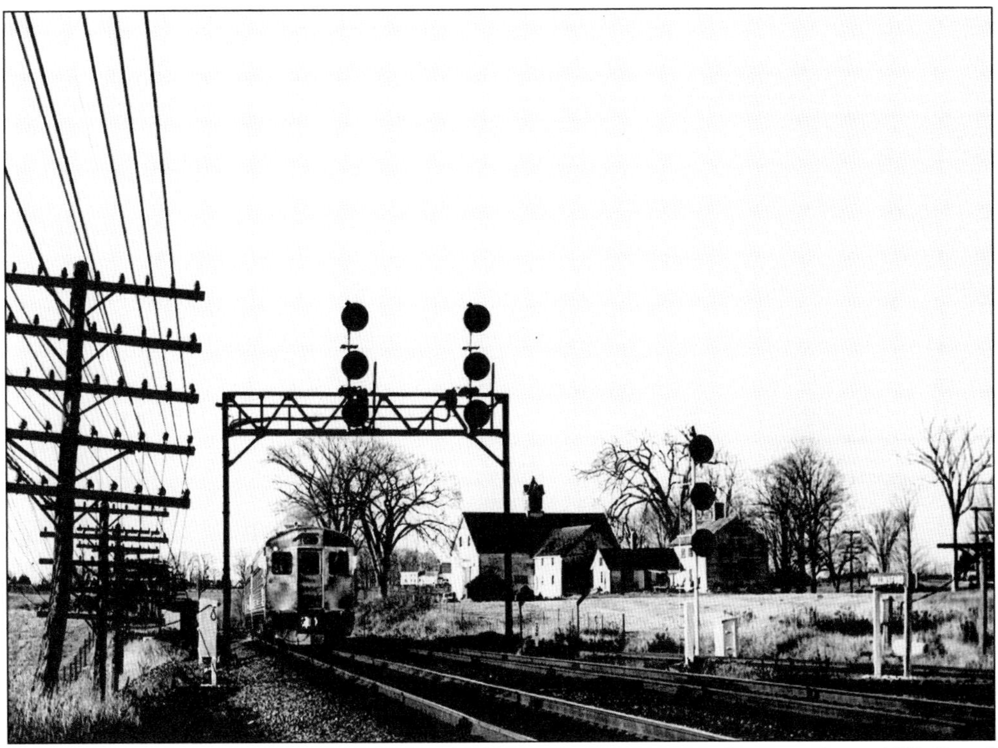

A pair of new RDC-1s run through Rollinsford Junction, New Hampshire, in this c. 1953 David K. Johnson photograph. The new units are covering the schedule of Boston–Portland train No. 103, the *Businessman*, which would depart Boston at 7:30 a.m. and arrive in Portland five stops later, at 9:55. The return trip provided a convenient 5:30 p.m. arrival in Boston.

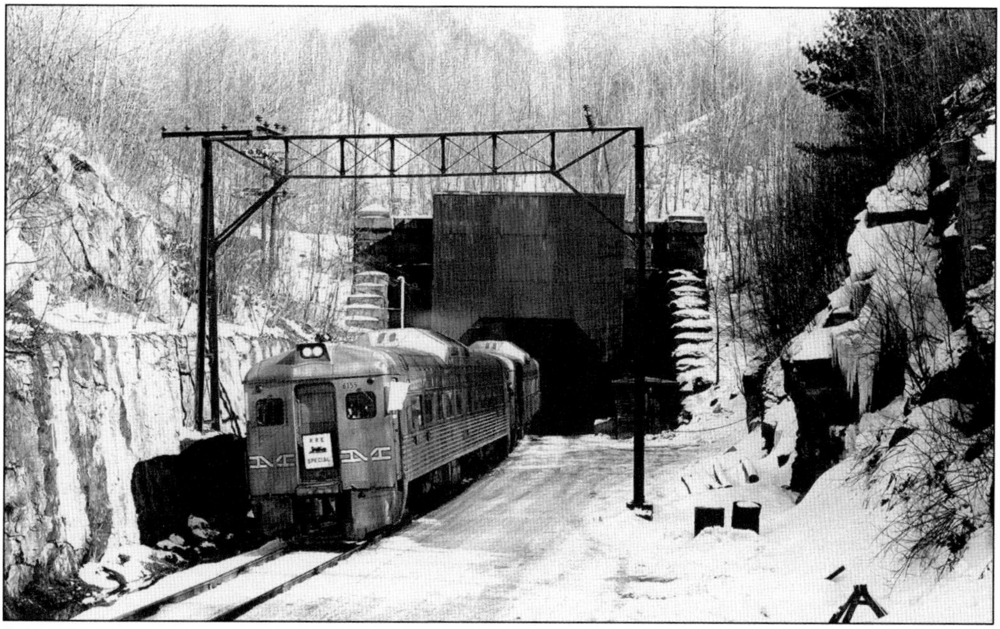

B&M RDC-1 No. 6155 leads the railroad enthusiast's annual snow train out of the west portal of Hoosac Tunnel at North Adams, Massachusetts, on February 24, 1973. By 1955, the B&M had placed 64 RDCs in service, largely in commuter runs.

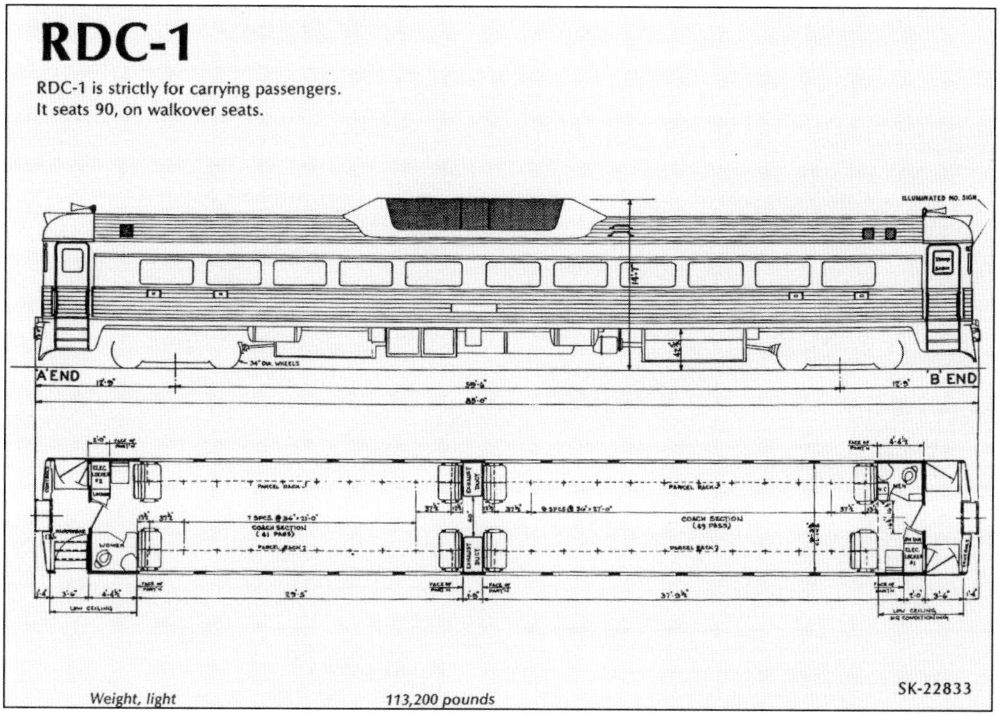

The RDC-1, whose plan is shown here, was a railcar strictly for carrying passengers. It seated 90 on walkover seats. In February 1956, orders included a pair of RDC-1s and RDC-2s to bring the fleet to 101. Two more RDC orders remained before the B&M's total of 109 Budd cars would be attained.

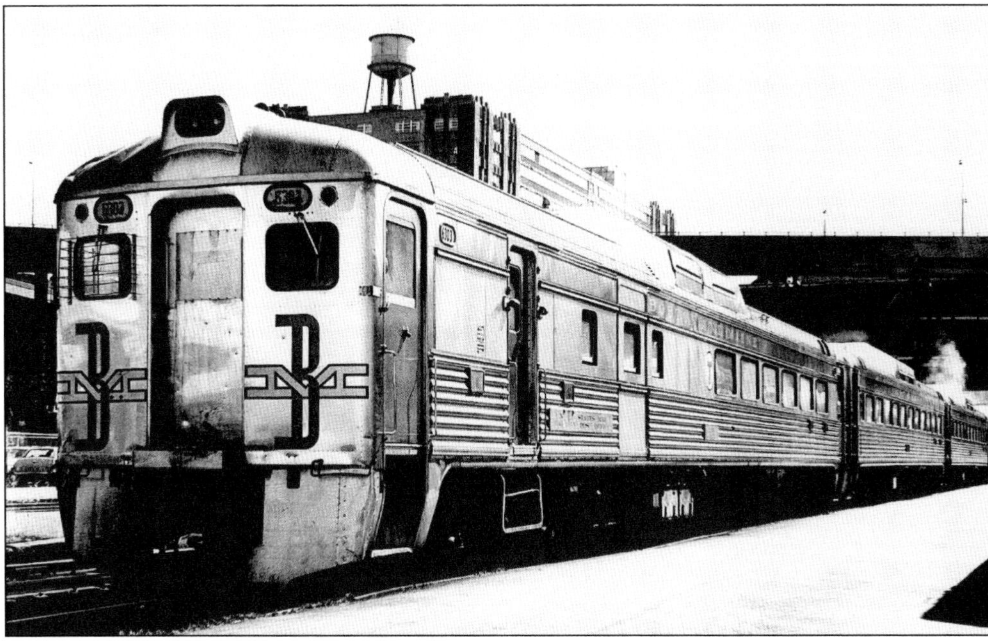

B&M RDC-3 No. 6303 is seen here at North Station on the first day of spring in 1975. This car was one of the final group purchased by the B&M. Late in 1978, it was converted to a steam generator car, and two years later, it was rebuilt by Morrison-Knudsen to a control-cab coach.

RDC-3

RDC-3 combines passengers, baggage-express, and mail, seating 49 passengers, with a 17 foot baggage-express compartment, separated by a bulkhead with a creep door from a 15 foot railway mail apartment.

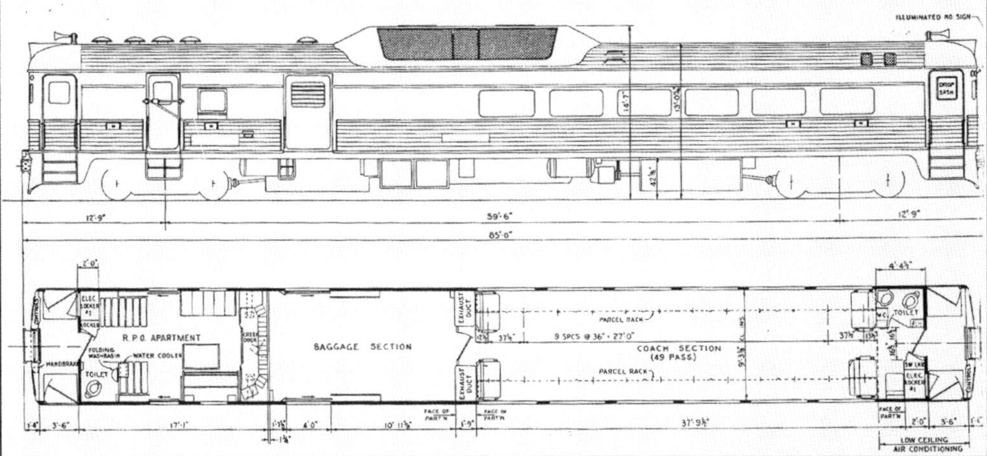

The RDC-3, whose plan is pictured here, combined passenger, baggage-express, and mail service, seating 49 passengers and including a 17-foot baggage-express compartment. This car was separated by two bulkheads. The 15-foot railway mail compartment had a creep door into the luggage section.

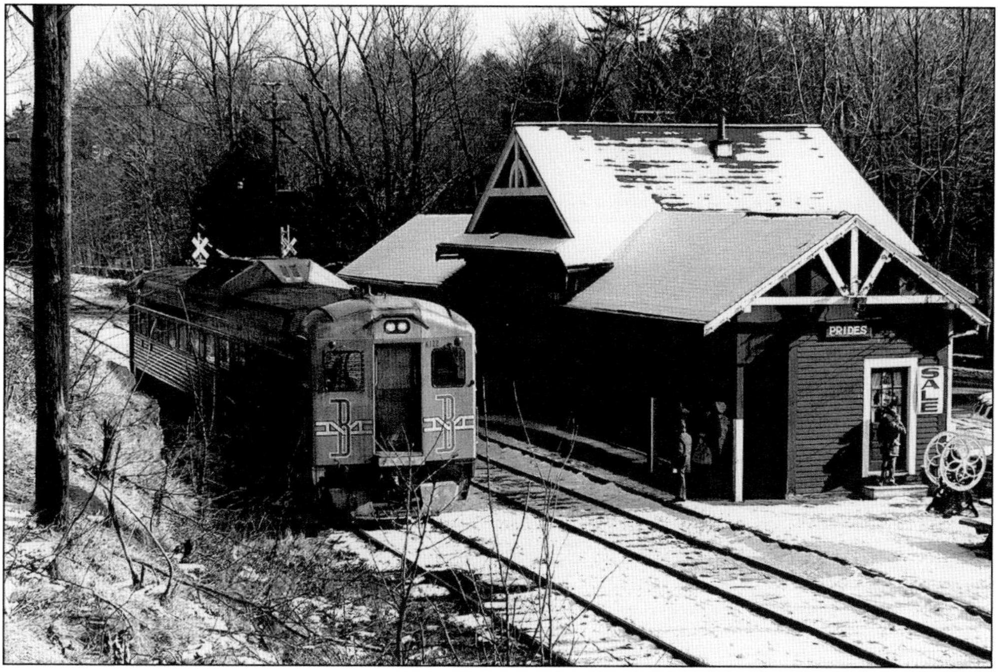

RDC-1 No. 6122 is seen at the rear of the former station building at Prides Crossing on the Gloucester branch in the 1940s. The building is now being used as the Prides Crossing General Store. The two platform benches have for decades been labeled "Republican" and "Democrat."

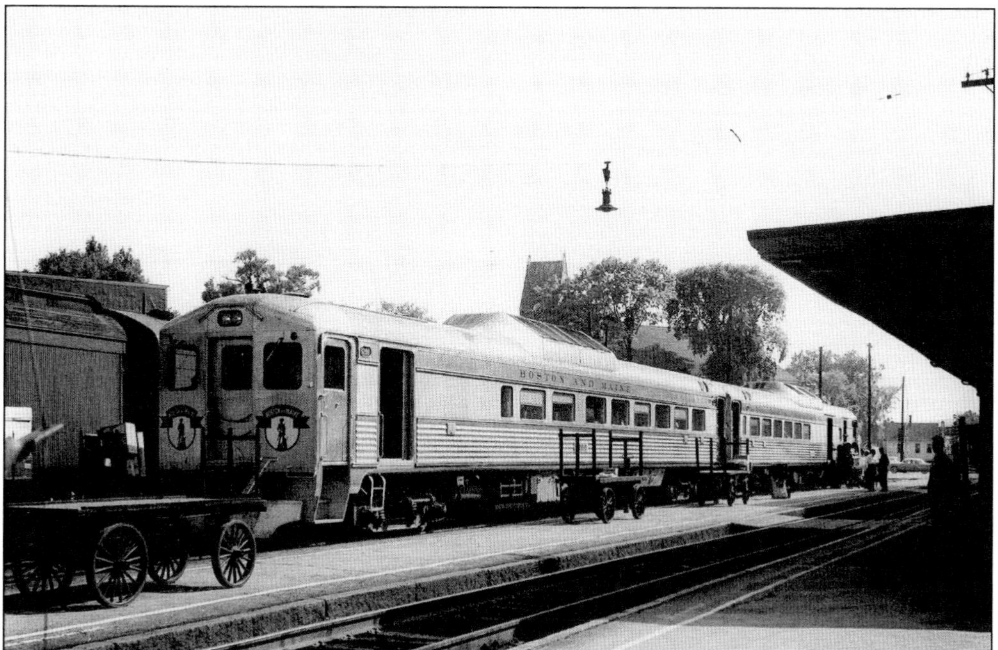

B&M RDC-2 No. 6200 and RDC-3 No. 6300 appear in Dover, New Hampshire, en route to Boston as train No. 168, the *Businessman*, during the mid-1950s.

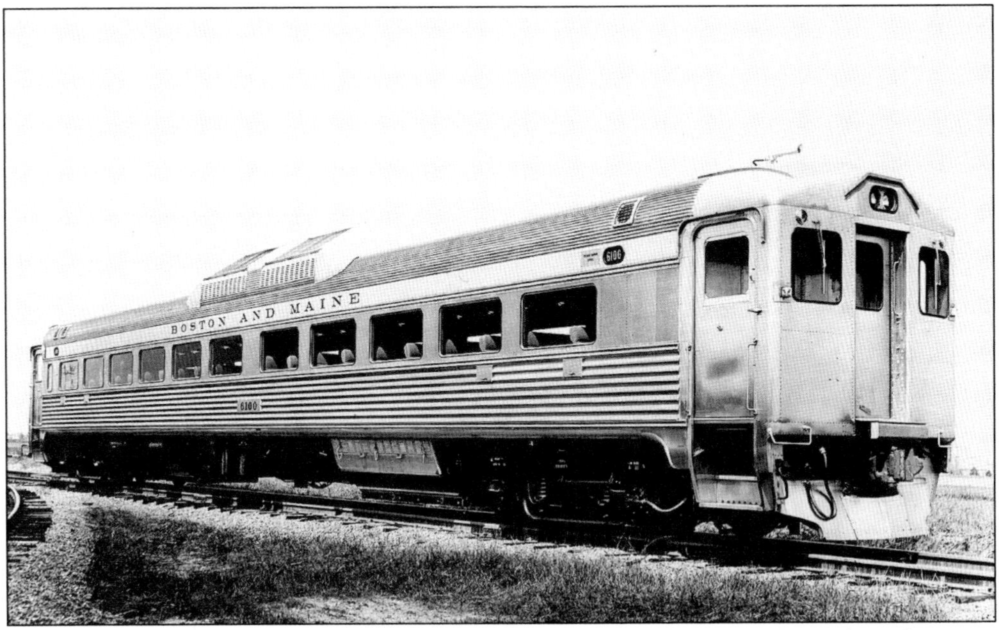

B&M No. 6100 rests proudly on a sidetrack in 1987. Note that there is no B&M logo shown, as it was a demonstrator car on display from the Budd Company. It was placed on the car after the photograph was taken, around the 1950s. Also note that the B&M did not buy Budd demonstrator No. 2960.

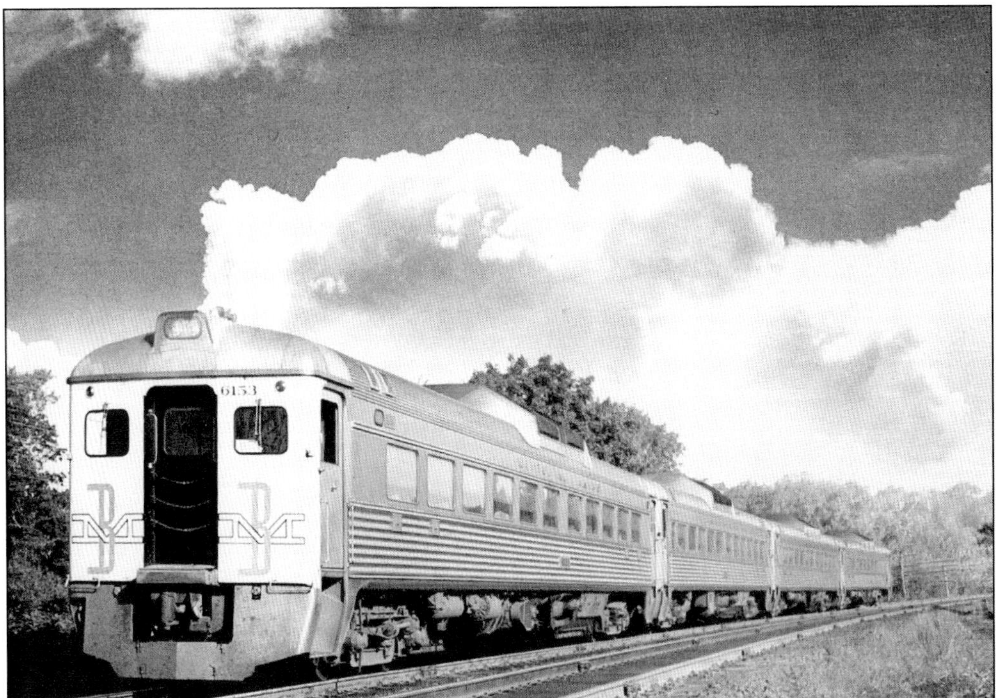

The B&M trains of Budd RDCs were known as the *Highliners*. The Boston and Maine Railroad had the largest fleet of air-conditioned, self-propelled, deluxe Budd *Highliners* in the world.

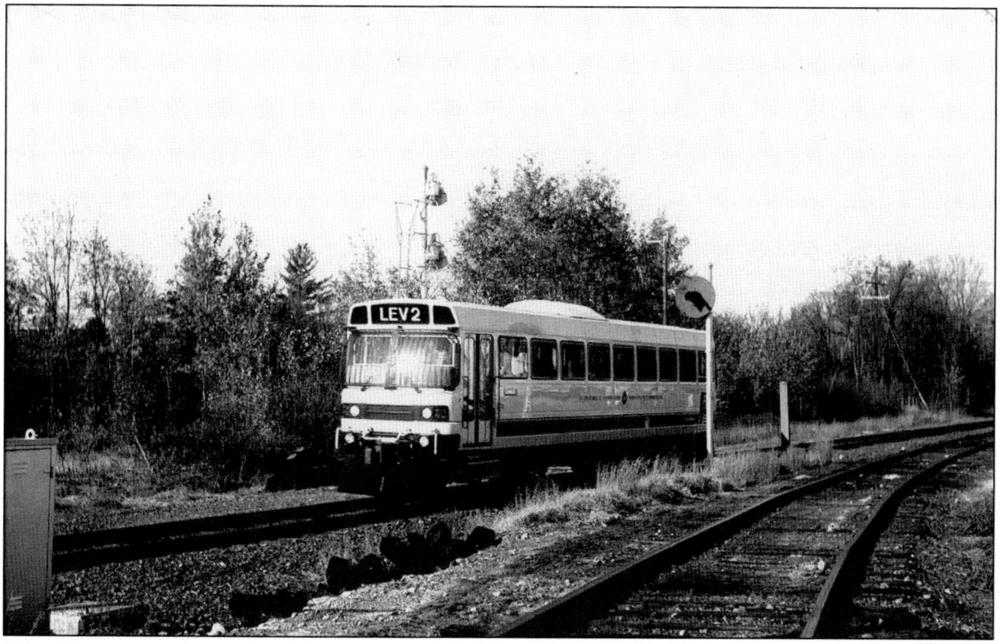

The LEV2 passes Bow Junction in New Hampshire during a special test run, its debut, on October 30, 1980. This vehicle was a two-axle, 56-seat marriage between the most advanced technologies of highway and rail transport industries and was capable of speeds up to 80 miles per hour.

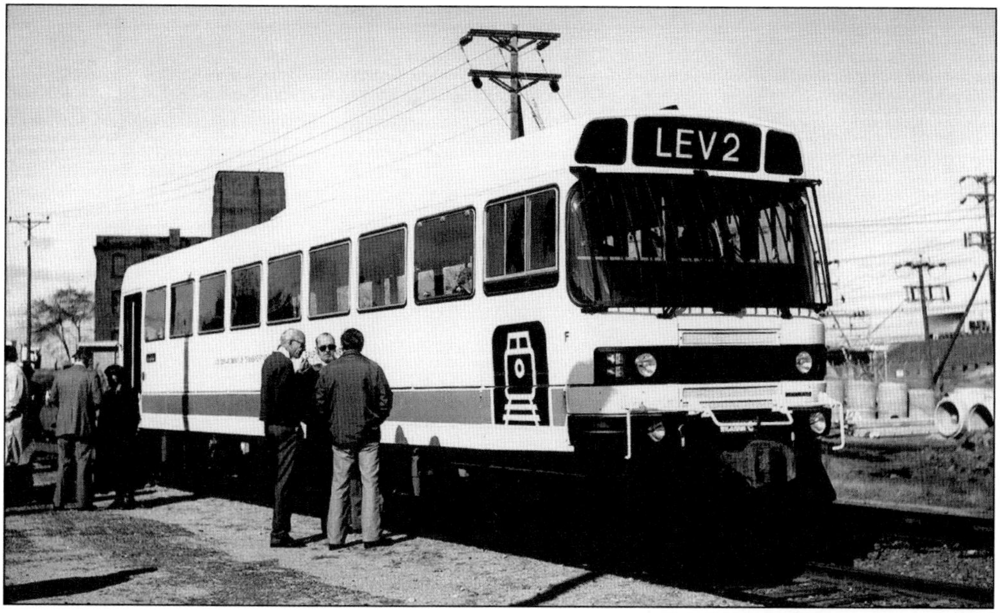

On October 30, 1980, the B&M ran the LEV2 from Boston to Concord, New Hampshire, for the benefit of Governor Gallen and various rail officials. This slightly longer version of the earlier LEV1, which had visited the B&M in 1979 for tests, began regular Concord–Lowell service on Monday, December 1, 1980. Here, the special waits at the Concord depot to return to Boston. Service lasted less than a year, terminating after the LEV was damaged in a highway crossing accident in 1981.

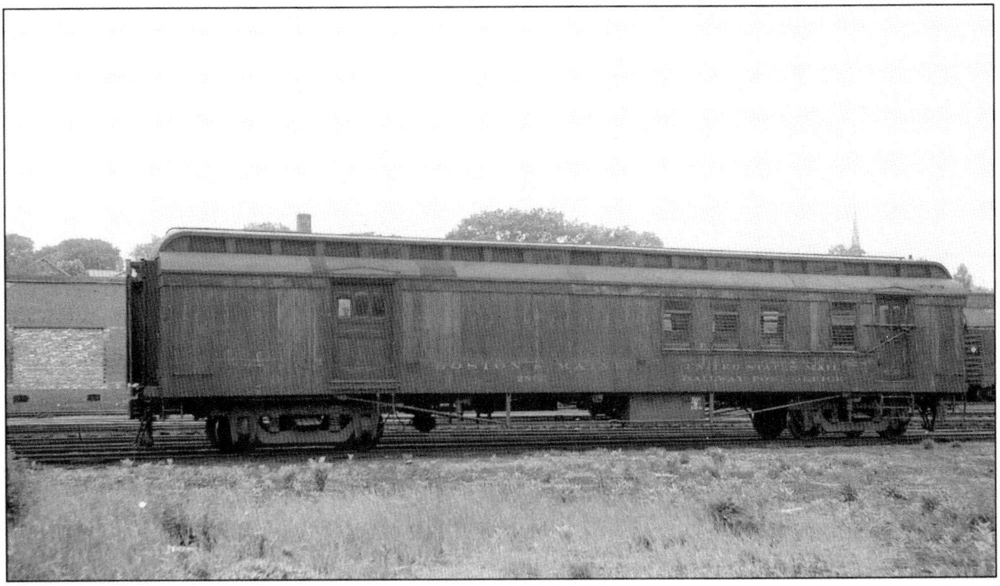

B&M all-wood U.S. baggage and U.S. mail car No. 2396, appears at Concord, New Hampshire, on May 31, 1952. The history of the rail post office (RPO) on the B&M began when the company procured nine full-mail wooden cars during the first decade of the 20th century. In 1911, Congressional law mandated that all railway post office cars be constructed of all steel or have a steel frame retrofitted under the existing wood frame.

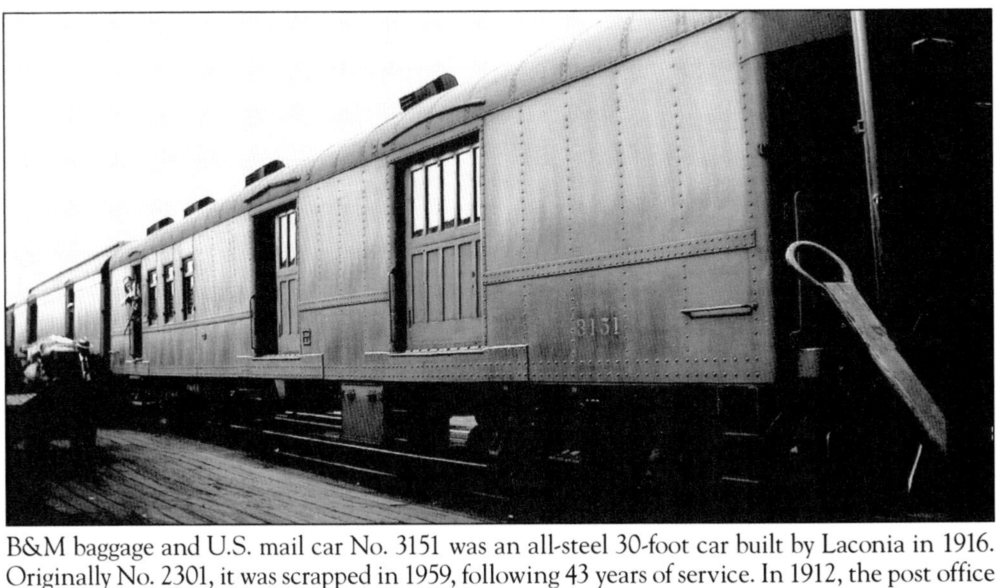

B&M baggage and U.S. mail car No. 3151 was an all-steel 30-foot car built by Laconia in 1916. Originally No. 2301, it was scrapped in 1959, following 43 years of service. In 1912, the post office published guidelines for the construction of steel cars for three compartment sizes, and in 1916, the law was amended to require that all cars on main-line routes be built of all-steel construction. This law ushered in the steel era on the Boston and Maine.

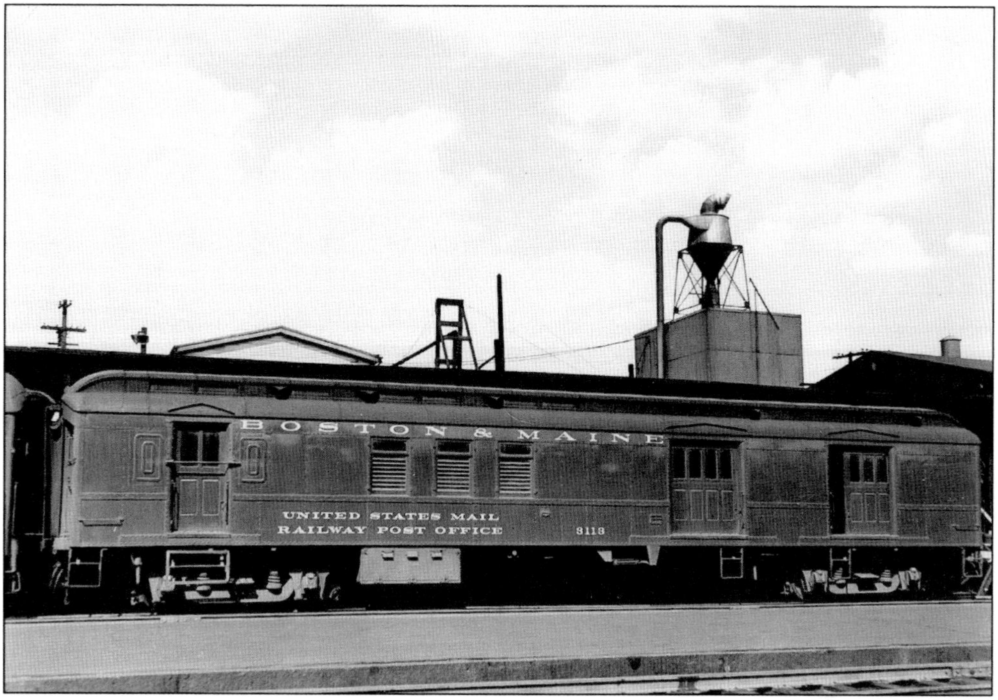

B&M baggage and U.S. mail car No. 3113 was part of a group of five all-steel cars with 30-foot mail compartments purchased from Osgood Bradley in 1929. No. 3113 saw service until 1929, when it was scrapped. This express car is seen at North Station in Boston on April 22, 1951.

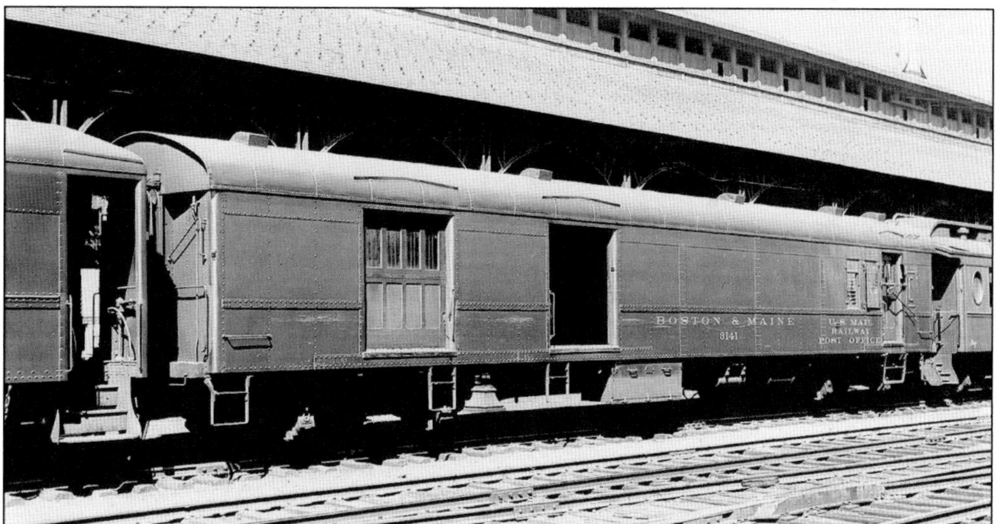

B&M baggage and U.S. mail car No. 3141, with a 15-foot mail compartment, is shown at Concord, New Hampshire, on July 29, 1947. The all-steel car was built in 1929 by the Osgood Bradley Company of Worcester, Massachusetts. It was rebuilt as baggage car No. 3289 in 1955 and finally scrapped in 1959. An important characteristic of car choice was the maximum width of the door opening. There were three major groupings of cars: those with four-foot, six-foot, and eight-foot openings. The history of these has been broken up into express-only cars, wooden baggage-express cars, and steel baggage cars.

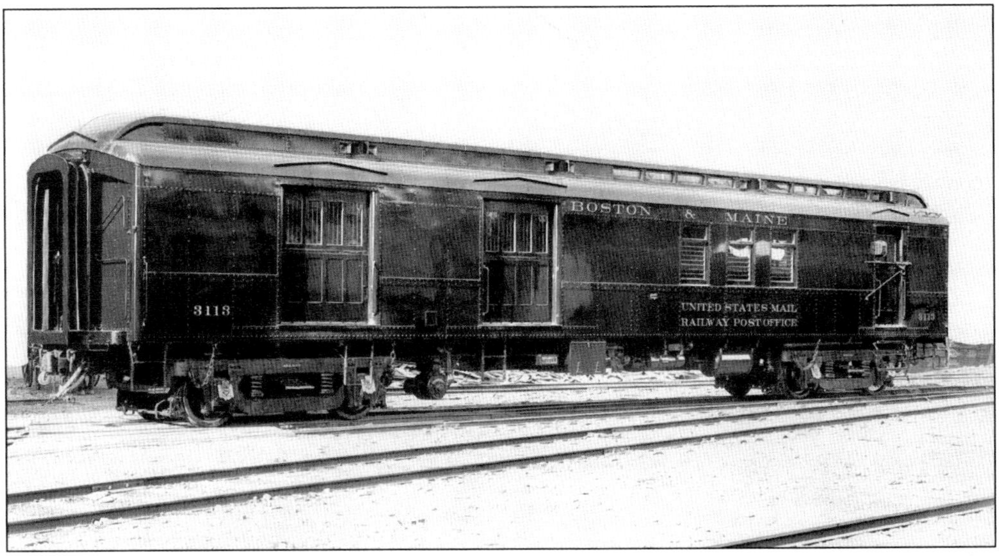

W448 Pullman/Worcester lot 6880 car No. 3113 was a 60-foot steel U.S. baggage-mail car. The 60-foot cars were dedicated completely to mail service and were all in Association of American Railroad Class MA. The railroad then procured 18 new all-steel 60-foot RPO cars from three different builders between 1914 and 1918, originally numbered 2282 to 2299. The new 60-foot wooden cars were converted over to 2900-series baggage cars, which always showed their heritage in their six-wheel trucks. Before the renumbering of the early 1920s, two of the new steel cars, including No. 3113, were converted into 30-foot compartment combines.

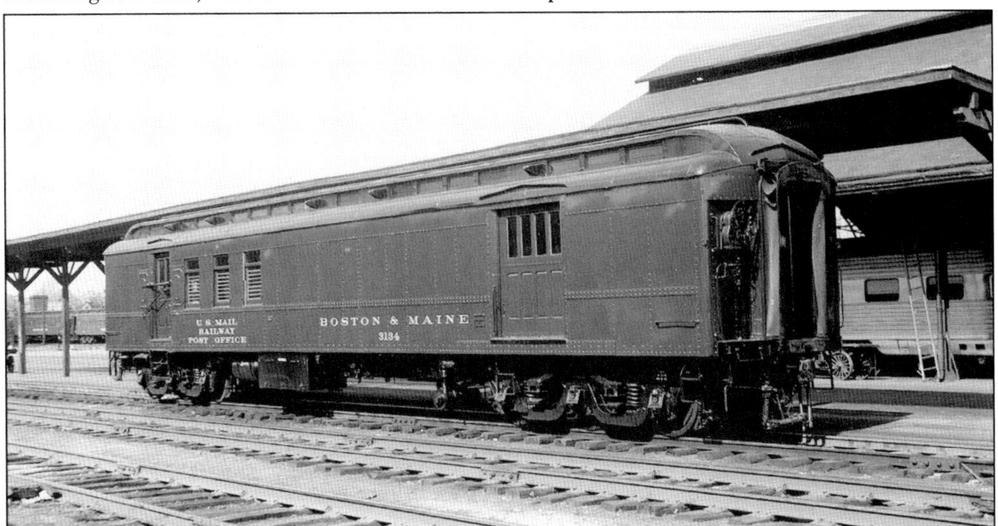

B&M baggage and U.S. mail car No. 3134 appears at Portland, Maine, on April 22, 1956. At one end of the car is a 30-foot mail compartment. The first two all-steel cars were purchased in 1916 from the Laconia Car Company and were assigned road numbers 2300 and 2301. These cars had a 70-foot overall length, which included a 40-foot baggage compartment. They rode on six-wheel trucks and were the longest RPO cars ever owned by the B&M. In the 1920s, they were renumbered 3150 and 3151. The two 60-foot cars that were rebuilt were Nos. 2302 and 2303, which became B&M Nos. 3100 and 3101. After the renumbering, all the Class MB steel cars became part of the 3100 series.

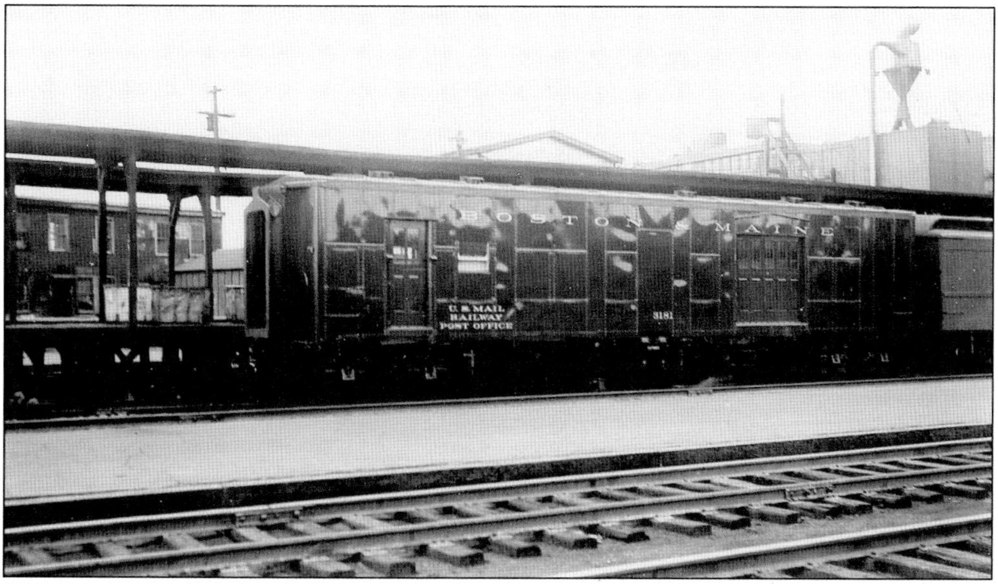

B&M baggage and U.S. mail car No. 3181 was a former army troop sleeper that, after World War II, was converted into an RPO with a 15-foot mail compartment. It is seen at Boston's North Station on April 9, 1949.

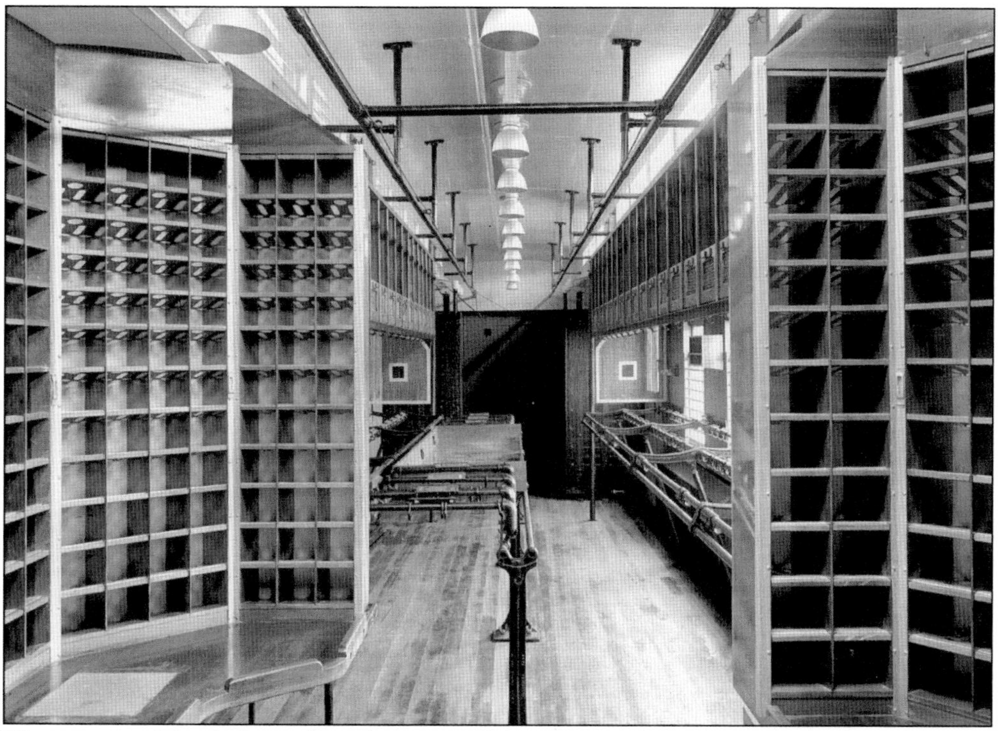

The interior of the 60-foot, all-steel W242 Pullman U.S. mail car, lot CO-5785, was typical of a mail car. Up to 14 postal workers could be assigned to sort the mail in this car. The safety of postal workers was a driving force in the government mandate to convert to all-steel construction.

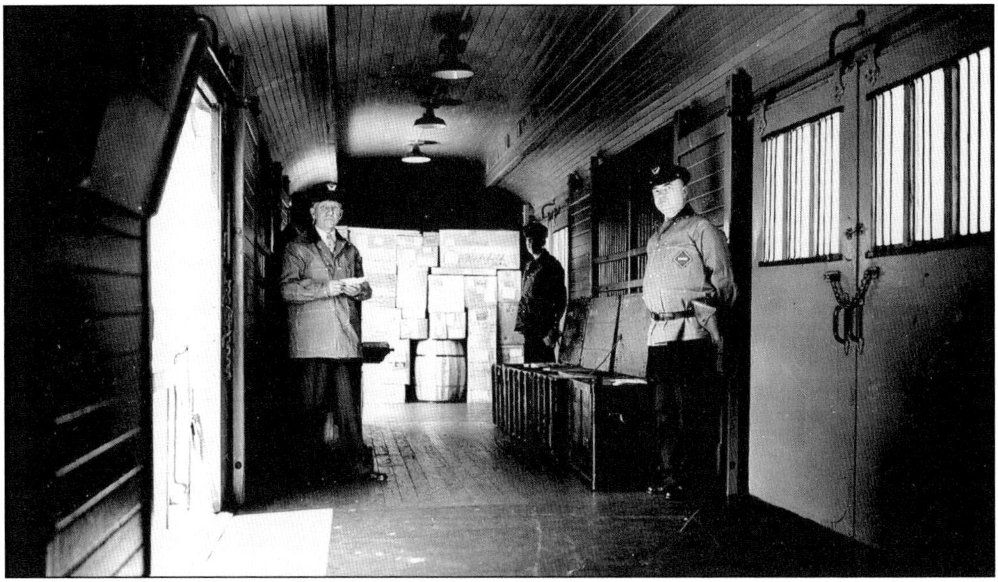

The wooden B&M baggage railway express car No. 2813 prepares to leave Boston's North Station on June 16, 1935. The three gentlemen seen inside the car are Railway Express Agency employees who will soon begin to sort the baggage and mail for delivery.

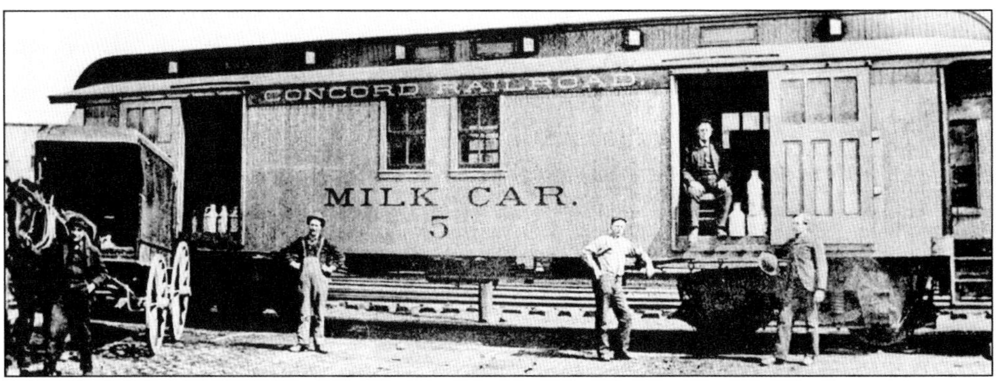

Concord Railroad milk car No. 5 is shown at Charlestown, Massachusetts, in the 1880s. The gentleman seated in the doorway is H. P. Hood. The milk car predecessor was the baggage car, running on many services in New England, especially on the branch trains during the mid-1880s. The train baggage man received the loaded cans at the way station and signed receipts, and the carload was delivered to the dairy in Boston. These cars were built by the Laconia Car Company, "Manufacturers of Railway Cars of Every Description."

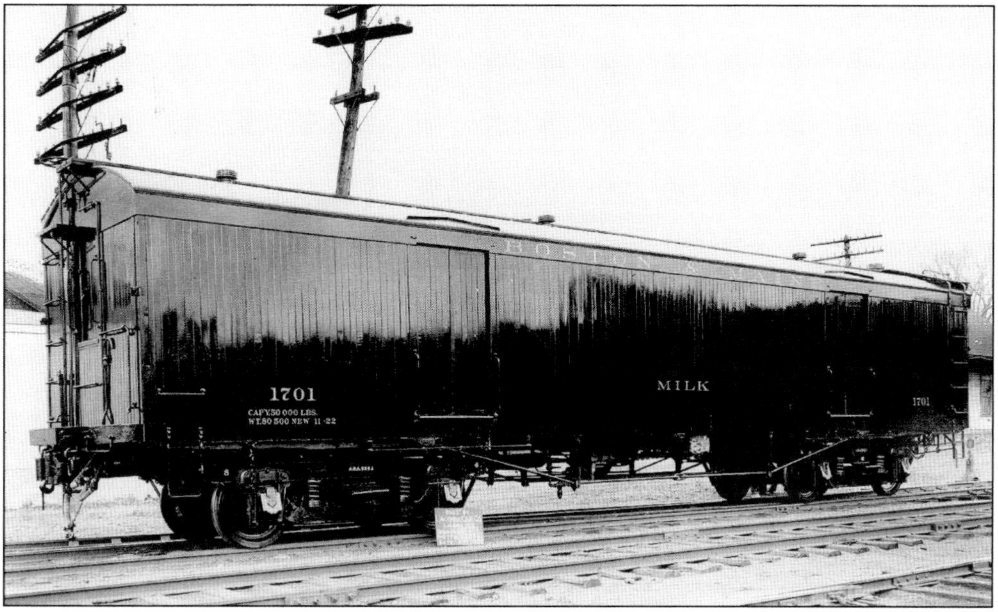

B&M milk car No. 1701 was one of 25 built about 1958 by the Laconia Car Company of Laconia, New Hampshire, designed for use in passenger or freight service. The two double doors on each side opened inward, and the car included Commonwealth four-wheel-type trucks with 36-inch rolled steel wheels. The length over the sills was 51 feet; the width over the side sheathing was 9 feet 11 inches; the height, rail to eaves, was 11 feet 6 inches; and the weight of the loaded car was 80,500 pounds.

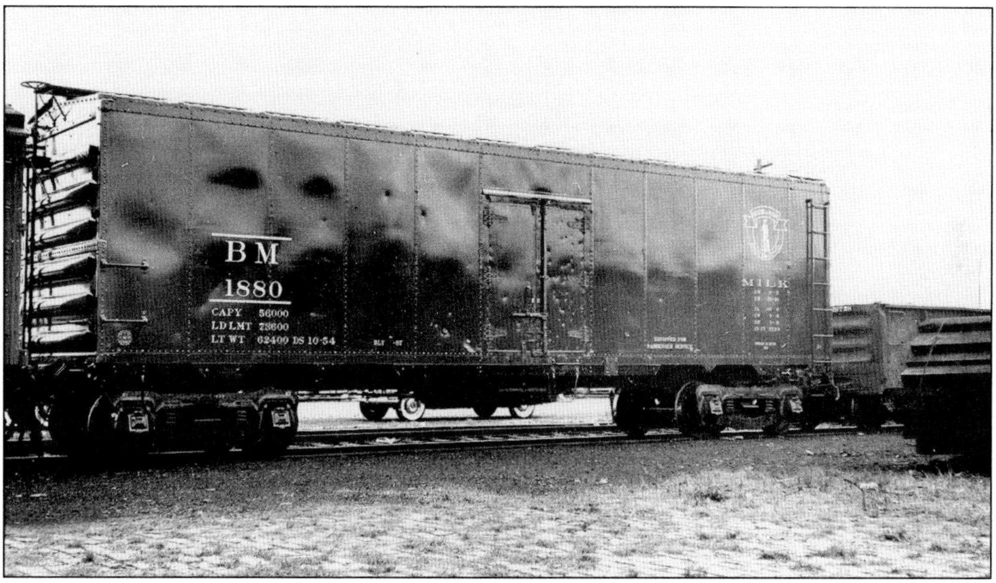

Built in 1937, B&M milk car No. 1880 is shown at Mystic Junction on November 1, 1954. With the rapid expansion of the milk industry, and the greater quantities of full-milk-can volume needed, baggage service rapidly became only an auxiliary mode limited to short, feeder lines or emergency needs of creameries or dealers. By 1960, the B&M's average baggage revenue had dwindled to $300 to $500 a month, primarily from jugs from the Central Vermont Railway via White River Junction, plus small interline amounts to the New Haven Railroad.

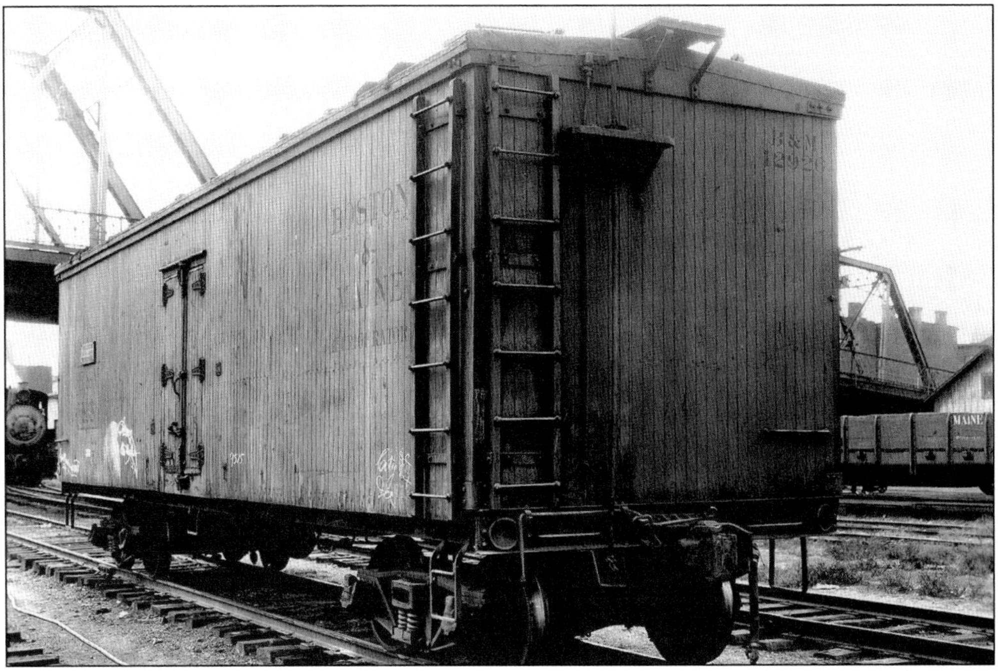

B&M refrigerator car No. 12926 sits in the yard at Troy, New York. Until about the 1950s, refrigerator cars all included ice bunkers on both ends. The cars themselves were costly to build and maintain and generally ran half of their mileage empty, though their owners sometimes succeeded in getting back-hauls of clean merchandise. Insulation and ice bunkers took up much of their interior space, so their cubic foot capacity was smaller than that of a comparable boxcar.

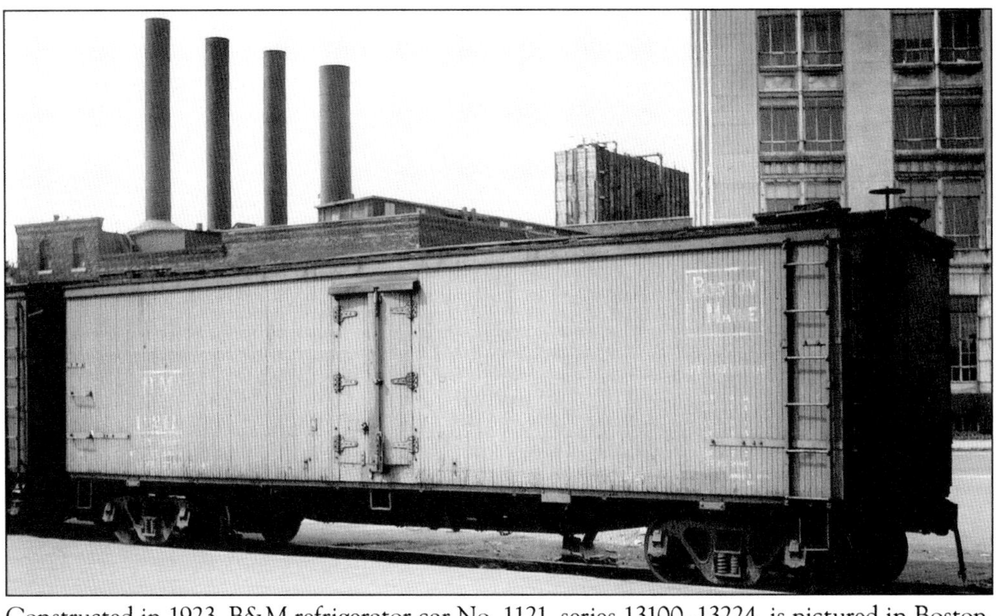

Constructed in 1923, B&M refrigerator car No. 1121, series 13100–13224, is pictured in Boston. Long strings of refrigerator cars traveling east from the Pacific Coast and north from Florida and the Gulf Coast carried fresh, ripe oranges, grapefruit, grapes, peaches, lettuce, and other perishables of field and grove to grocery stores in every part of New England.

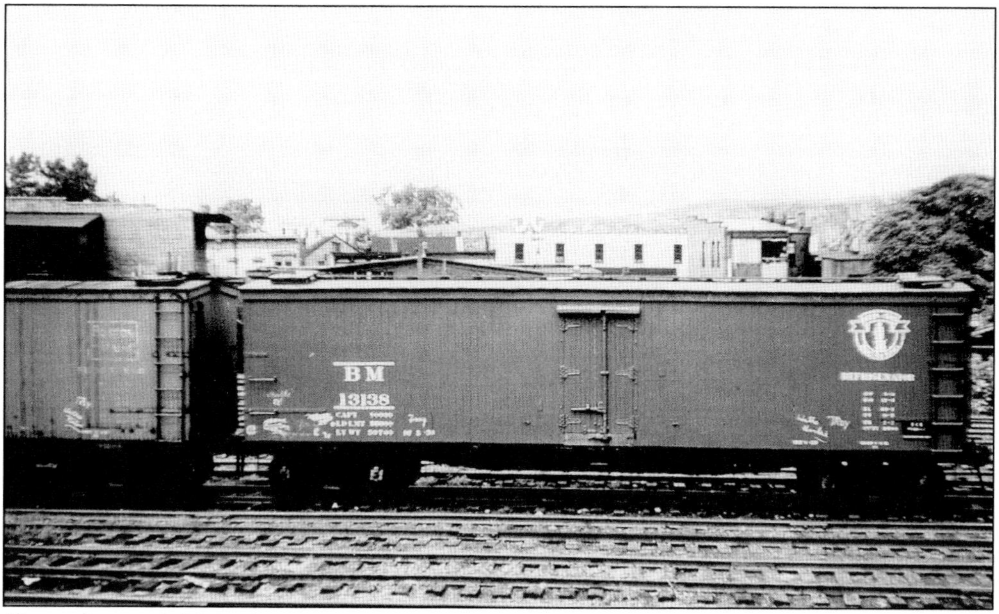

Shown here is B&M refrigerator car No. 13138, series 13100–13224, at Troy, New York, on July 30, 1950. To keep perishables fresh, railroads had to provide icing decks at frequent intervals. In many cases, these decks also had to be supplied with ice and salt hauled from a considerable distance in nonrevenue cars.

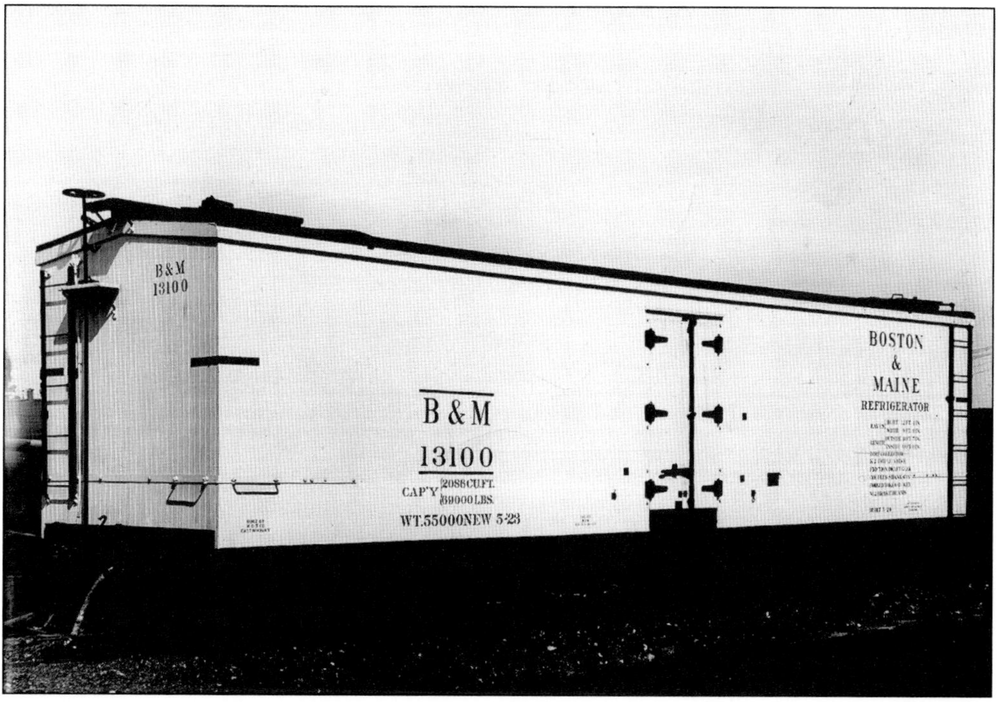

B&M refrigerator car No. 13100 was used as a demonstrator car. Before the company bought any new cars, officials examined the latest on the market. During the mid-1900s, mechanical refrigeration supplanted ice refrigeration. The mechanical refrigeration units proved their worth in replacing the armies of railroad employees who were no longer needed to re-ice the cars.

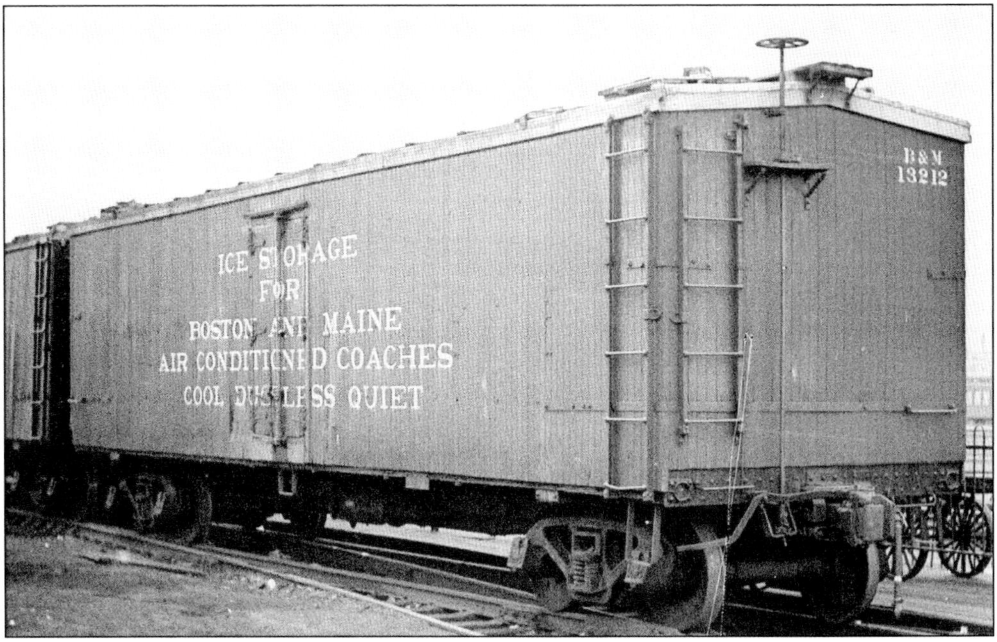

B&M ice-storage boxcar No. 13212 appears at North Station in Boston. Block ice was typically used in early-1930s air-conditioned diners and coaches.

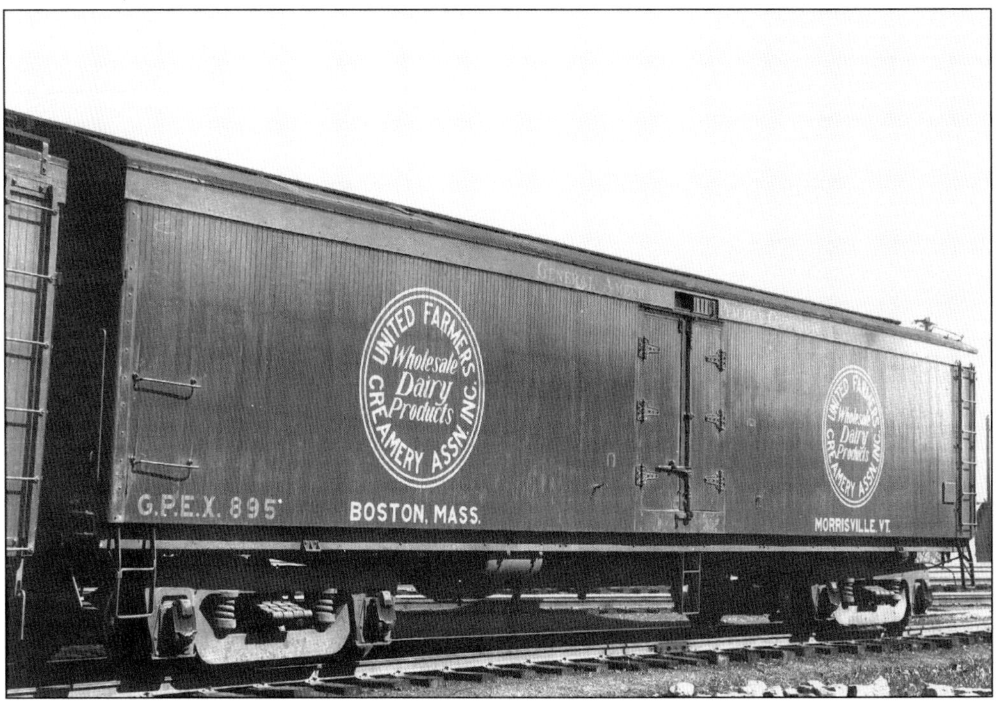

United Farmer's Creamery Association milk car No. GPEX 895 carried wholesale dairy products. In early refrigerator cars, it was difficult to maintain constant temperatures while under way; they required frequent re-icing and sometimes the use of salt in the bunkers to promote lower temperatures except in winter, when charcoal heaters were often needed to prevent perishable cargoes from freezing.

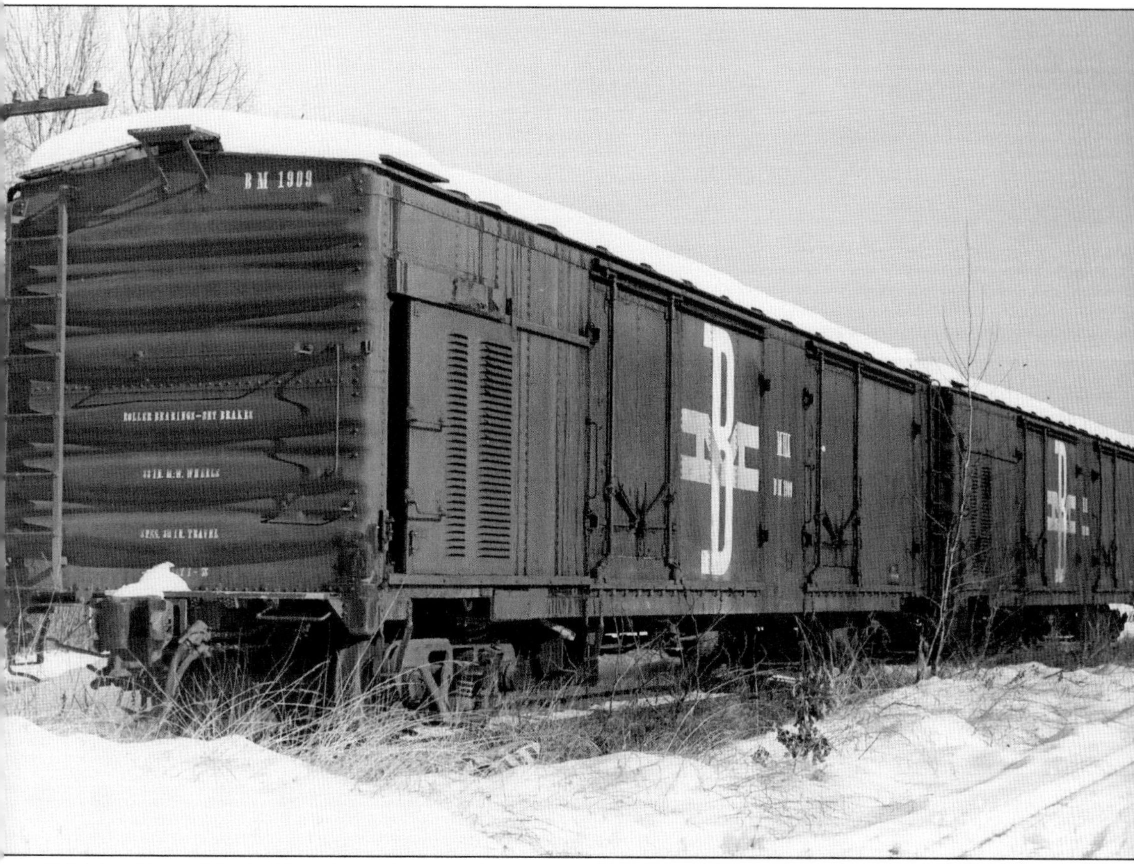

B&M milk car No. 1909 is shown here at East Deerfield, Massachusetts. By 1925, the railroad had 89 insulated milk cars, with 64 in this B&M series being built about 1917. These cars averaged 50 feet long with two doors per side.

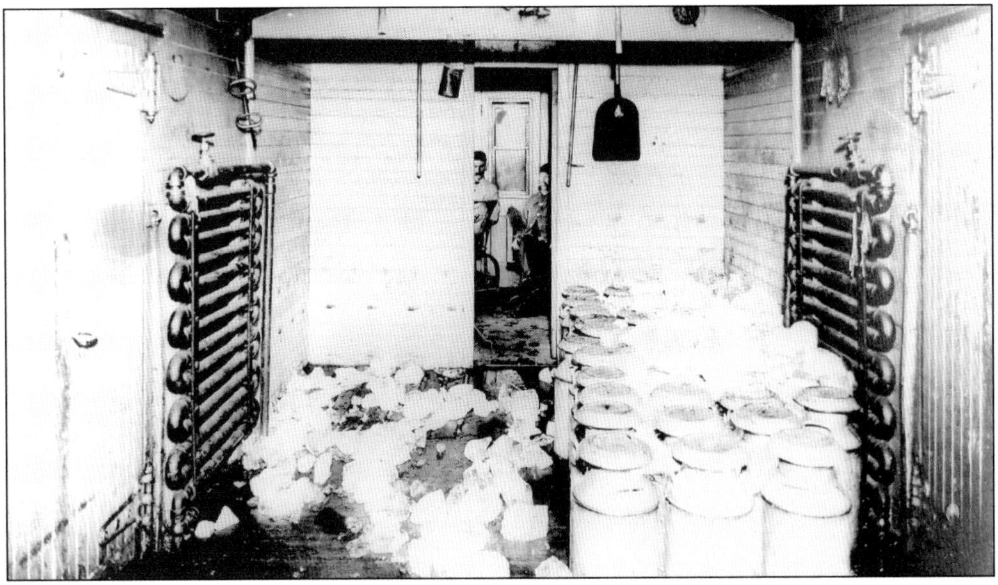

In this B&M milk car, the milk containers and ice occupy much of the space, while an office appears in the rear. The 40-quart cans were loaded in two tiers, one on another and braced in a specified manner using two-by-four-inch timbers and 40D or 50D heavy nails for nailing the braces to the floor and side walls. The milk train supplied the Boston market beginning in 1838 and ending on August 31, 1970. By 1930, over 93 percent of the milk was handled on these trains. Their rise in importance and ultimate decline is an interesting part of railroad history.

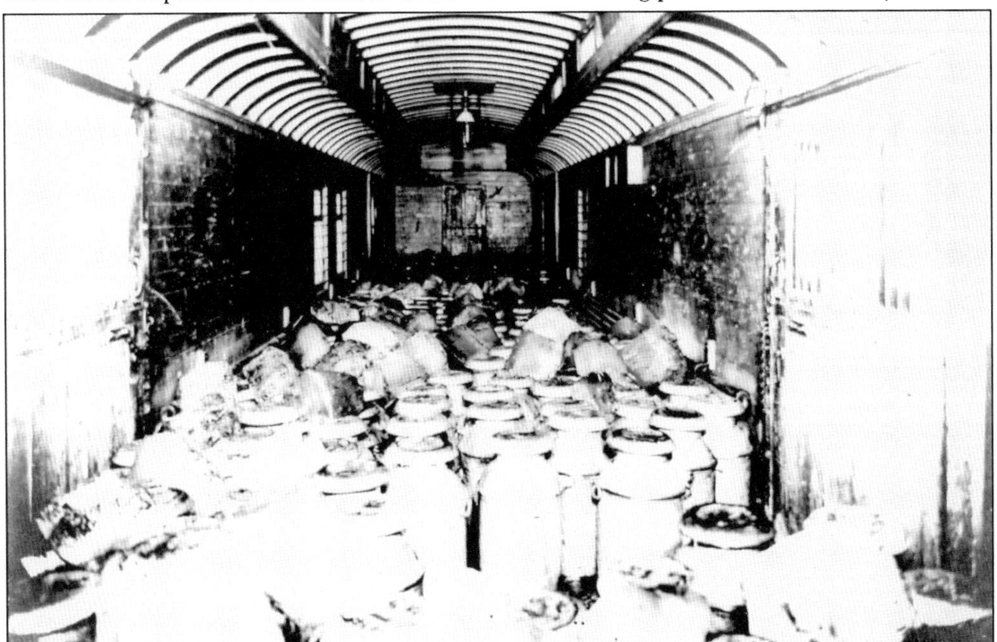

Milk containers are stored in ice in this view of the car interior. The B&M was considered a leading national milk handler during its peak years. Milk car operations required more time, care, and concern than any other single commodity that was hauled in greater volumes or that yielded higher revenues per hundred weight.

Two

FREIGHT AND WORK TRAINS

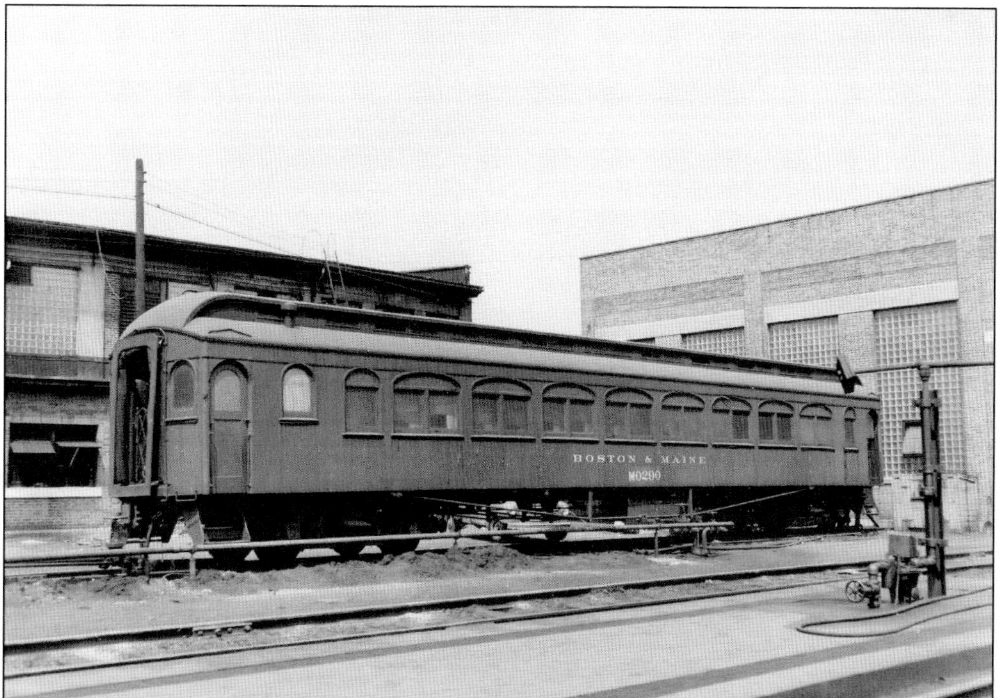

B&M instruction car No. MO290 is located at the B&M engine terminal on June 21, 1953. In the mid-1800s, a work train usually consisted of an old locomotive, a string of flatcars (platform cars), and a large gang of men. The first change was likely the addition of a tool car, which provided shelter and a place to store the tools.

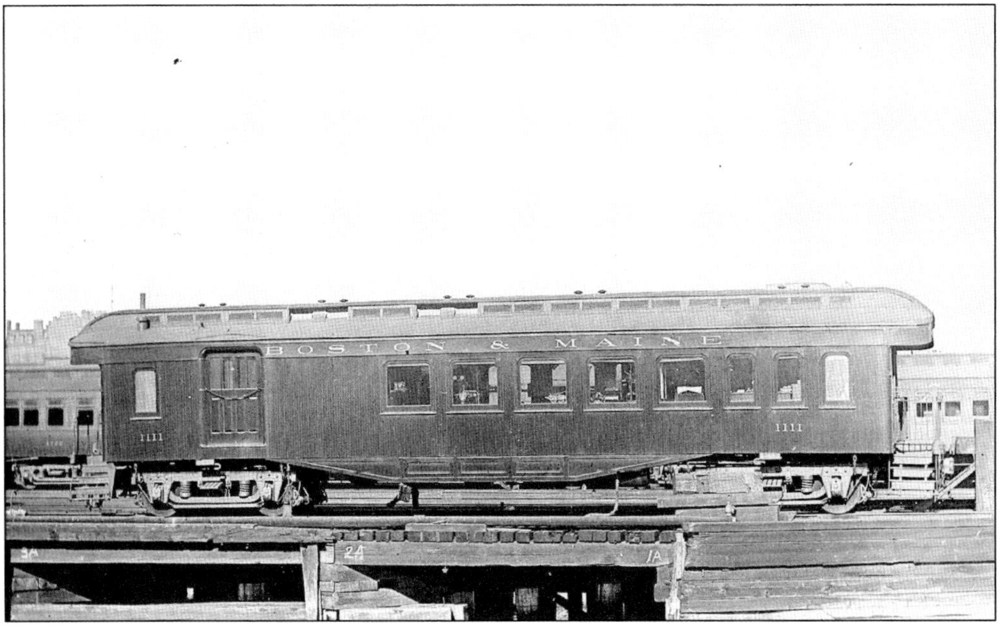

B&M air-brake instruction car No. 1111 was originally Worcester, Nashua and Portland No. 399, R/N 599. This car was destroyed on August 16, 1937, at the Billerica Shops in Billerica, Massachusetts.

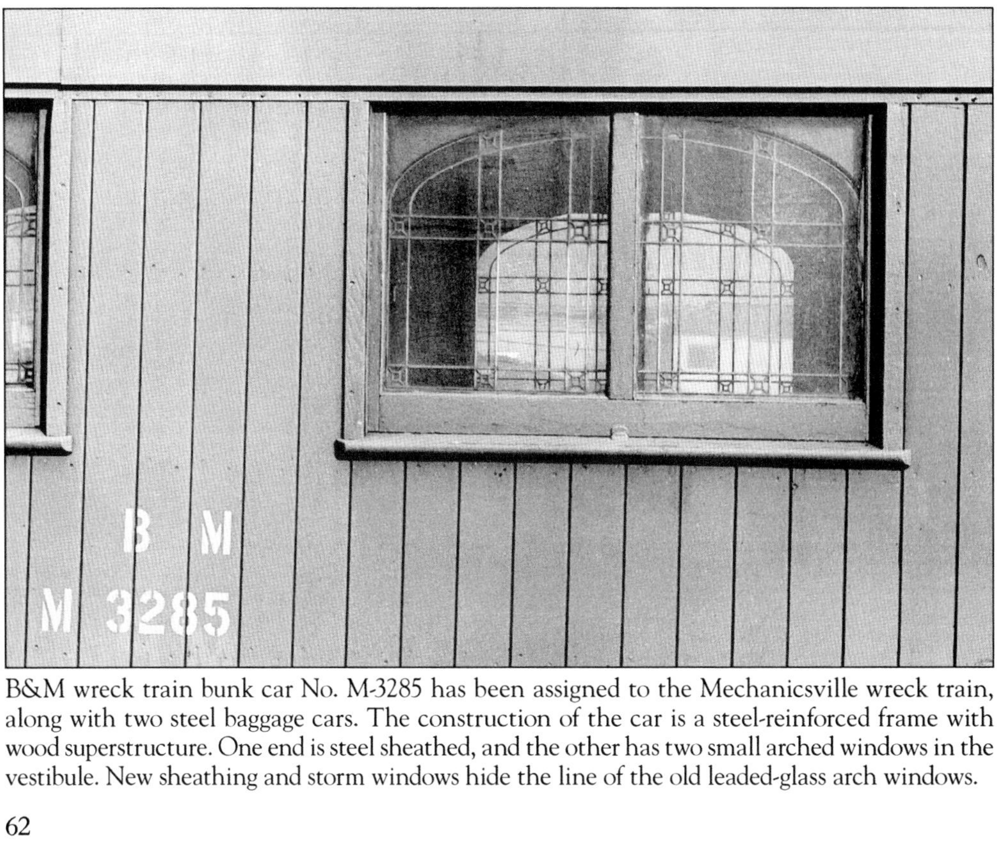

B&M wreck train bunk car No. M-3285 has been assigned to the Mechanicsville wreck train, along with two steel baggage cars. The construction of the car is a steel-reinforced frame with wood superstructure. One end is steel sheathed, and the other has two small arched windows in the vestibule. New sheathing and storm windows hide the line of the old leaded-glass arch windows.

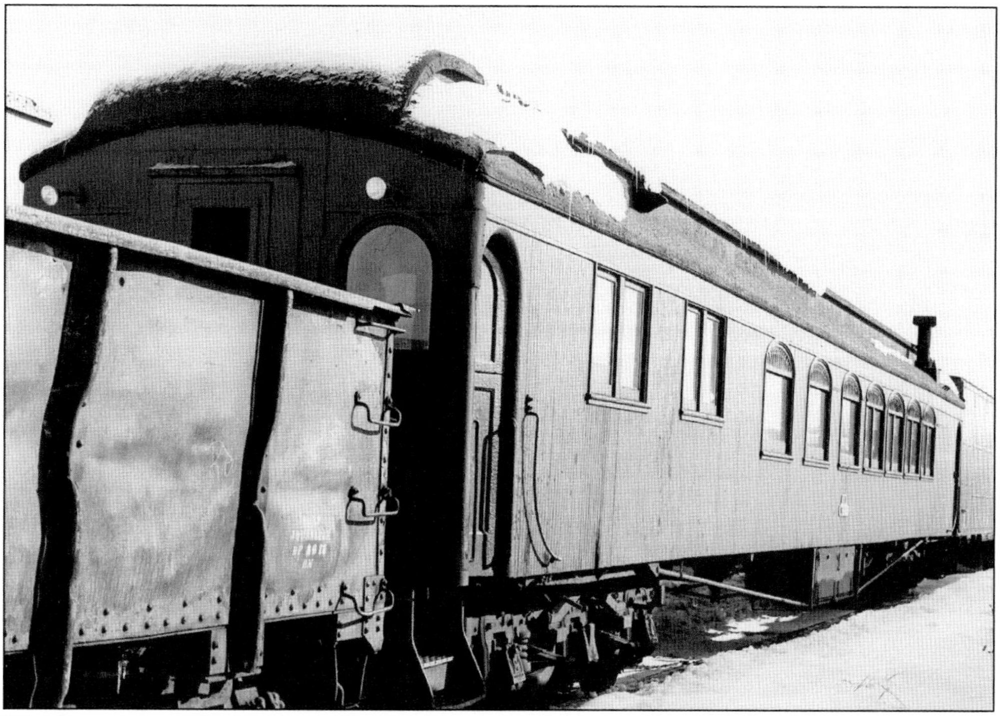

Wrecker train car No. M-3288 is shown in East Deerfield, Massachusetts, on December 28, 1975.

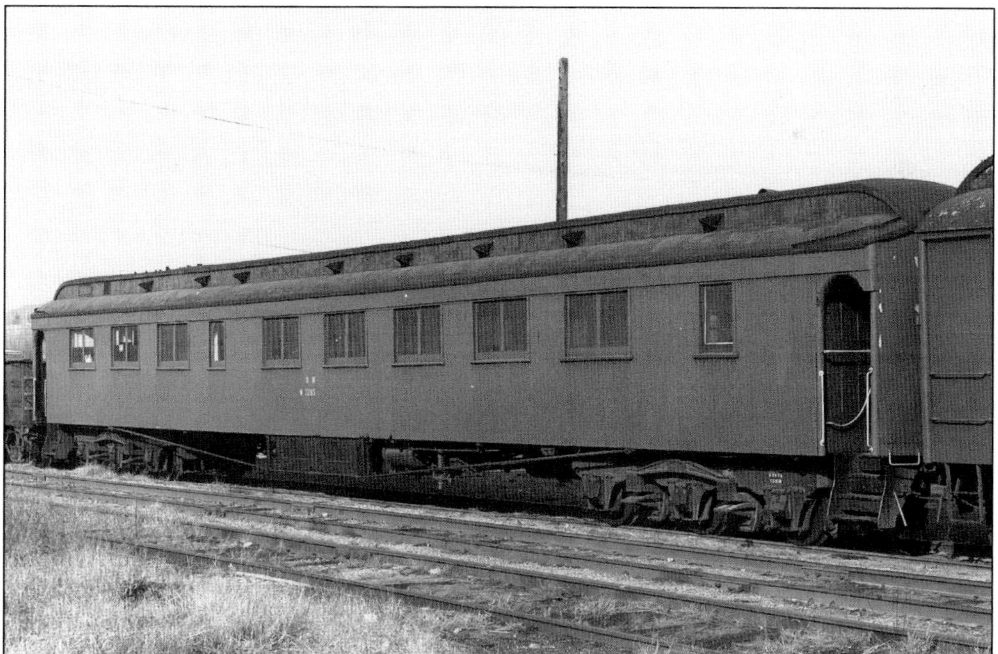

B&M wrecker train bunk and kitchen car No. M-3285 is pictured on November 20, 1975.

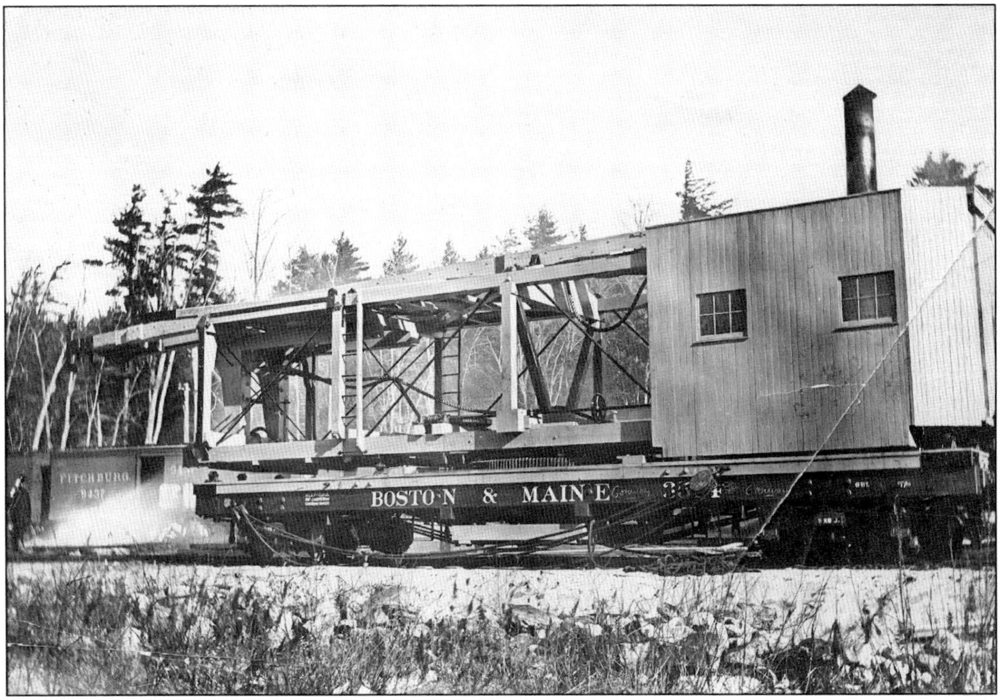

The B&M pile driver was built at the Sanbornville Railroad Shops, Sanbornville, New Hampshire, in 1905.

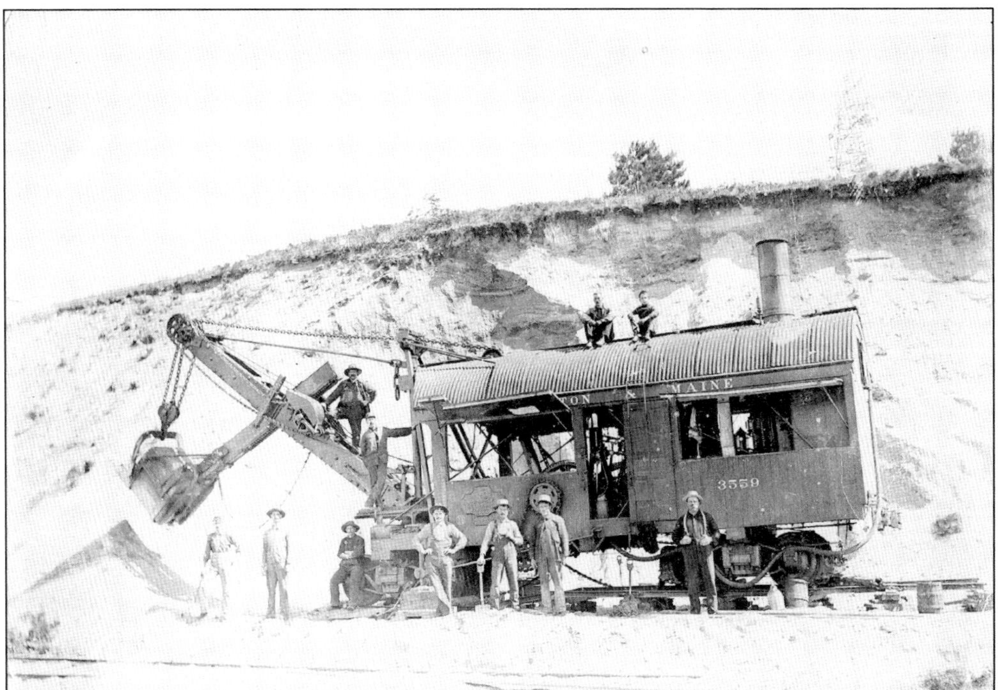

B&M steam shovel No. 3559 was constructed by the B&M in 1901.

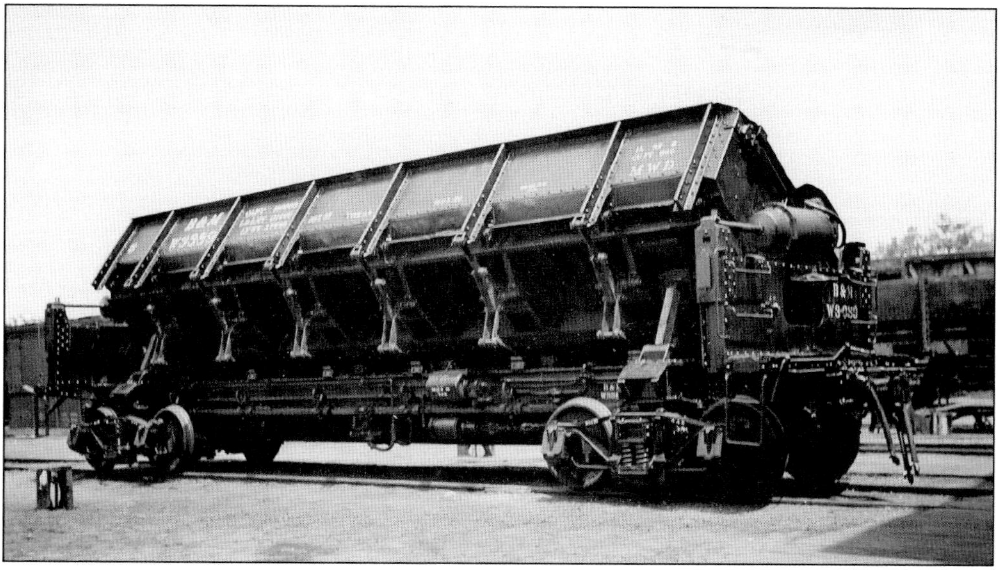

This side dump car was built by the Clark Car Company.

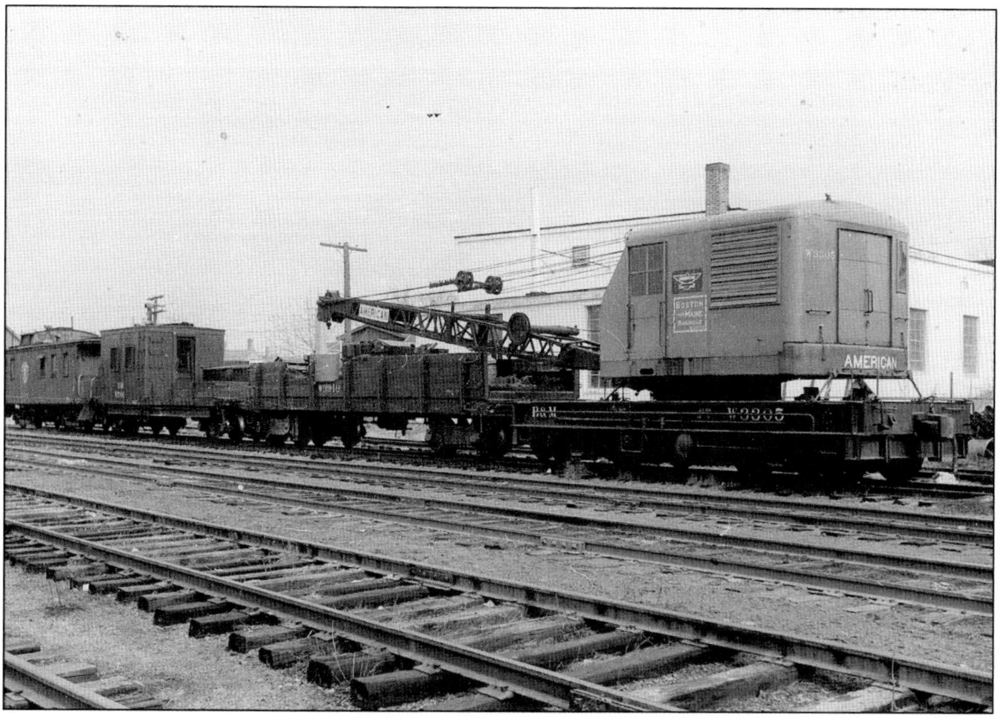

Most of the excavators, such as No. 3305, saw far more service as cranes than as excavators. This common type of work train was used to support track renewal, and its center was the crawler crane on its flatcar. After work was completed, the same train was used to pick up used material, either for reuse or scrap.

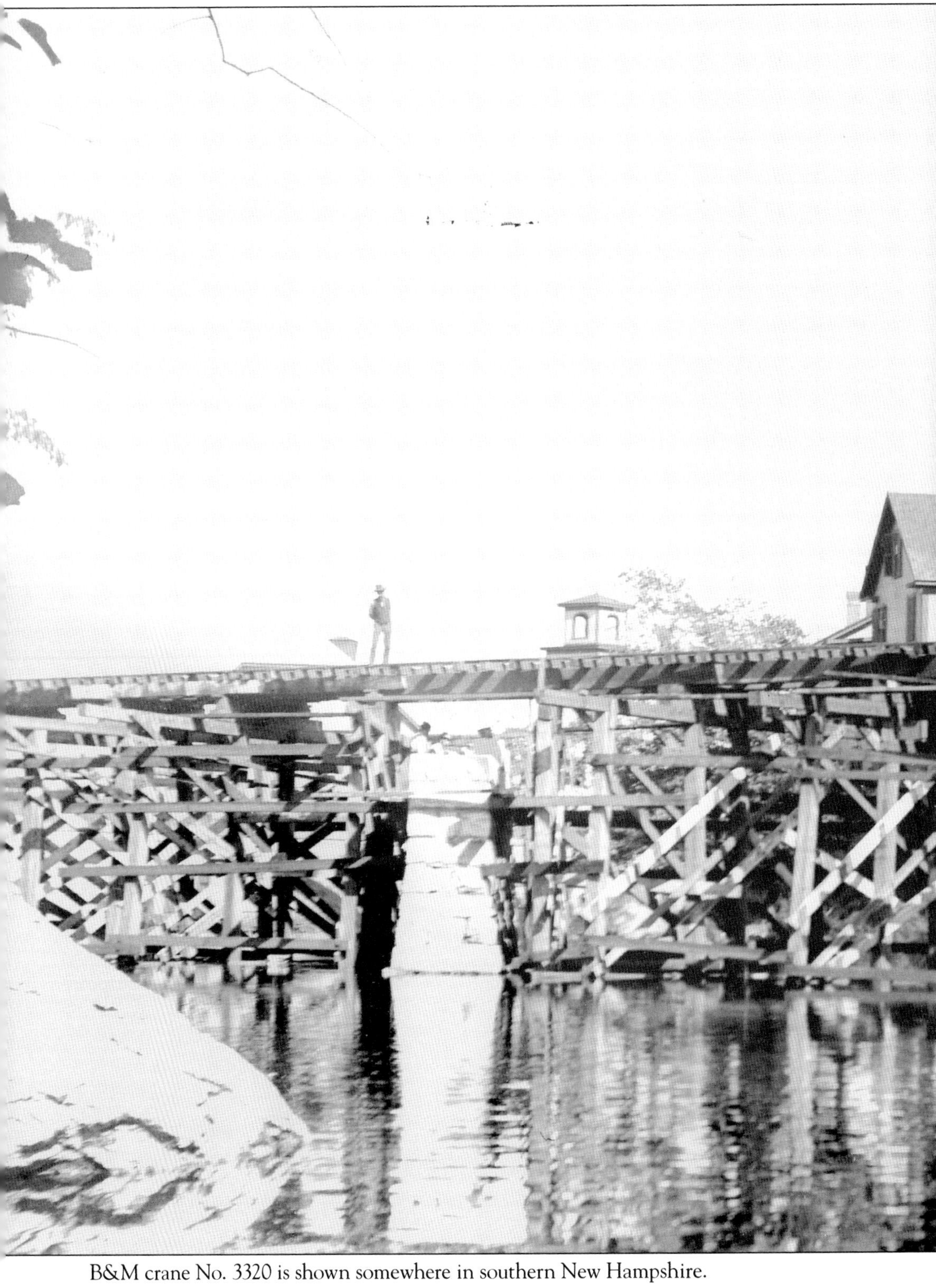

B&M crane No. 3320 is shown somewhere in southern New Hampshire.

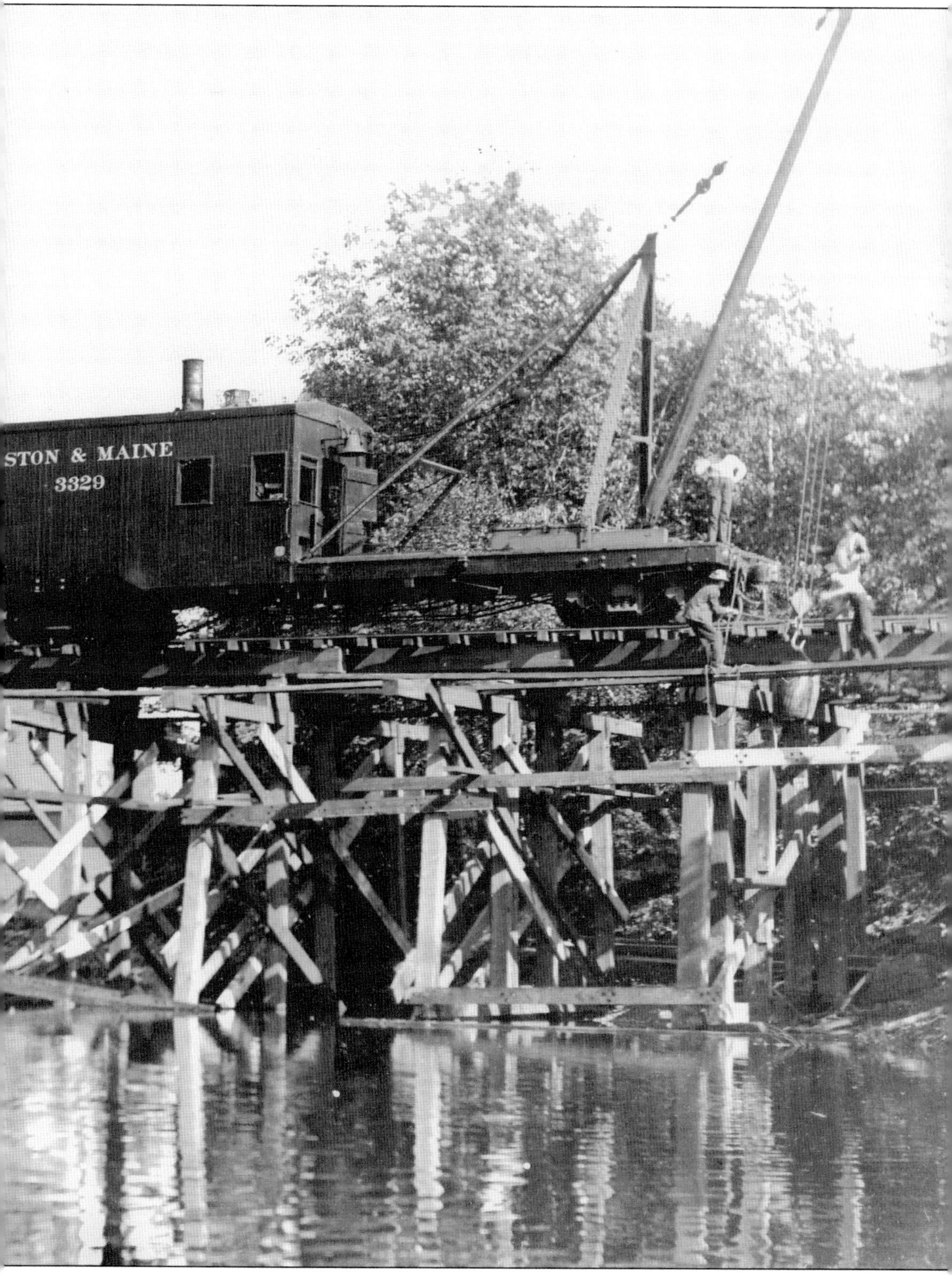
STON & MAINE
3329

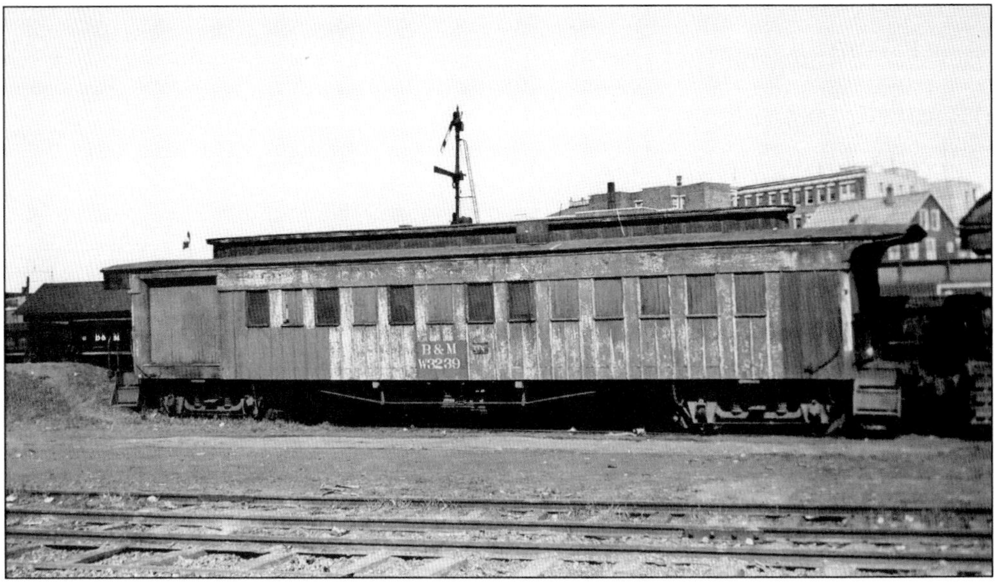

Pictured here is B&M maintenance-of-way car No. W-3239, which had been converted from passenger car No. 67 in 1896. It was destroyed at Salem, Massachusetts, in July 1939. In the 1870s and 1880s, other types of work equipment appeared such as pile drivers, derricks, snowplows, flangers, spreaders, ditchers, and dump cars. With the advent of all this specialized equipment, work trains took on a different personality and purpose.

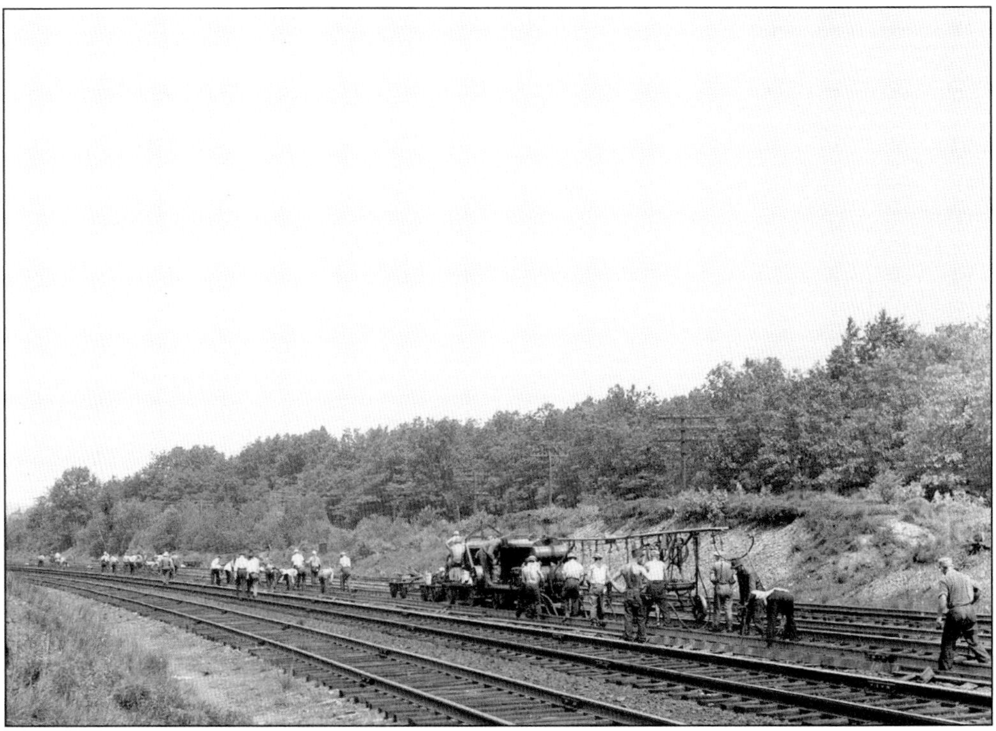

A B&M gang lays new rail between Ayer and Fitchburg, Massachusetts, on July 7, 1940.

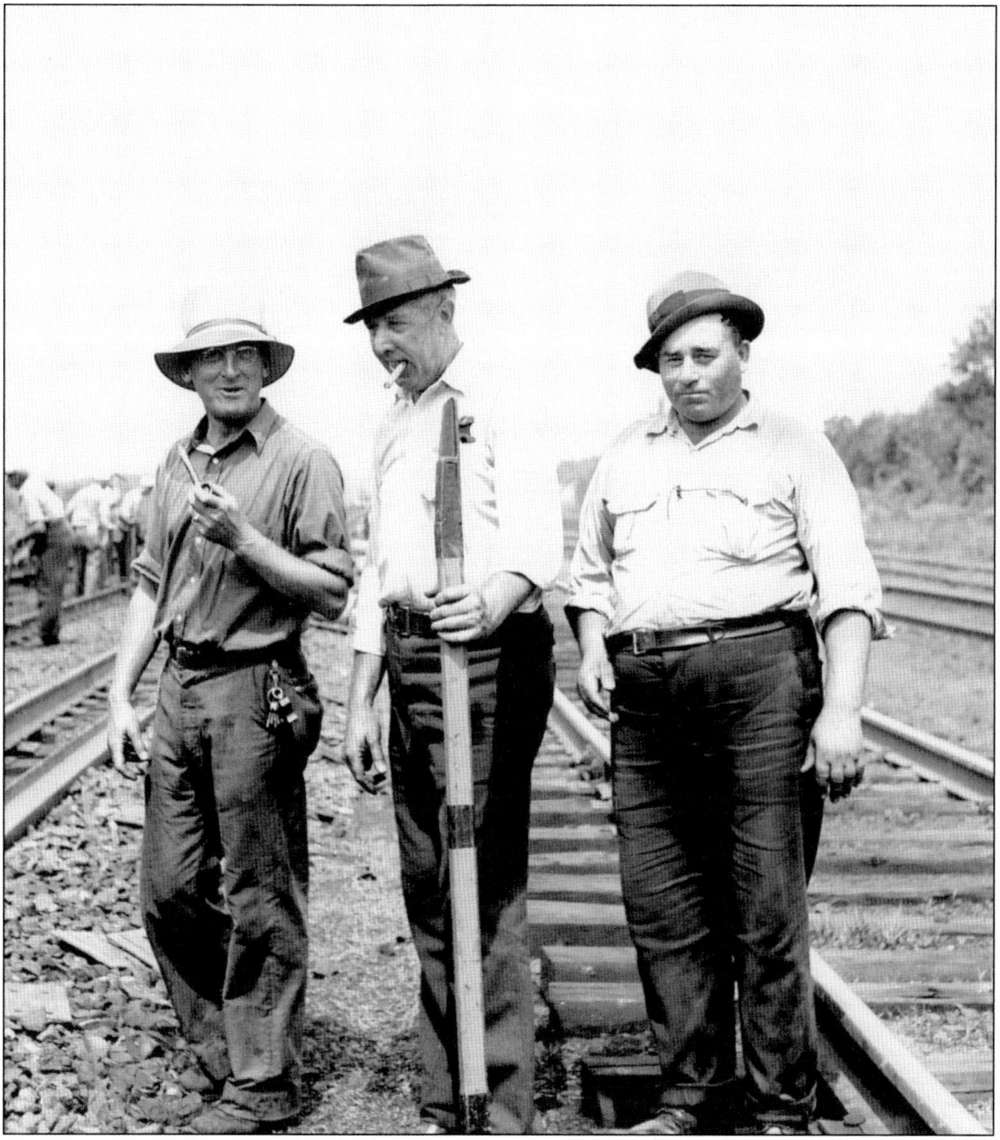

A B&M steel gang works at Fitchburg, Massachusetts, on July 7, 1940. They are, from left to right, Mr. Hosley, Mr. Molloy, and Mr. Daleo.

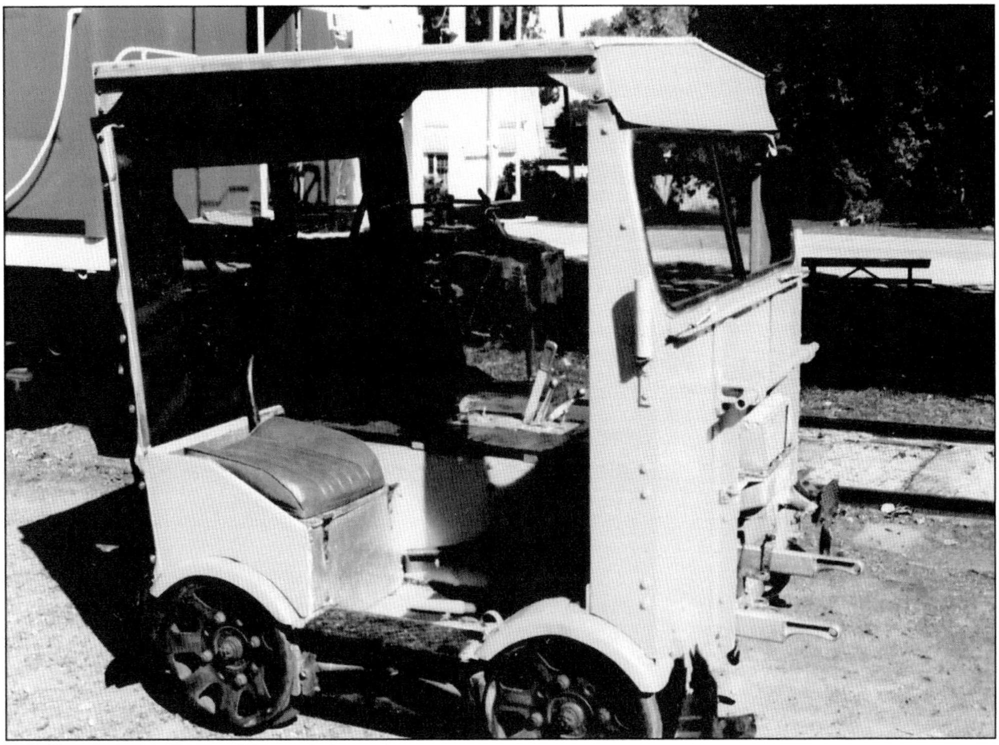
The maintenance and inspection motorized railcar was seen only occasionally, when railroad officials toured the line to inspect the condition of the property, especially the right-of-way.

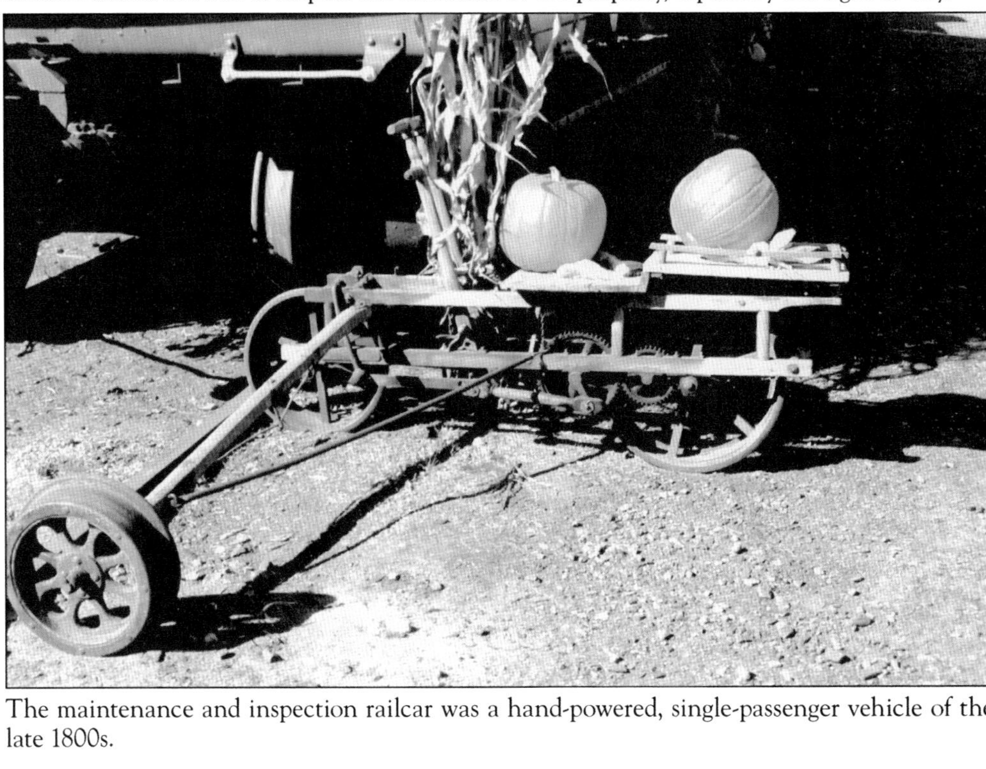
The maintenance and inspection railcar was a hand-powered, single-passenger vehicle of the late 1800s.

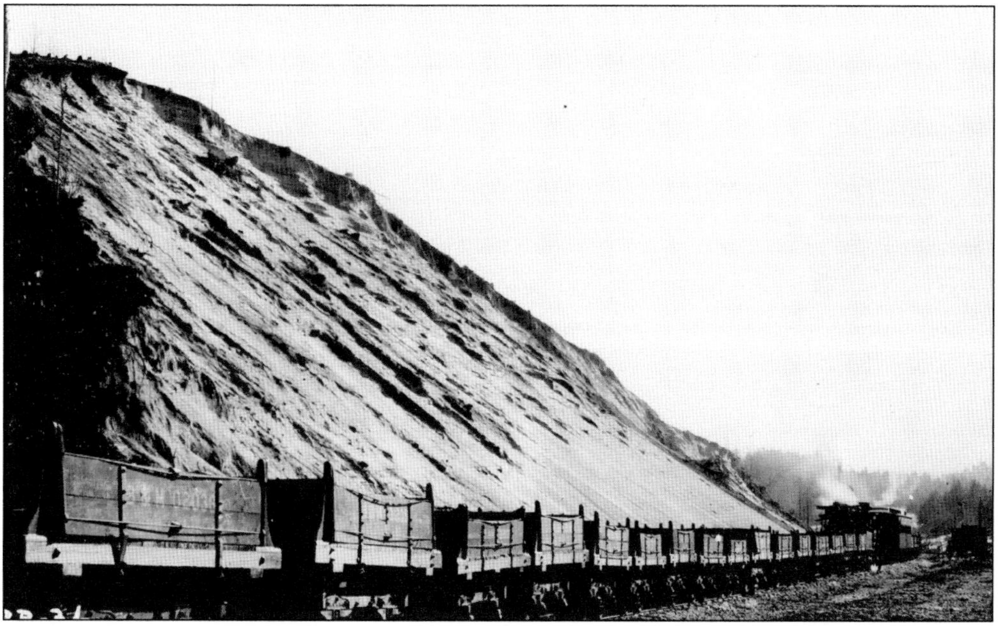

B&M ore-sand cars were used conveniently to move large amounts of earth from one area to another, as seen in this late-1800s or early-1900s photograph taken in Antrim, New Hampshire.

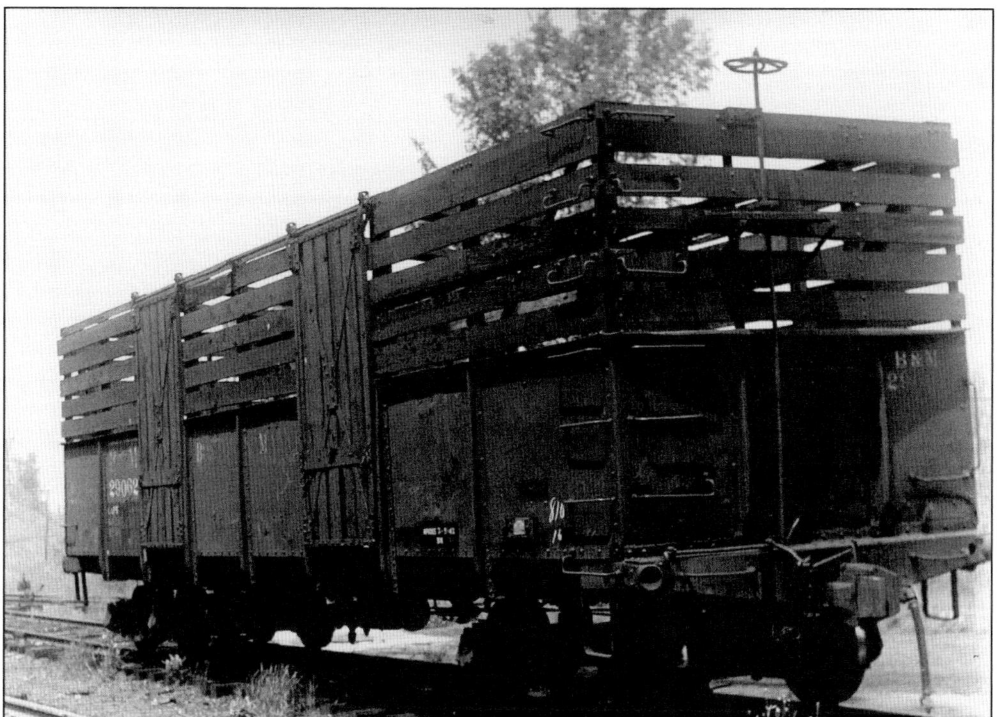

B&M pulpwood car No. 29062, series 29000–29099, appears in Littleton, New Hampshire, in June 1943. These cars were built primarily for the paper industry, which was prevalent in the White Mountains.

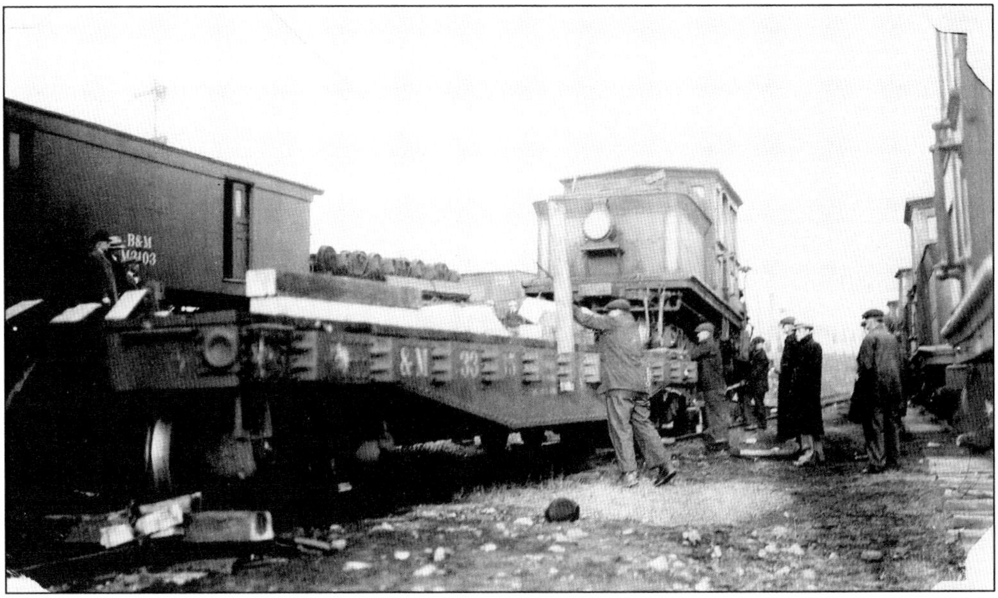

A B&M flatcar from the series 33501–33796 is pictured at West Lynn, Massachusetts, in 1928. These cars, ranging from 36 feet in length to 50 feet or more, hauled a variety of loads such as tractors and farm machinery, wooden utilities poles, lumber and logs, and large-diameter pipeline and galvanized culvert pipes. Being loaded on the flatcar is a narrow-gauge locomotive from the Boston, Revere Beach and Lynn Railroad on its way to be scrapped.

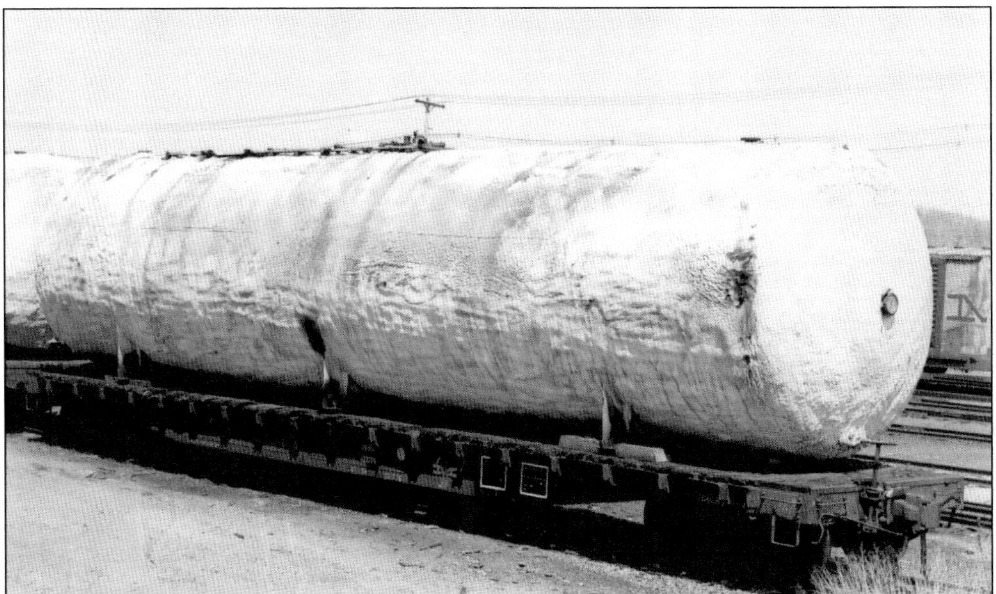

Seen at Concord, New Hampshire, B&M flatcar No. 34008, series 34000–34089, is undoubtedly transporting a boiler from Lincoln.

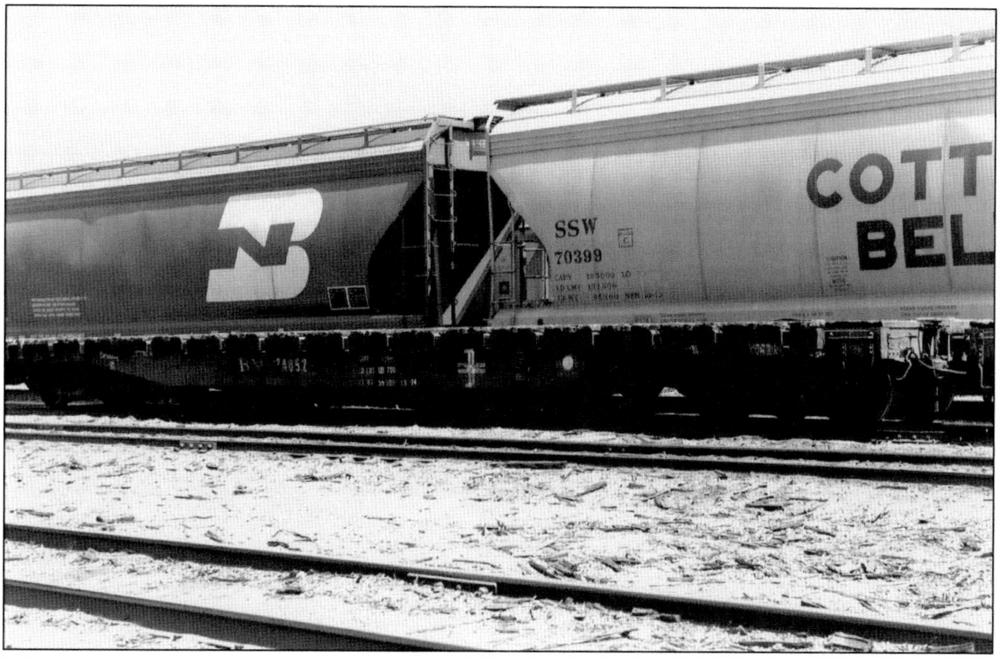

B&M flatcar No. 34052 appears at Nashua, New Hampshire, on May 9, 1981. Note the brake wheel in its down position.

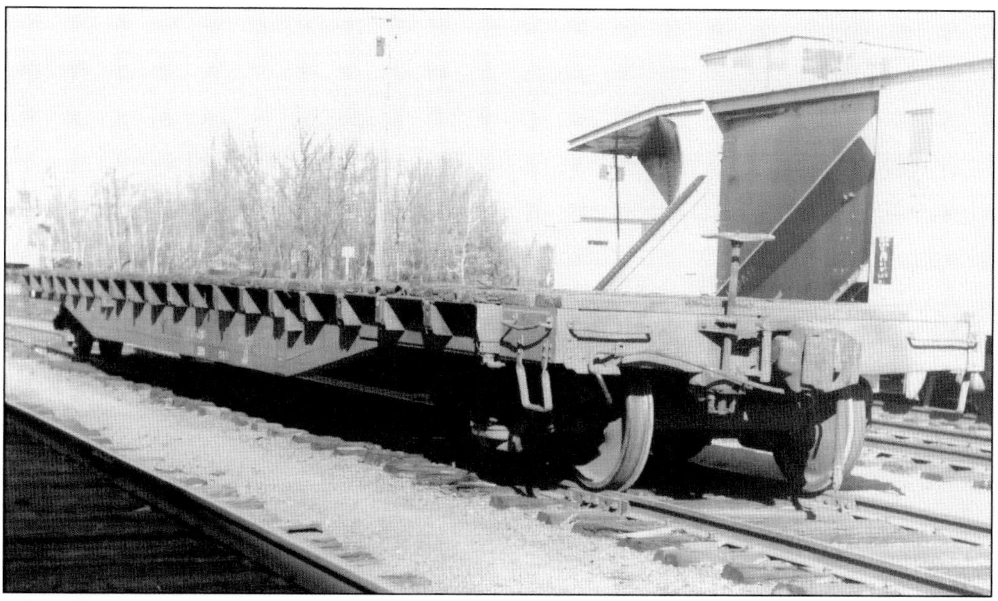

B&M flatcar No. 34074 is pictured at Nashua, New Hampshire, on February 2, 1980. Empty idler flatcars were sometimes placed at one or both ends of the weighted car to take care of the overhanging load.

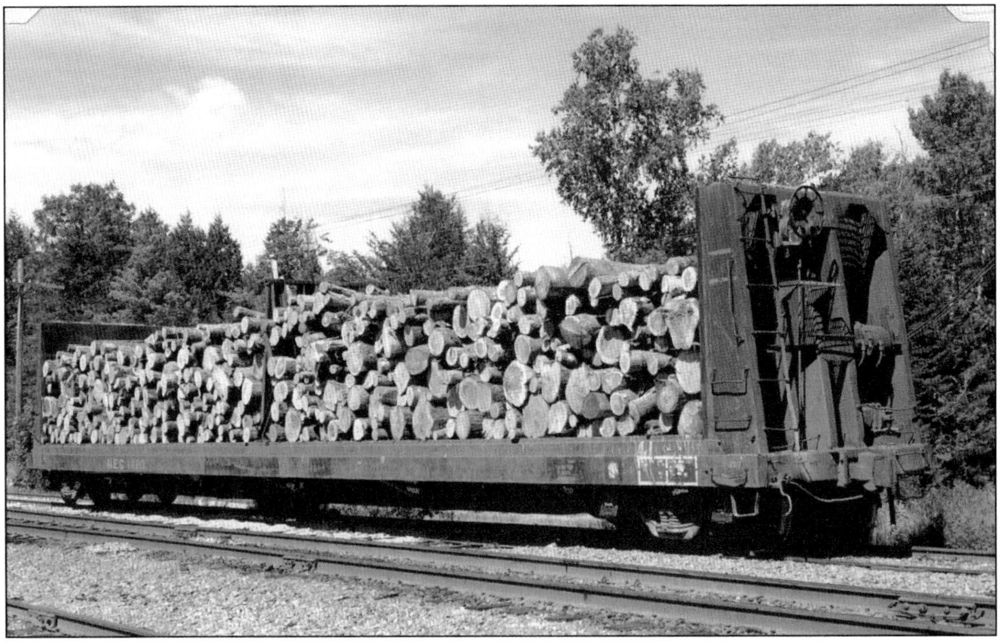

Bulkhead flats, such as MEC flatcar No. 1420, series 1400–1599, were commonly used to haul lumber, sheetrock, wallboard, and pulpwood.

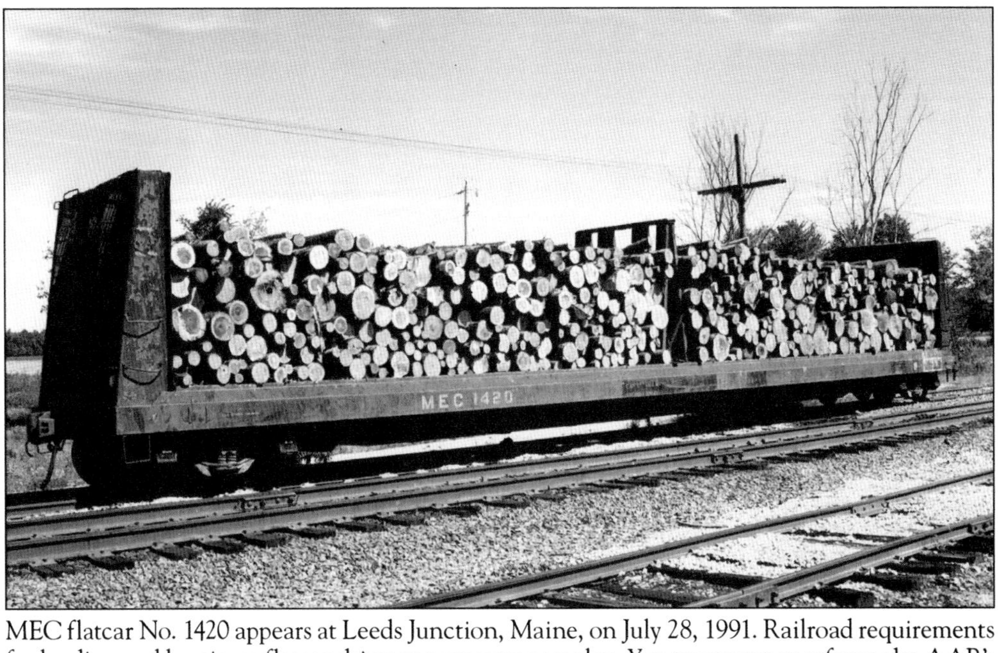

MEC flatcar No. 1420 appears at Leeds Junction, Maine, on July 28, 1991. Railroad requirements for loading and bracing a flatcar shipment are very complex. You may want to refer to the AAR's "Rules Governing the Loading of Open Top Cars" to ensure that your model railroad loads are tied down securely in an approved manner.

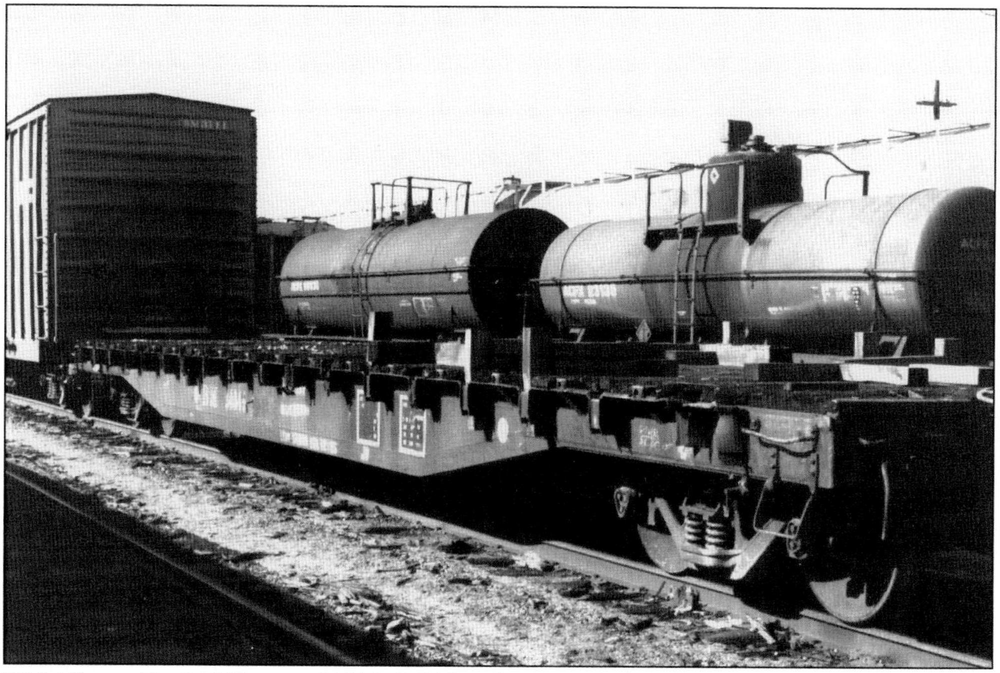

B&M flatcar No. 34045, series 34000–34089, is shown at Nashua, New Hampshire, on August 20, 1983. Flatcars have many uses, including transporting fuel over the rail.

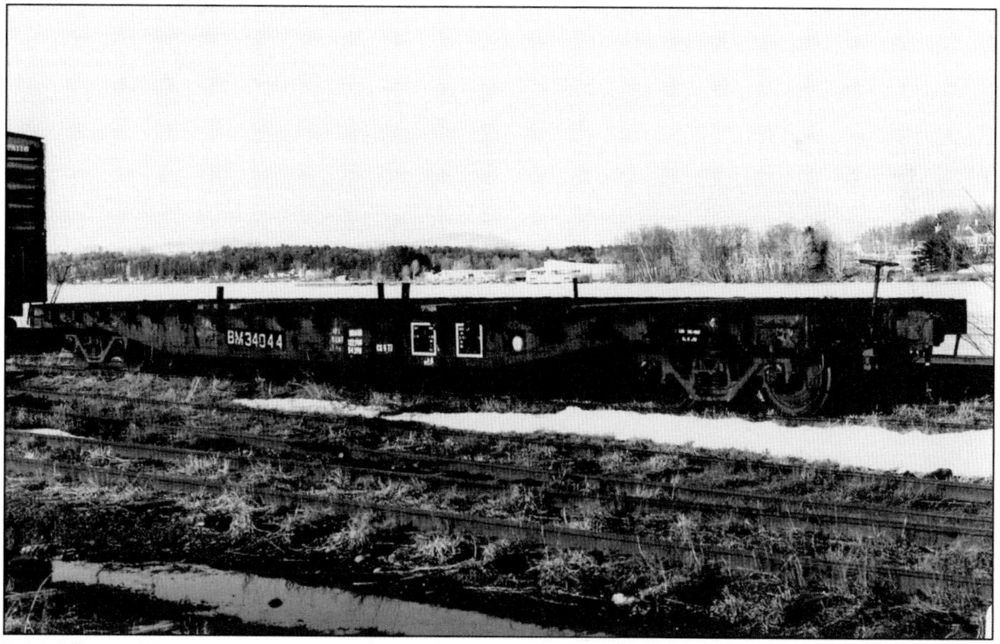

B&M flatcar No. 24044, series 34000–34089, waits on a sidetrack for future use at Lakeport, New Hampshire, on March 24, 1984. In the background, Paugus Bay is frozen over.

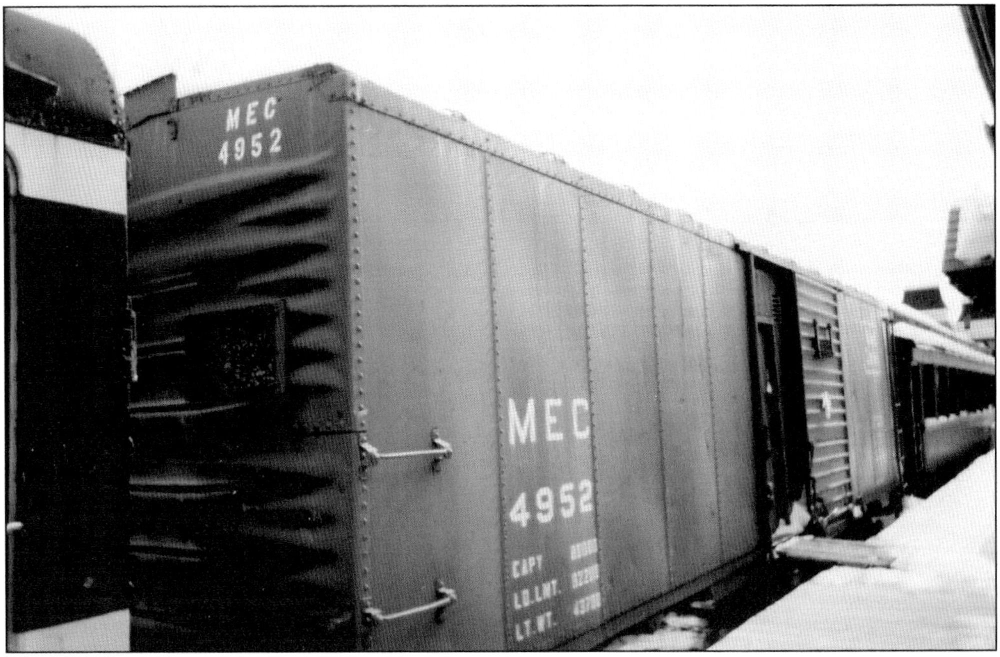

MEC boxcar No. 4952 was built in 1937. The boxcar had it advantages. It was easy to load from the line-side platform and could carry virtually anything and protect it from the elements.

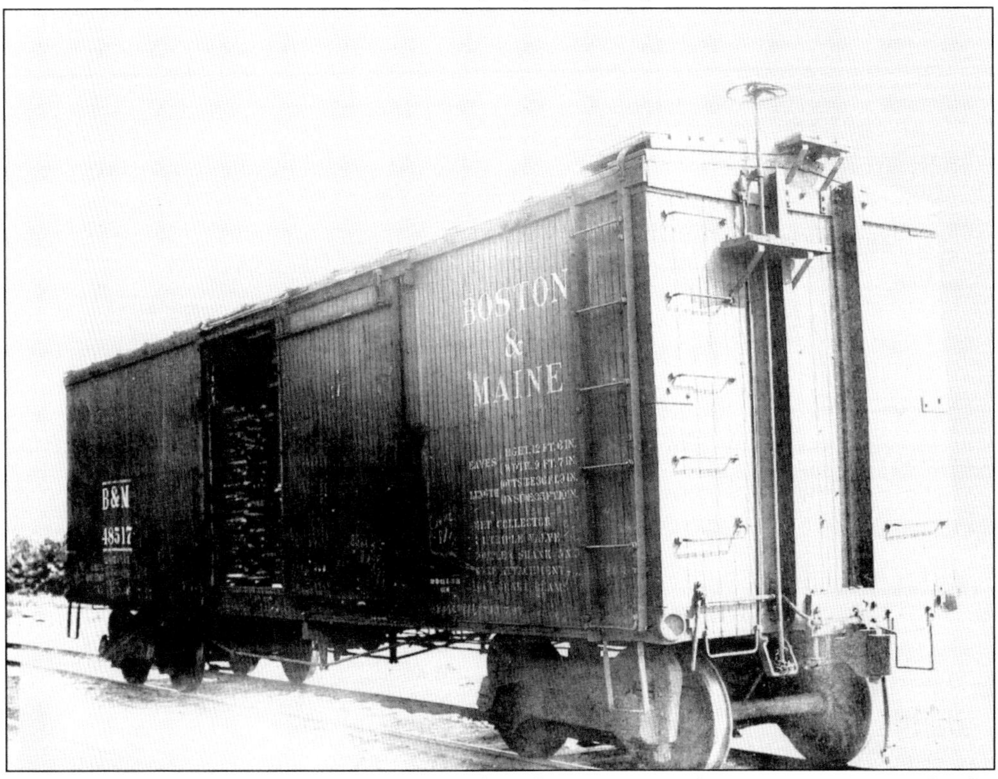

Here, B&M boxcar No. 48517 is located at Burleyville, New Hampshire, on June 27, 1929. By the 1920s, most boxcars had grown to 40 feet in length with a capacity of about 50 tons.

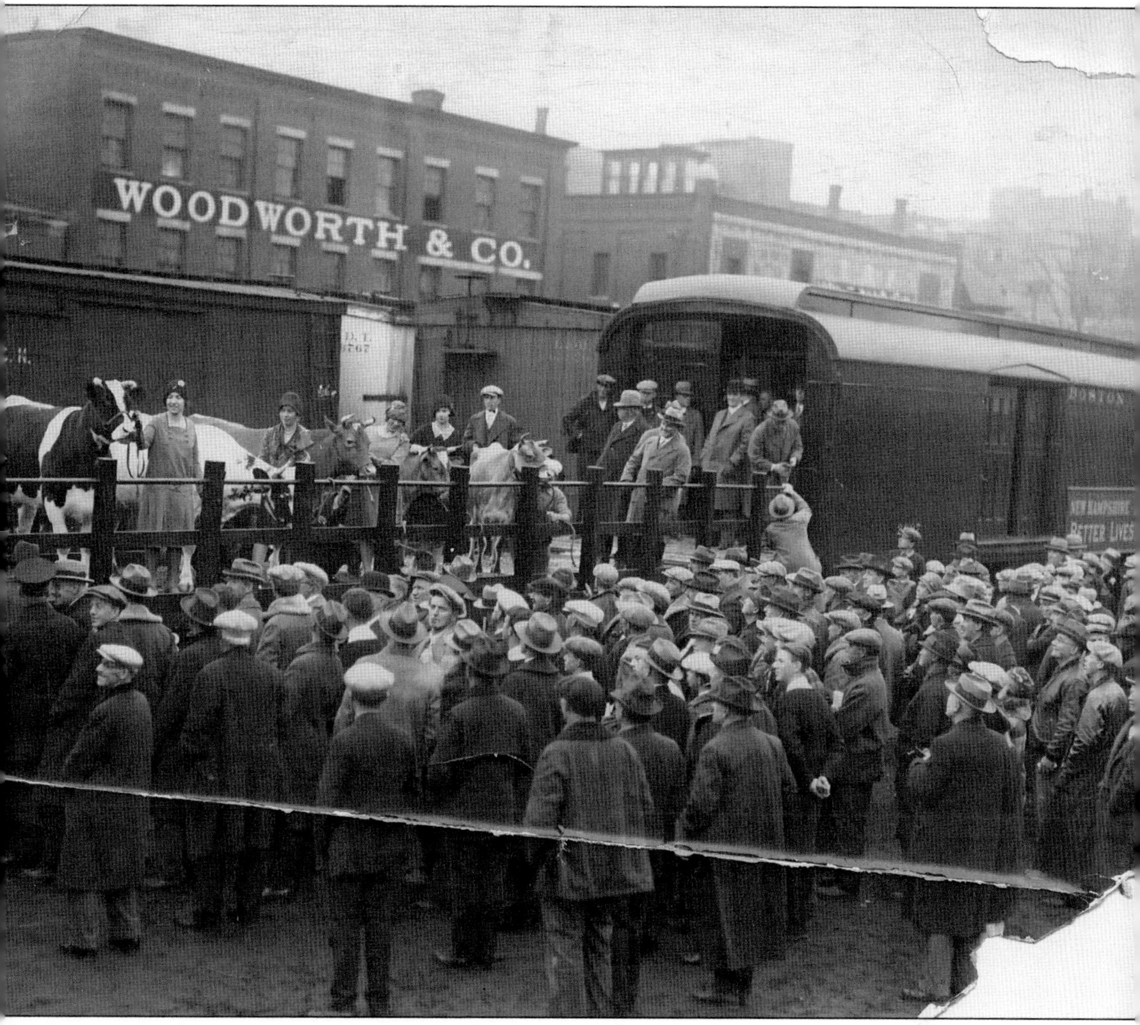

During the first week of May 1928, the B&M ran a New Hampshire "Better Livestock" train. Among the equipment employed for this train was wooden horse car No. 2687. Evident in this scene at Concord, New Hampshire, is the car's end-loading feature. Judging by the size of the crowd, this was a very popular event.

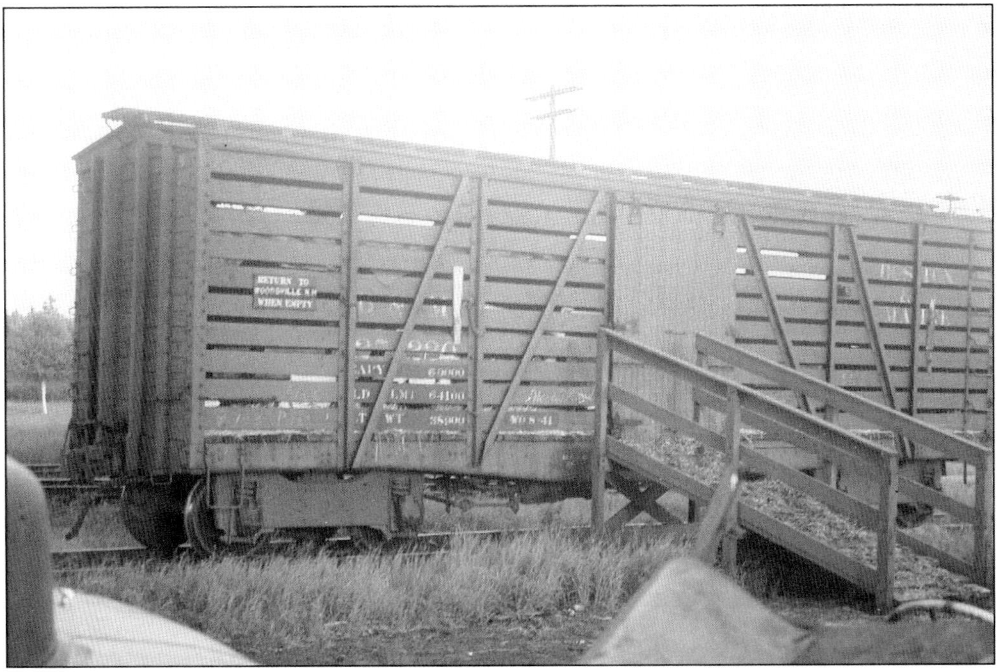

A B&M stock car from the series 27200–27239, built in 1923, is shown here at Coos Junction, New Hampshire, in May 1943. The farming and cattle industry was very strong in the North Country, so it was necessary to move many heads of cattle via the rail system.

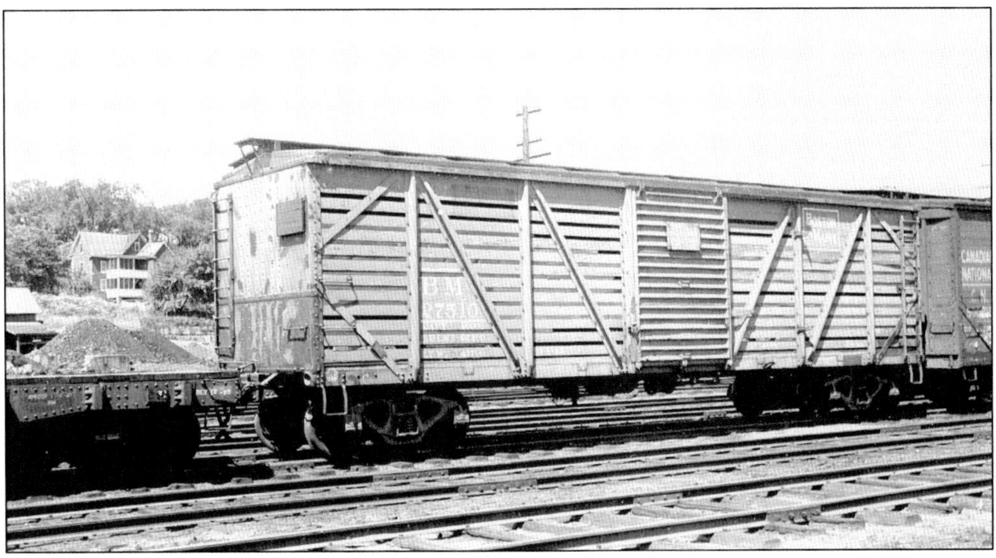

A B&M stock car from the series 27500–27514 (converted from 72000-series cars in 1945) appears at Concord, New Hampshire, on July 29, 1947. It was reconverted to a boxcar in 1956.

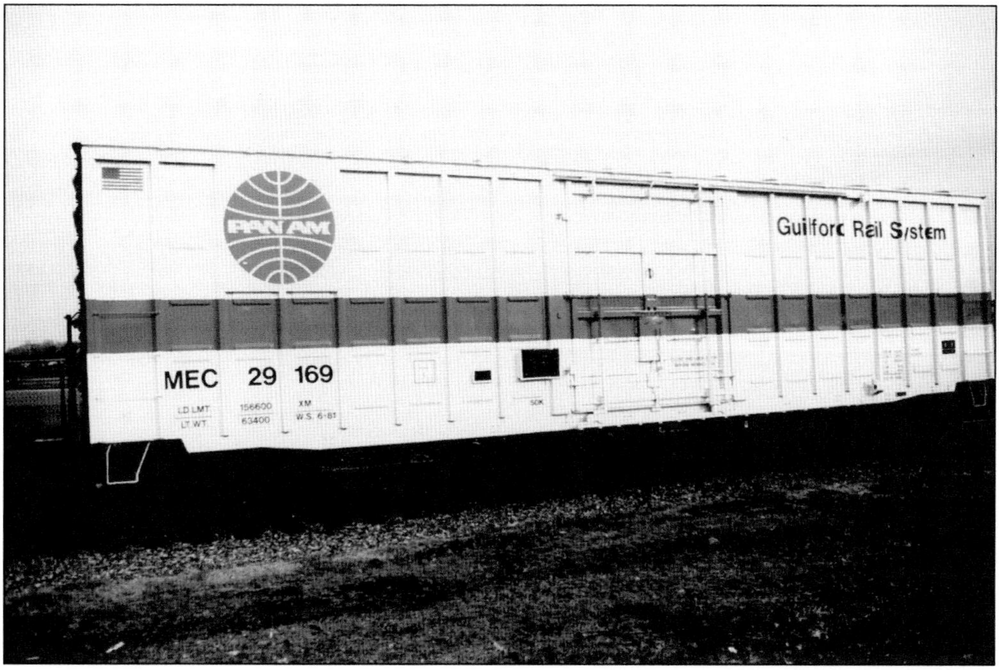

The Guilford Rail System B&M No. 339, MEC 229169, is shown in Portsmouth, New Hampshire, on December 16, 1998. The most popular car of this era was the standard 40-foot boxcar adopted by the U.S. Railway Administration, which took over the railroads during World War I.

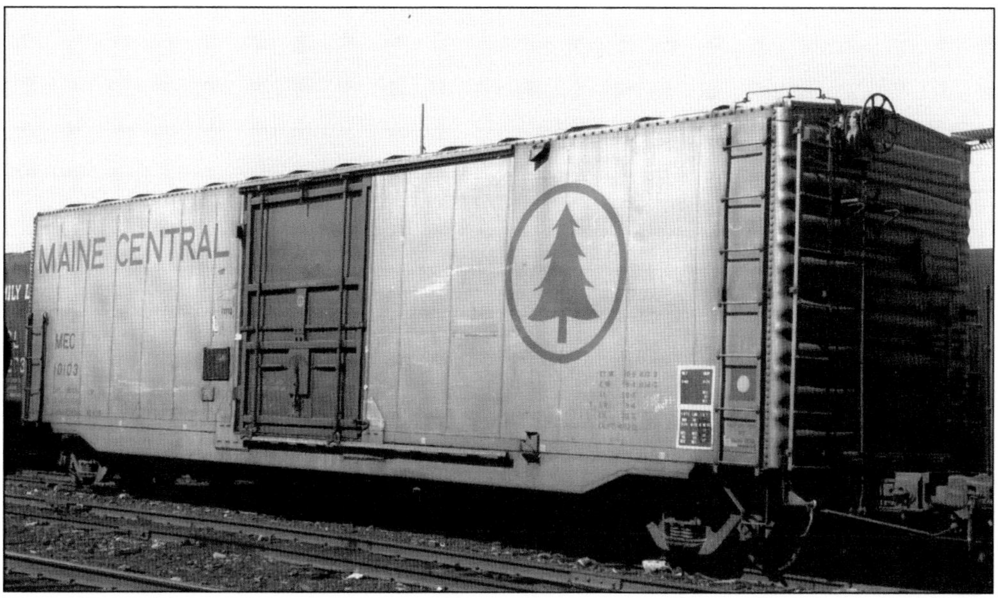

Maine Central boxcar No. 10103, series 10100–10199, is pictured in Lawrence, Massachusetts, on August 20, 1983.

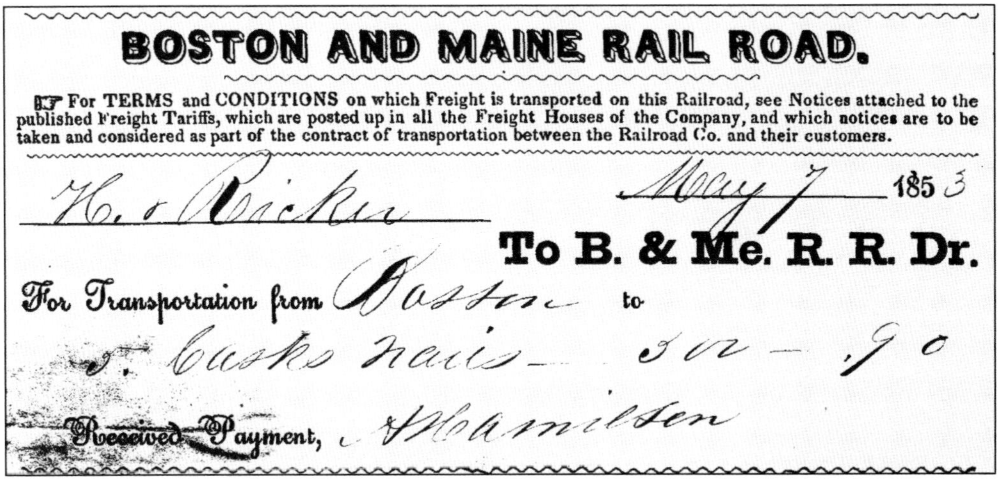

BOSTON AND MAINE RAIL ROAD.

For TERMS and CONDITIONS on which Freight is transported on this Railroad, see Notices attached to the published Freight Tariffs, which are posted up in all the Freight Houses of the Company, and which notices are to be taken and considered as part of the contract of transportation between the Railroad Co. and their customers.

May 7 1853

To B. & Me. R. R. Dr.

For Transportation from Boston to

Casks Nails

Received Payment,

This receipt records a shipment from Boston on May 7, 1853. It reads, "For Terms and Conditions on which Freight is transported on this Railroad, see Notices attached to the published Freight Tariffs, which are posted up in all the Freight Houses of the Company, and which notices are to be taken and considered as part of the contract of transportation between the Railroad Co. and their customers."

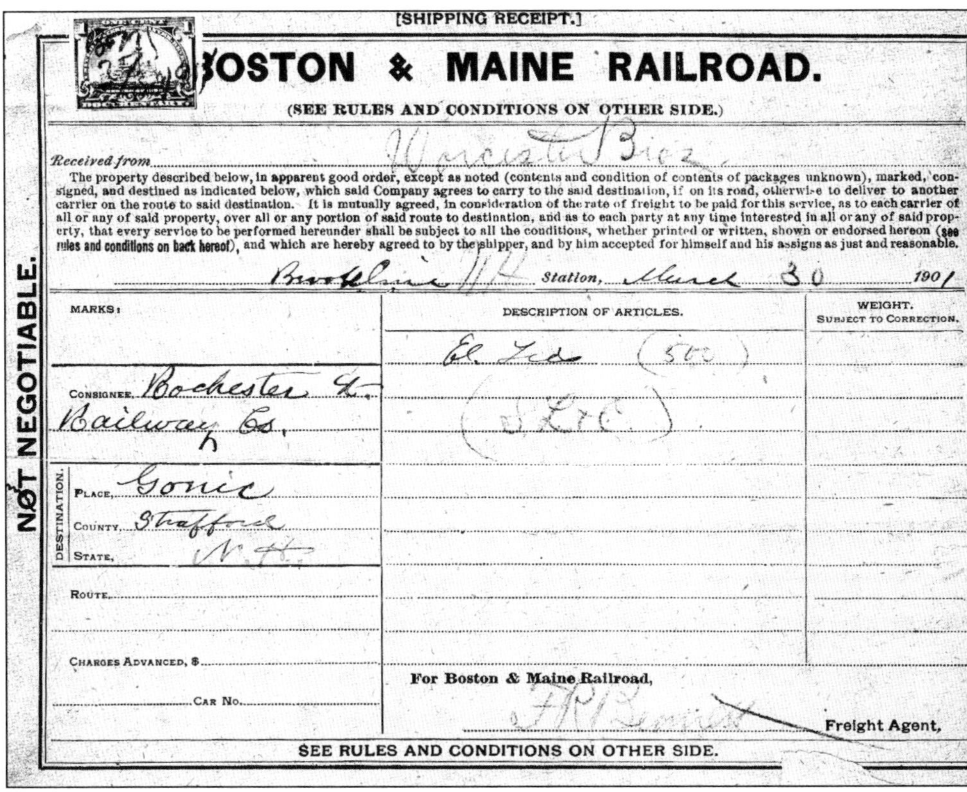

[SHIPPING RECEIPT.]

BOSTON & MAINE RAILROAD.

(SEE RULES AND CONDITIONS ON OTHER SIDE.)

NOT NEGOTIABLE.

Received from

The property described below, in apparent good order, except as noted (contents and condition of contents of packages unknown), marked, consigned, and destined as indicated below, which said Company agrees to carry to the said destination, if on its road, otherwise to deliver to another carrier on the route to said destination. It is mutually agreed, in consideration of the rate of freight to be paid for this service, as to each carrier of all or any of said property, over all or any portion of said route to destination, and as to each party at any time interested in all or any of said property, that every service to be performed hereunder shall be subject to all the conditions, whether printed or written, shown or endorsed hereon (see rules and conditions on back hereof), and which are hereby agreed to by the shipper, and by him accepted for himself and his assigns as just and reasonable.

Station, March 30 1901

MARKS: | DESCRIPTION OF ARTICLES. | WEIGHT. SUBJECT TO CORRECTION.

CONSIGNEE, Rochester St. Railway Co.

DESTINATION. PLACE, Gonic COUNTY, Strafford STATE, N. H.

ROUTE,

CHARGES ADVANCED, $

CAR NO.

For Boston & Maine Railroad,

Freight Agent,

SEE RULES AND CONDITIONS ON OTHER SIDE.

Shown here is a shipping receipt dated March 30, 1901.

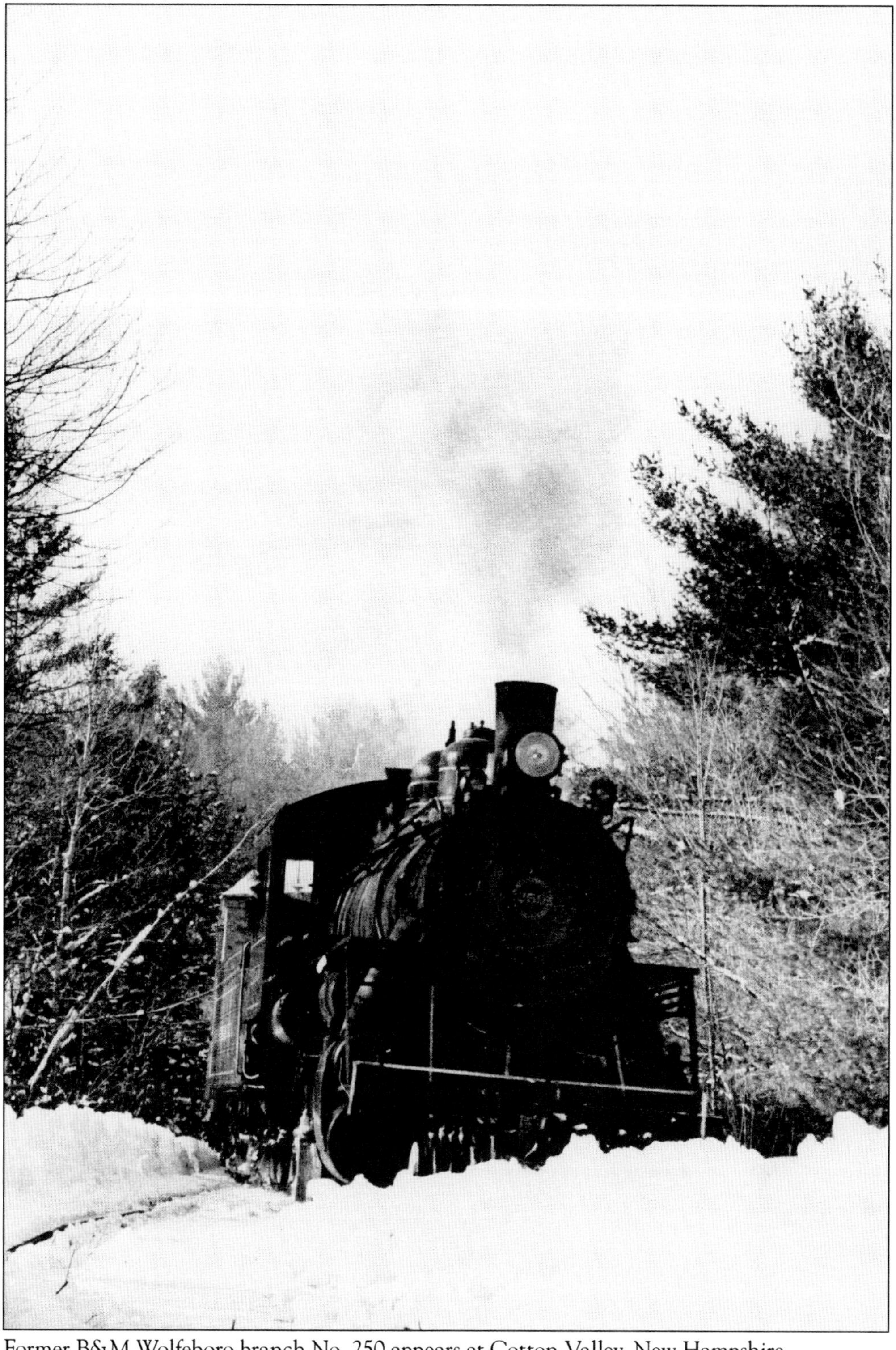

Former B&M Wolfeboro branch No. 250 appears at Cotton Valley, New Hampshire.

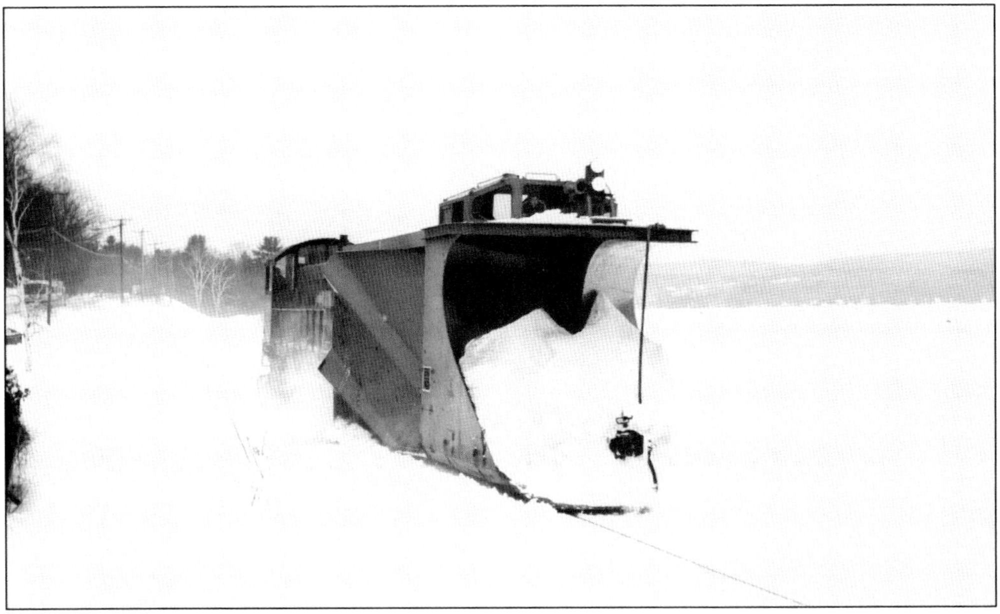

North Stratford Railroad No. 1008 and B&M plow W-3750 moves snow on the shore of Lake Winnipesaukee at Laconia, New Hampshire, on January 30, 1982. This is a Brent Michiels photograph.

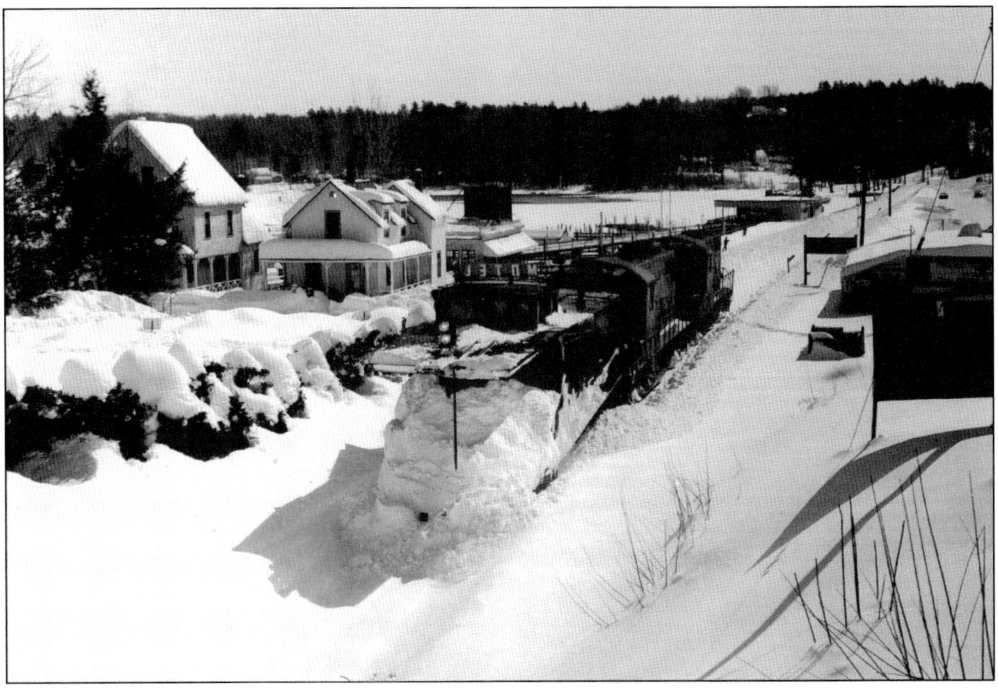

B&M equipment plows in front of the footbridge at the Weirs in Laconia, New Hampshire, in March 1969. Looking south down the track, we see the Weirs station and Lake Winnipesaukee.

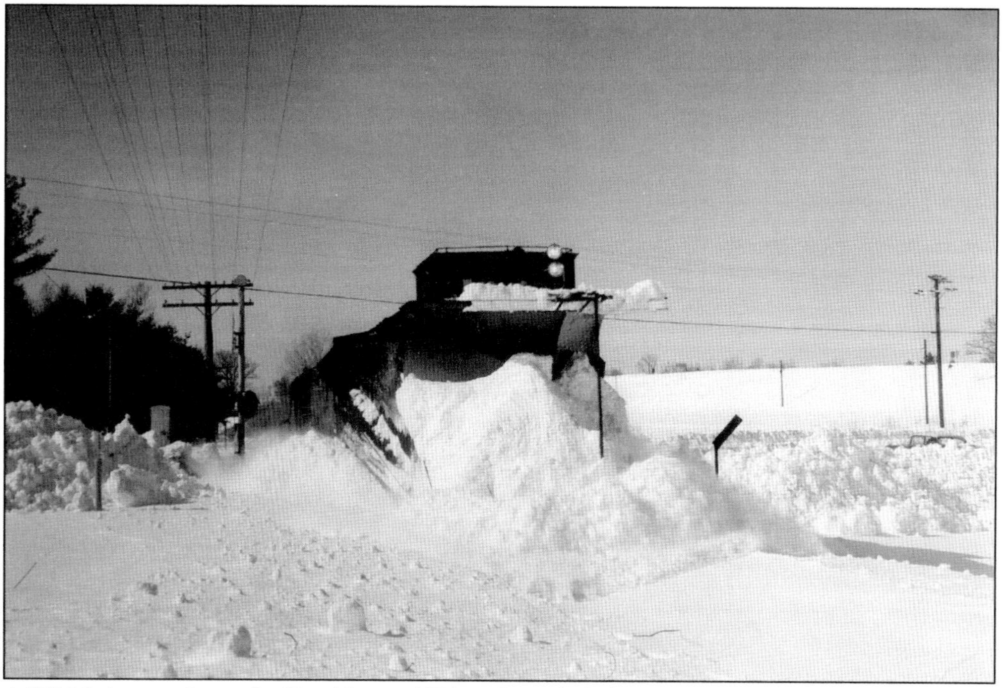

A B&M plow works on the Franklin and Tilton branch, Tilton, New Hampshire, in March 1969. It is not unusual to have more than 50 inches of snow in central New Hampshire.

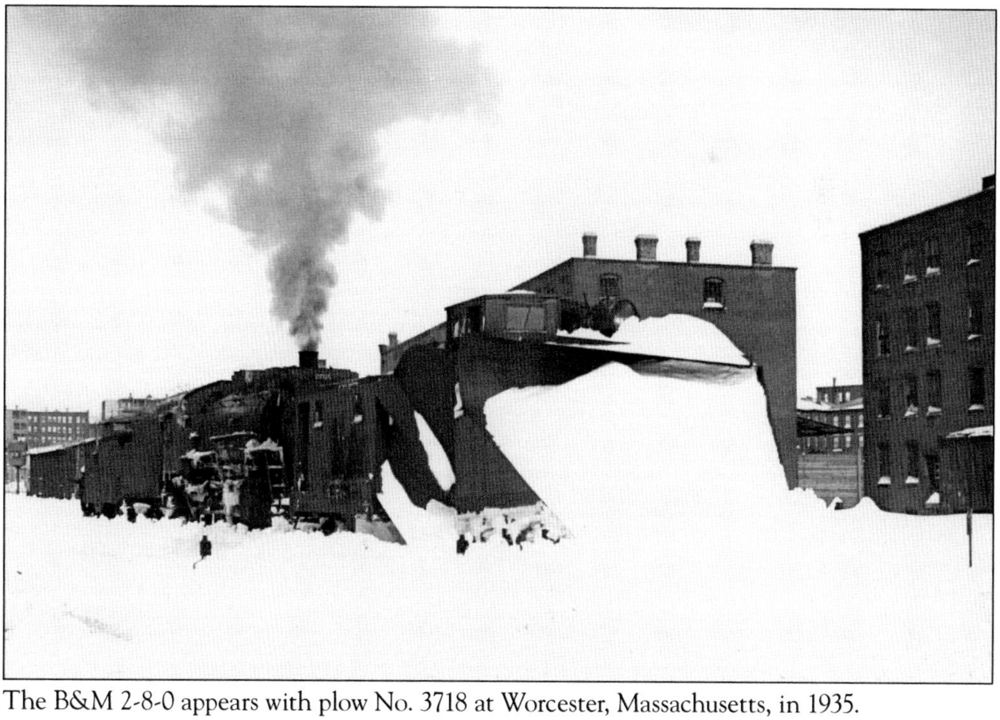

The B&M 2-8-0 appears with plow No. 3718 at Worcester, Massachusetts, in 1935.

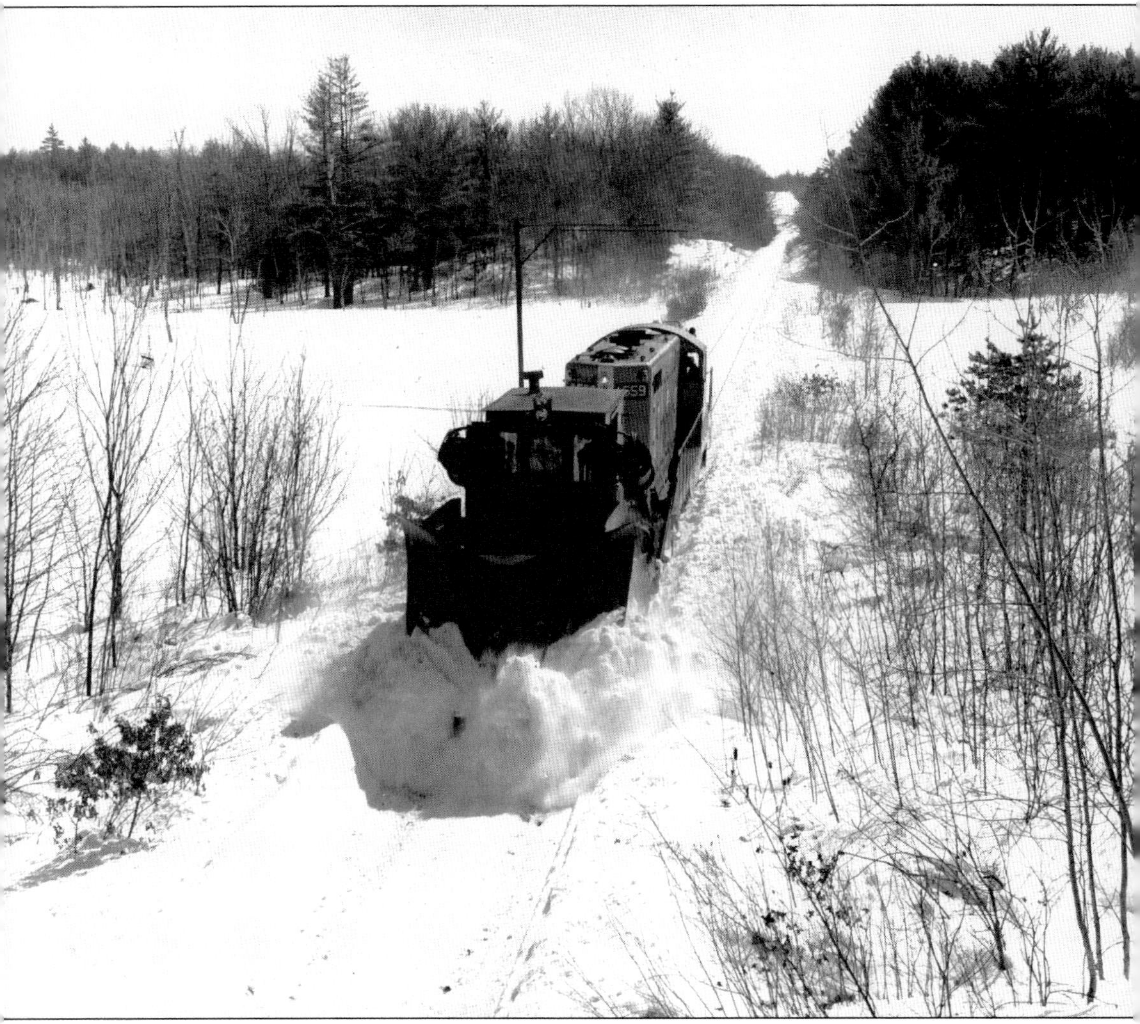

B&M GP-7 No. 1559 pushes Jordan Spreader W-3593. The winter of 1968–1969 was an exceptionally severe one in New Hampshire, and the spreaders were in almost constant use, attempting to maintain service throughout the system. Here, a spreader breaks trail about one mile north of Windham.

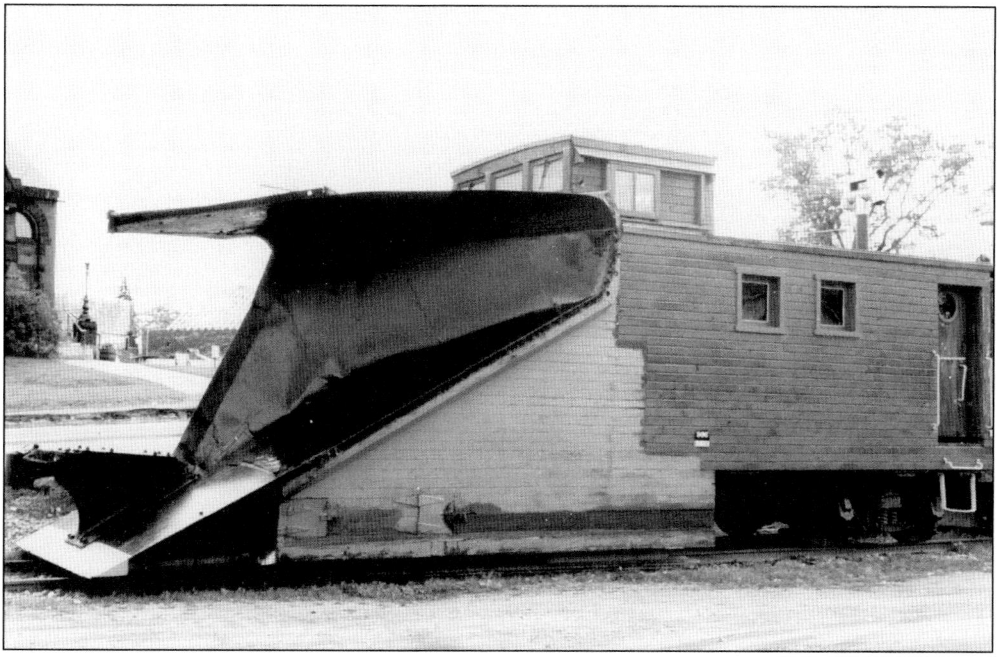

An old wooden Russell snowplow, used extensively by the B&M, is being restored at the Tilton freight house.

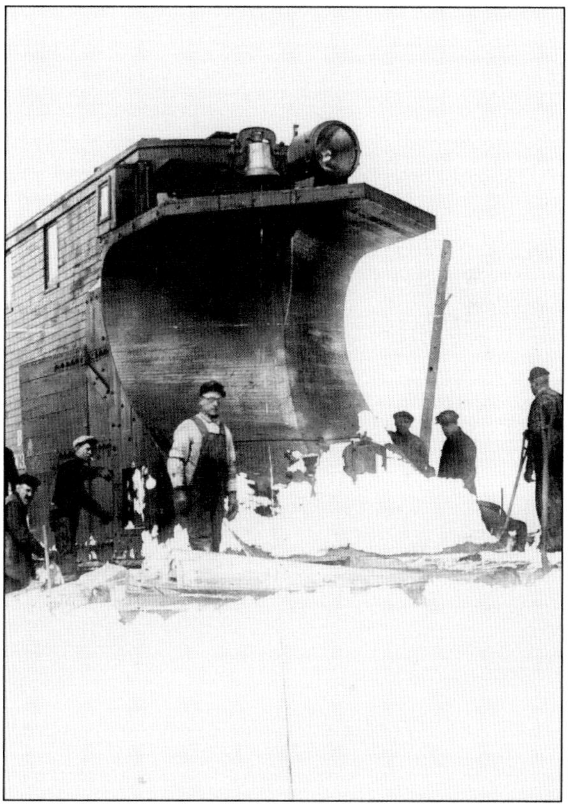

This is a closeup view of the snowplow in the previous image. Note the new smokestack and wipers on the cupola front windows. This derailed plow on the B&M's Belmont branch rests next to the bridge over the Winnipesaukee River in East Tilton, New Hampshire, on March 9, 1926. Snow-removal operations were temporarily suspended after the plow departed from the right-of-way.

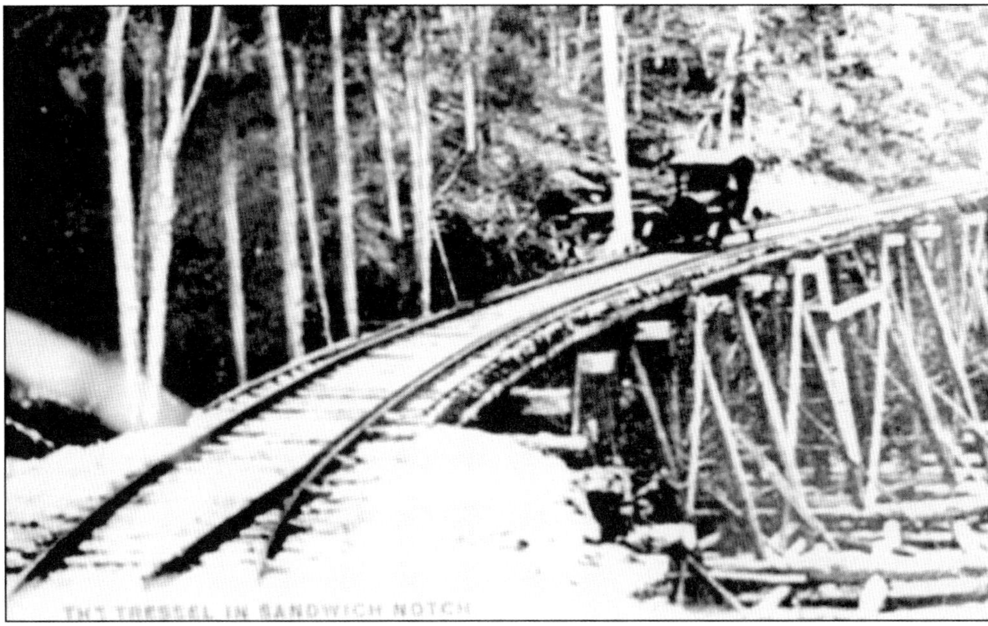

This trestle, shown in the early 1900s, was located in Sandwich Notch for use by the lumber and timber business. Because the logging operation moved through the woods as trees were harvested and new stands were marked for cutting, the railway track tended to be temporary.

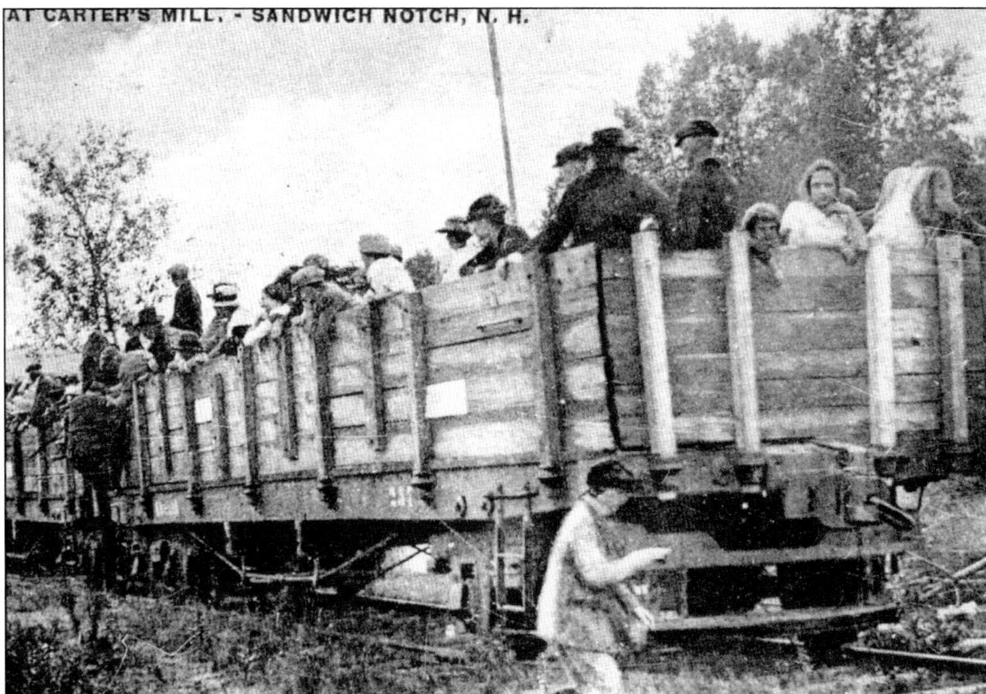

Workers travel to Carter's Mill in Sandwich Notch, New Hampshire. The B&M shared the environment in New Hampshire with 16 logging railroads built in the White Mountains during the late 19th and early 20th centuries. These roads answered the growing demand for timber, as after 1890, the White Mountain pulp and paper industry hit full stride.

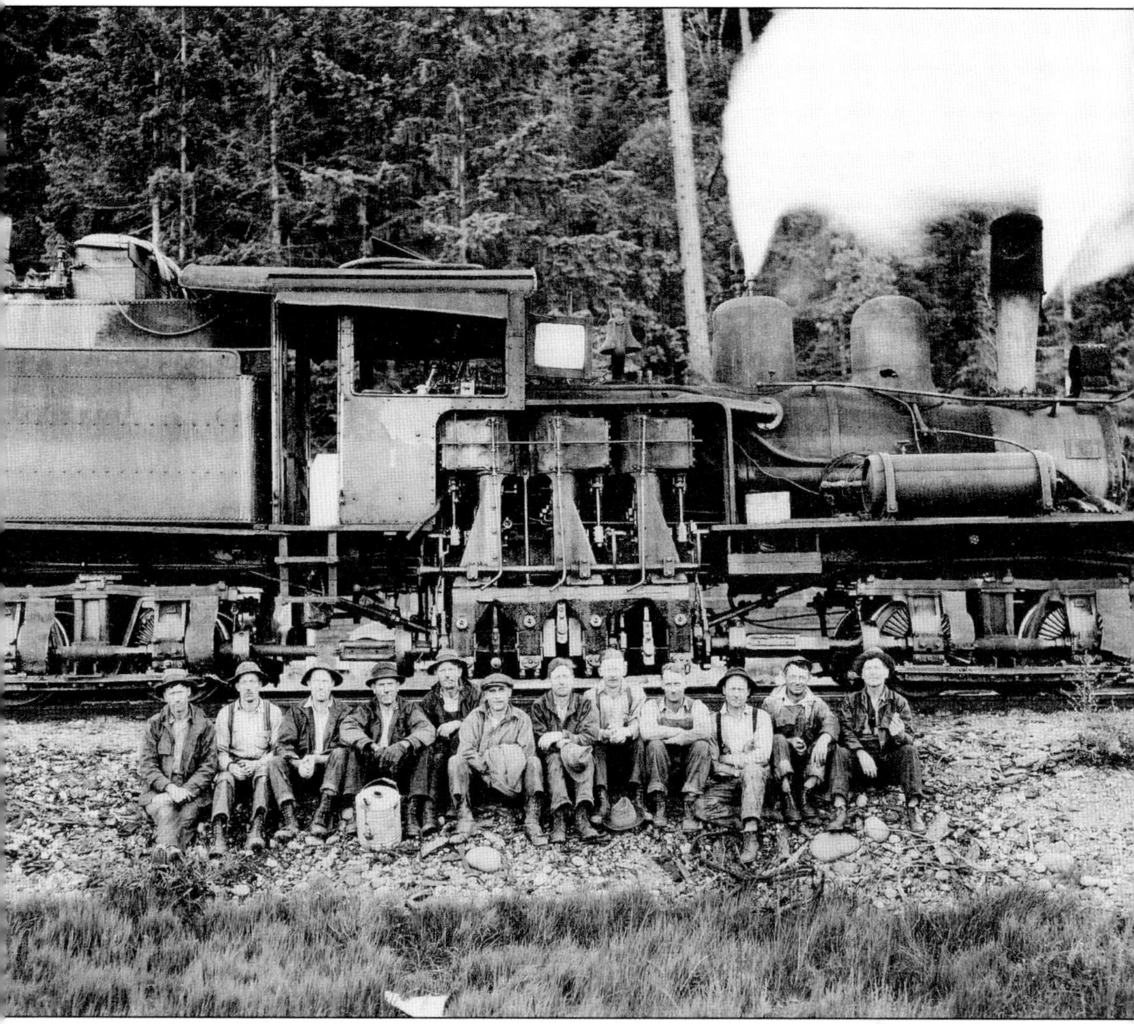

A logging crew poses in front of its locomotive lumber train for a restful moment on the Beebe River Railroad in Sandwich Notch, New Hampshire. The story of the area's logging railroads begins in 1867, when the state sold off its remaining land in the White Mountains.

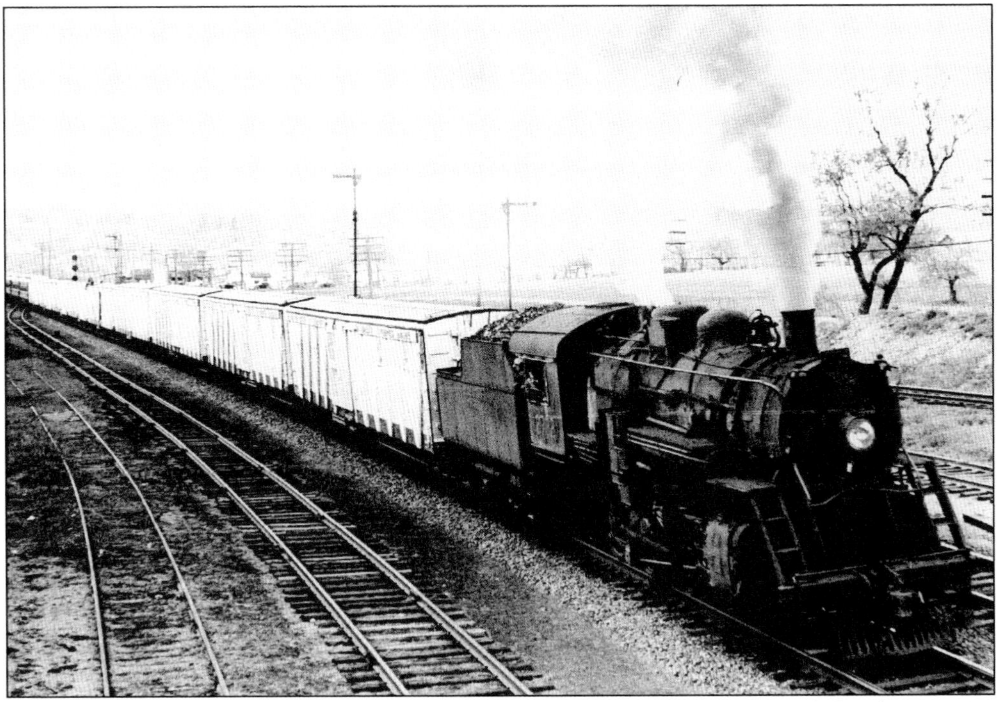

The Ringling Brothers and Barnum & Bailey Circus train's first section arrives behind B&M K8c 2-8-0 No. 2732 on the hill crossing the freight cutoff, headed for East Somerville, Massachusetts, in May 1938

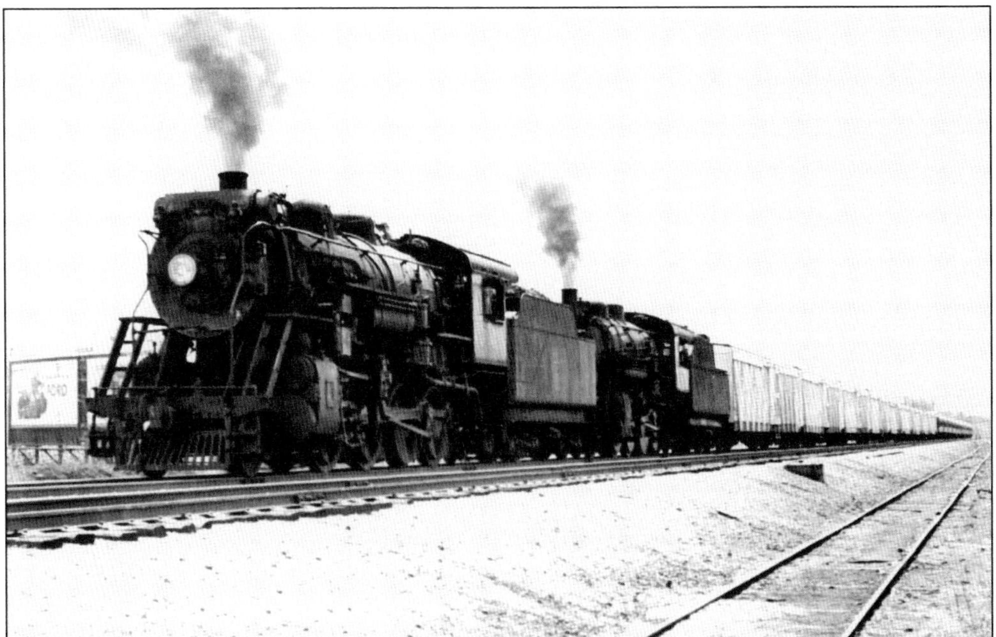

The second section of the circus train leaves Worcester up the hill at Greendale behind the double-headed K-Class 2-8-0. The firemen would earn their pay this day in May 1938.

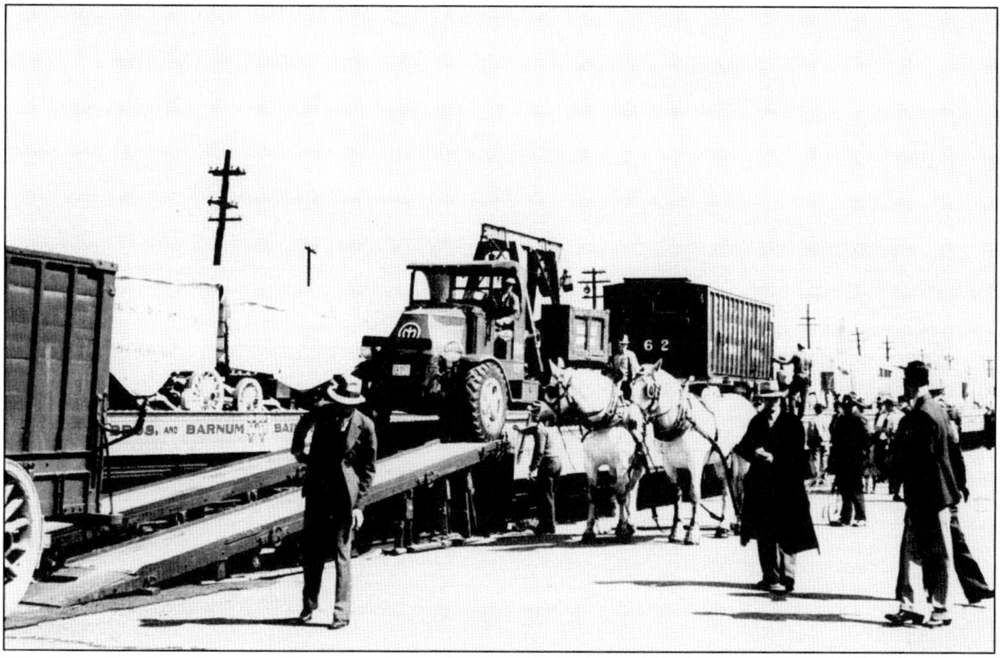

The Ringling Brothers and Barnum & Bailey Circus train unloads in East Somerville, complete with Mack truck, draft horses, and colorful circus wagons. Lots of people arrived to watch the parade shape up for the march uptown to the Boston Garden in May 1938.

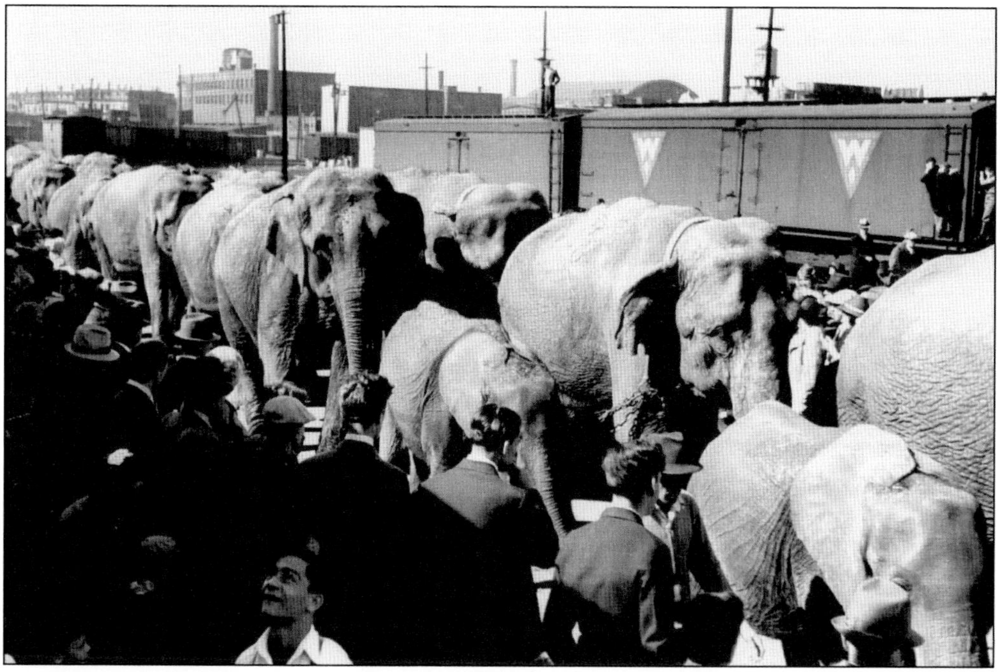

The B&M Ringling Brothers and Barnum & Bailey Circus train is pictured in East Somerville, Massachusetts. The elephants joined in the parade, and the Whiting milk cars brought up the rear. The previous four photographs were taken as the circus traveled by rail from Worcester to Boston via the B&M in May 1938.

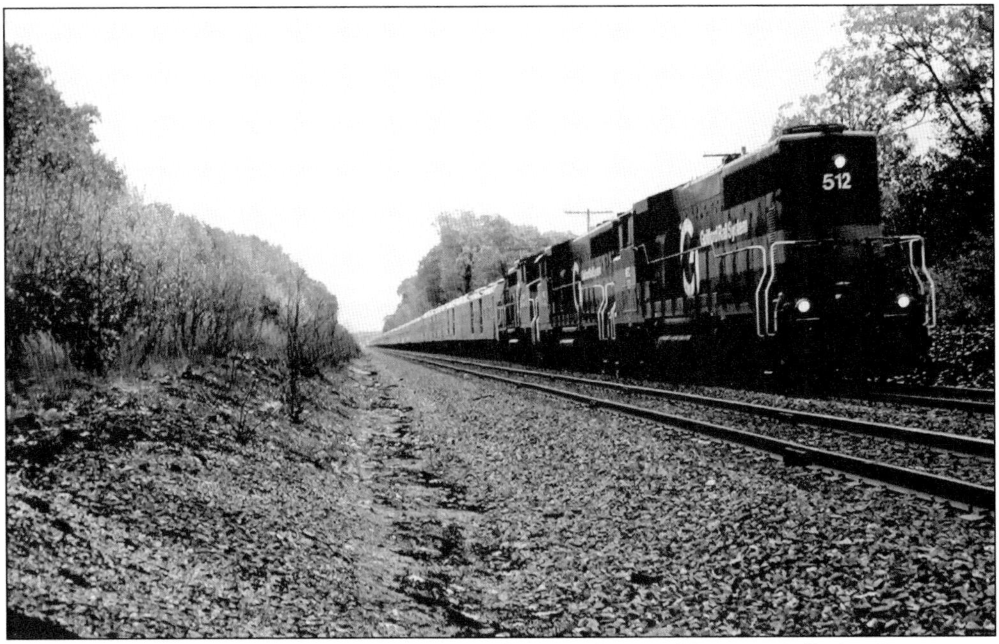

Guilford Rail System No. 512 travels on the Ringling Brothers and Barnum & Bailey Circus train from Manchester, New Hampshire, on October 27, 2003.

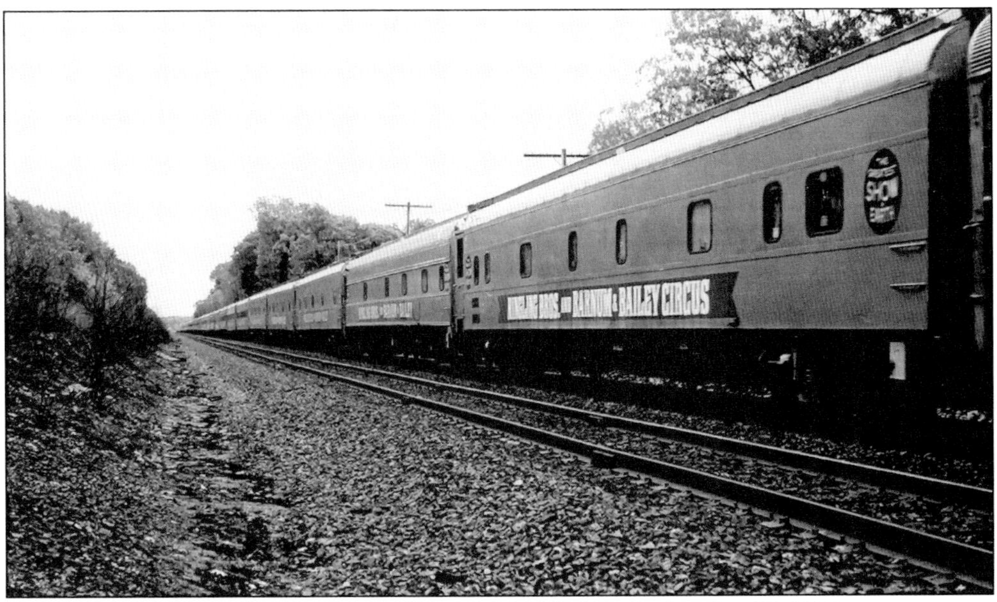

The Guilford Rail System circus cars appear in Manchester on October 27, 2003.

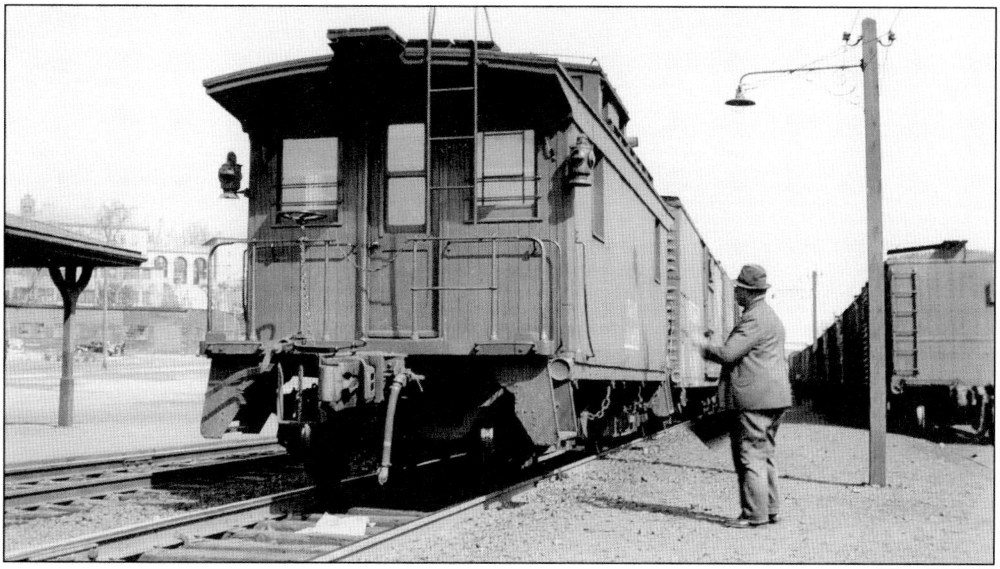

B&M caboose No. 104619 is shown at Tufts College station, Medford, Massachusetts, in 1939. The caboose served many purposes but most importantly was the watchtower to monitor both the train and personnel en route. The crews' toolboxes stored the parts and general maintenance equipment required when the car malfunctioned, for instance hot boxes and dragging equipment.

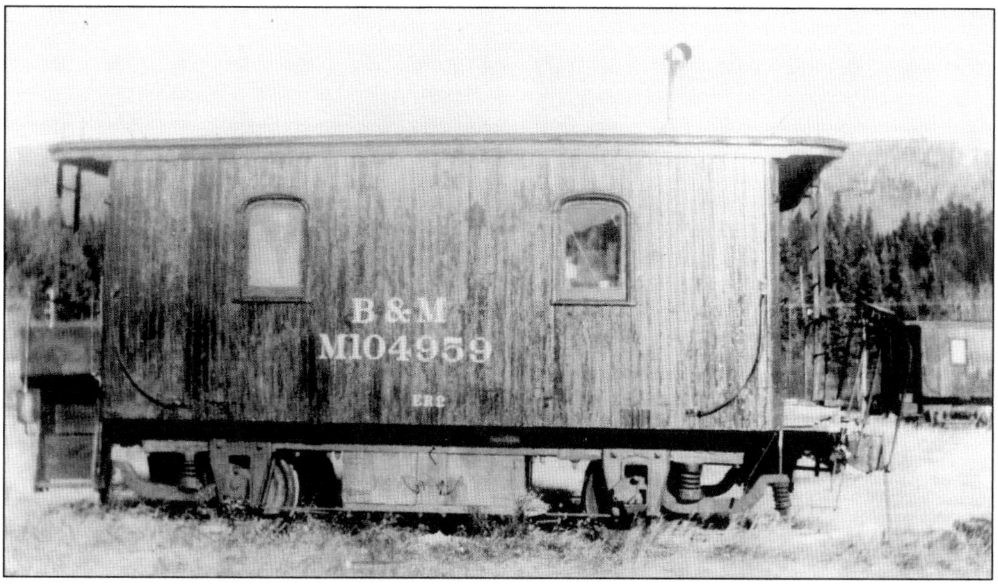

B&M four-wheel caboose No. 104959 is used as the Fabyan's yard office during the 1920s. Prior to this time, it bore the number 4959, but when the "10" was added to all caboose cars, this last remaining one was repainted and renumbered. The caboose was the rear-end protector for the train. A train was created only when the rear markers were hung from the caboose; otherwise, without markers, it was just a collection of cars. The caboose became a home away from home, serving as an eatery and bunkhouse if the crew could not return without laying over.

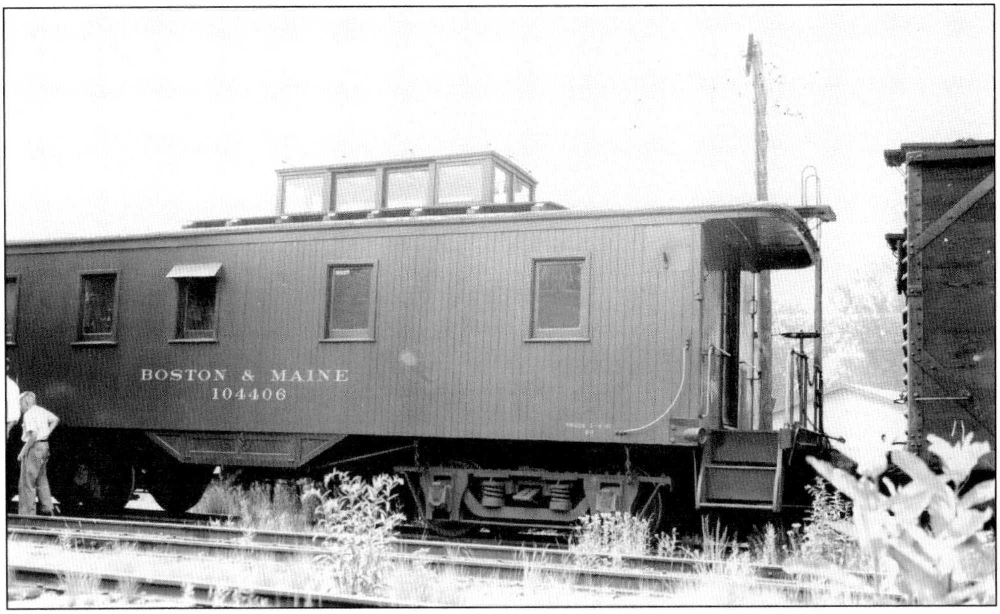

B&M caboose No. 104406 takes an railroad excursion trip in Hillboro, New Hampshire, on June 29, 1947. The classic caboose was developed in the 1860s as a combination of boxcar and passenger car features, along with a few unique innovations like the rooftop cupola.

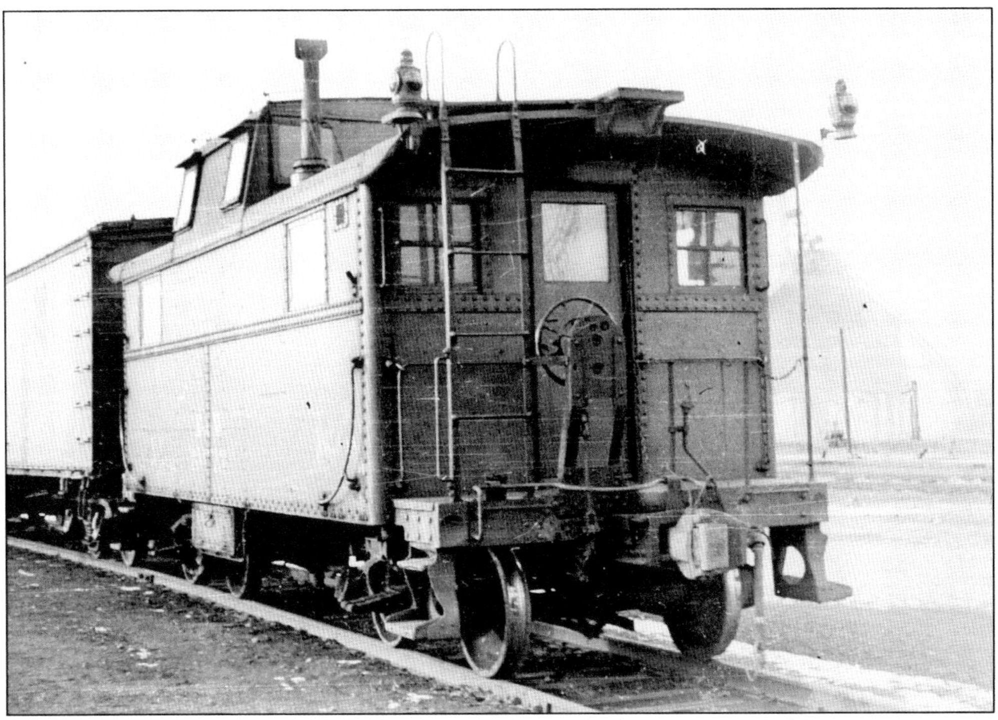

B&M caboose No. 134173, the *Pathfinder*, is shown in Charlestown, Massachusetts.

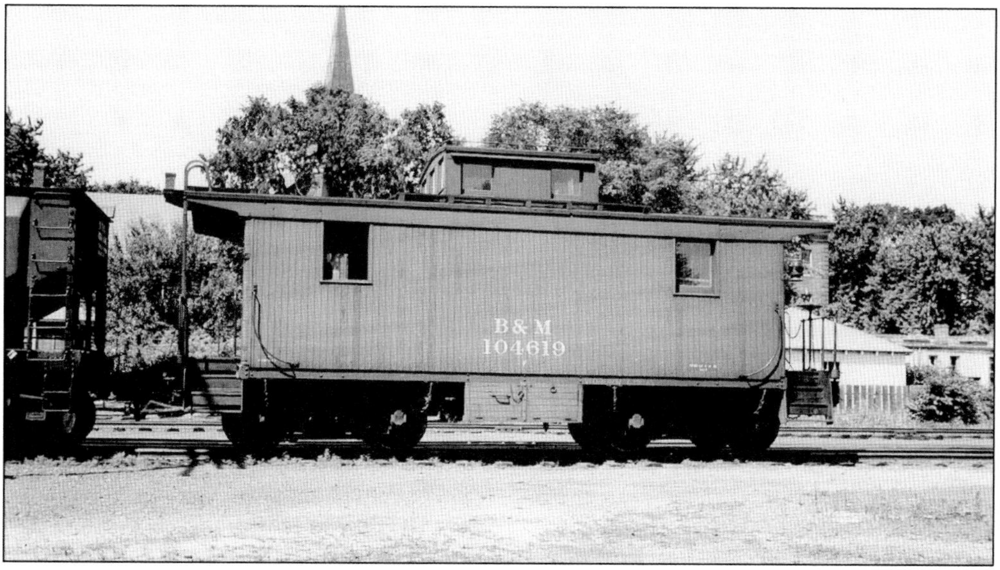

B&M caboose No. 104619 travels on the New Hampshire division at Woburn, Massachusetts, in 1939. Today, cabooses are a rare sight, having been replaced by the technology of the 1980s in the form of FRED (flashing rear-end device), a box with a blinking light that rides in the rear coupler of the last car. One can occasionally see cabooses in some local-freight and work-train services.

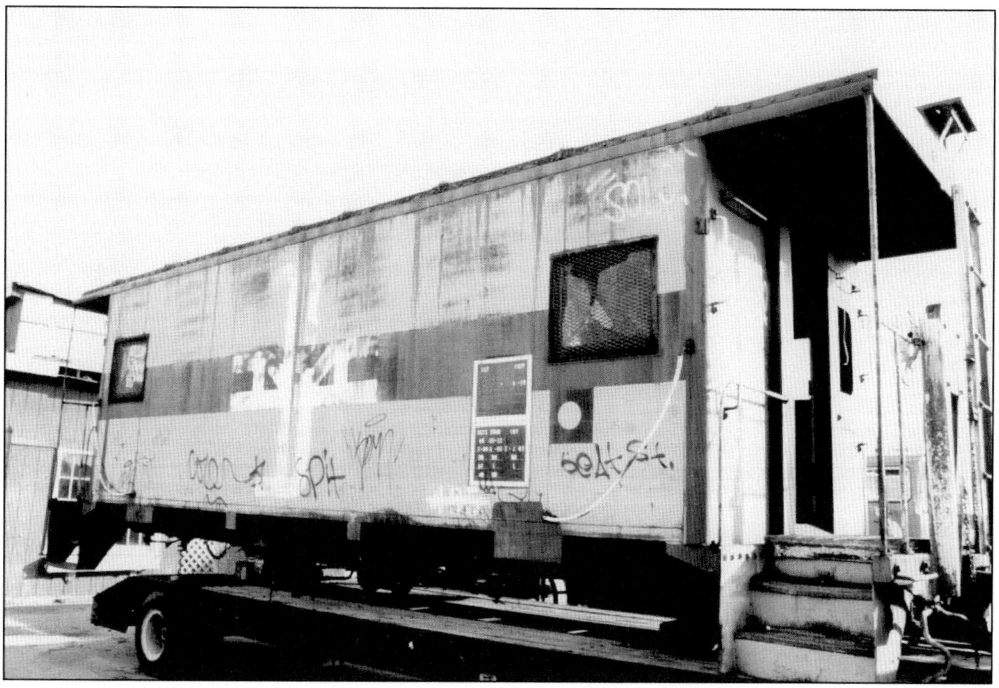

B&M caboose No. 495 sits on a flatbed trailer in front of Line Lumber, just north of the railroad overpass on Route 1 near the Hampton–North Hampton town line. The color specifications remained mostly the same from the beginning of the 20th century up until the mid-1950s, when the all-steel cars were painted blue. It was customary that "off-the-shelf" maroon paint was generally used to distinguish it from bright red on the ends.

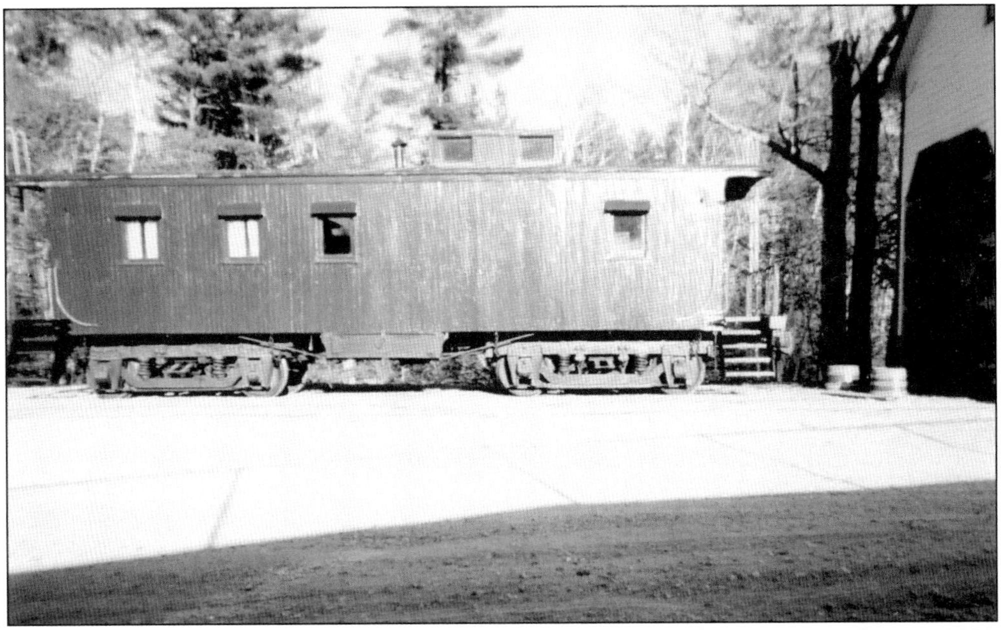

B&M caboose No. 104082 appears at Clark's Trading Post in Lincoln, New Hampshire, in 2001. Red was used for visibility, the same reason fire trucks are painted red. When a buggy was shopped, a bright red (signal) was applied to the ends. This tint quickly faded to a caboose red when the sun's rays took their toll.

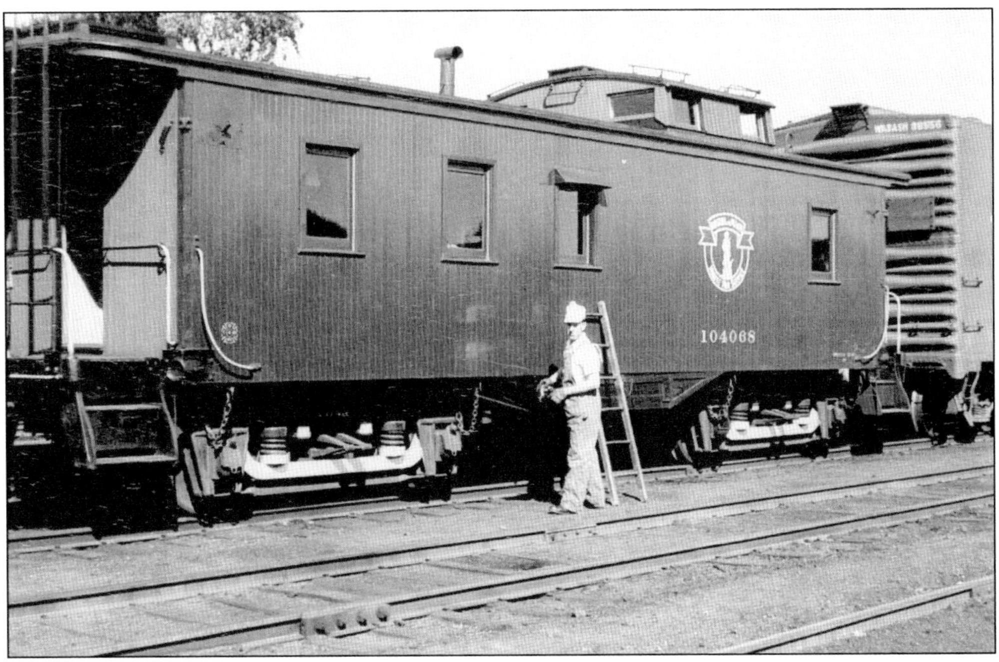

Shown here is B&M caboose No. 104068. The freight conductor, taking care of the caboose of the Lawrence–Dover local, is seen before traveling to Lawrence, Massachusetts. Many of the modifications made to the caboose were reflected in the purchase of new equipment.

Three

BEYOND THE RAIL

BUSES, TRUCKS, BOATS, AND WORKSHOPS

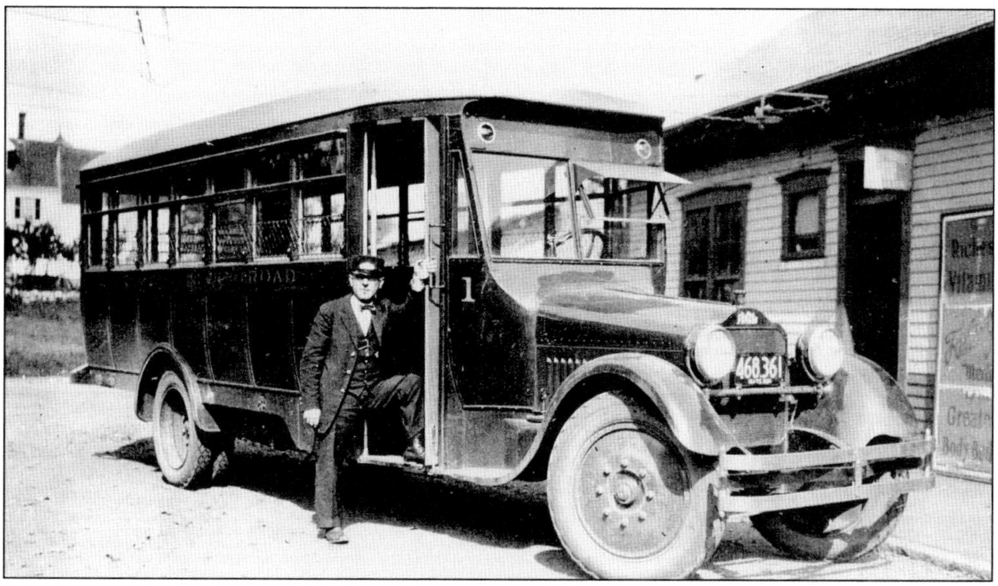

B&M bus No. 1, shown at Ashburnham, Massachusetts, in 1924, was built by the White Motor Company. The bus operator pictured at the door is Lee Scribner. The story of the B&M Transportation Company starts with this White Model 50-A bus seating 25 passengers, with a streetcar-type body. No. 1 was owned and lettered by the B&M, predating the formation of the railroad bus subsidiary. The small size of the bus was matched by the length of the initial route: 2.6 miles from Ashburnham to South Ashburnham, Massachusetts.

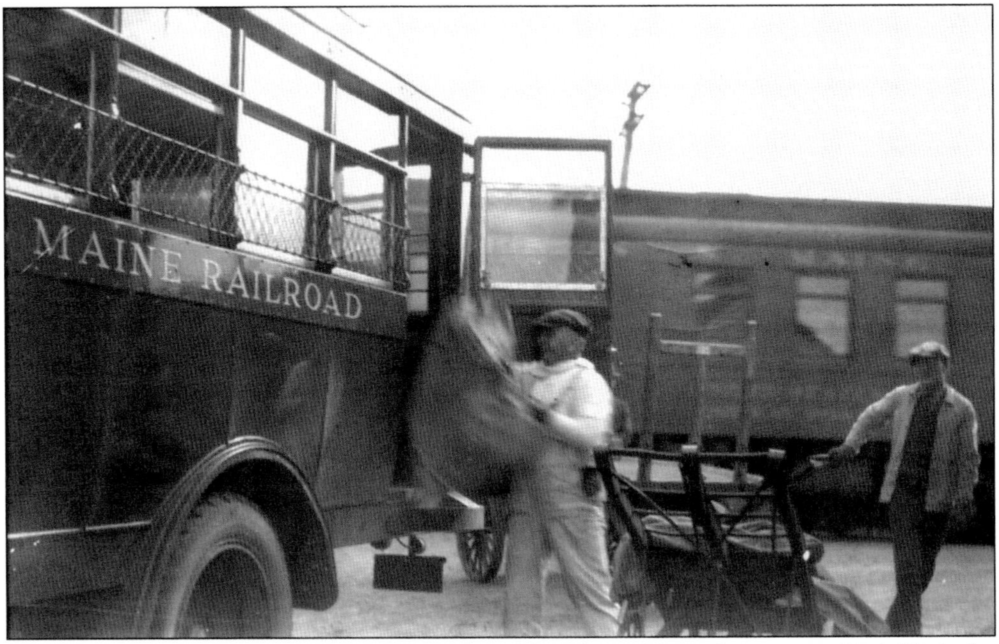

Mail is loaded into B&M bus No. 1 at South Ashburnham, Massachusetts, in 1924. With the knowledge of operating a bus line, the B&M formed the Boston and Maine Transportation Company on November 15, 1924, incorporating under the laws of the commonwealth of Massachusetts. Organized by Howard A. Fritch, the company grew and eventually offered interstate, local, and city service throughout New England. The first endeavor of the new company was to take over the discontinued services of the Portsmouth Electric Railway, a B&M subsidiary, on May 17, 1925. The Portsmouth trolley company was one of two city lines owned by the B&M, the other being the Concord (New Hampshire) Street Railway. When the Portsmouth system shut down, some of its trolley equipment migrated to Concord until it, too, ceased operations.

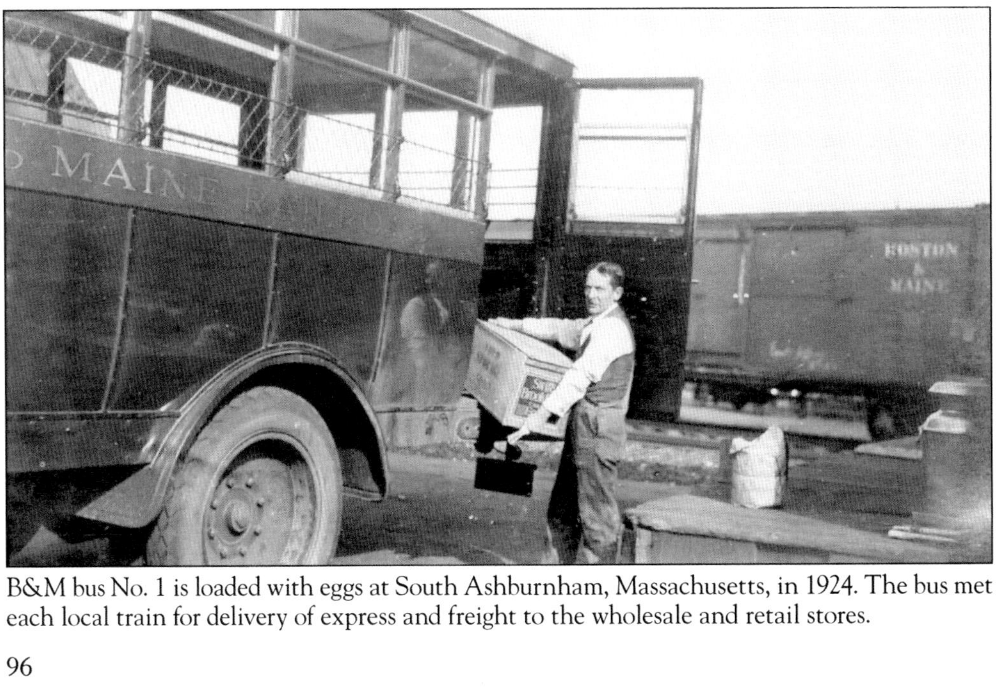

B&M bus No. 1 is loaded with eggs at South Ashburnham, Massachusetts, in 1924. The bus met each local train for delivery of express and freight to the wholesale and retail stores.

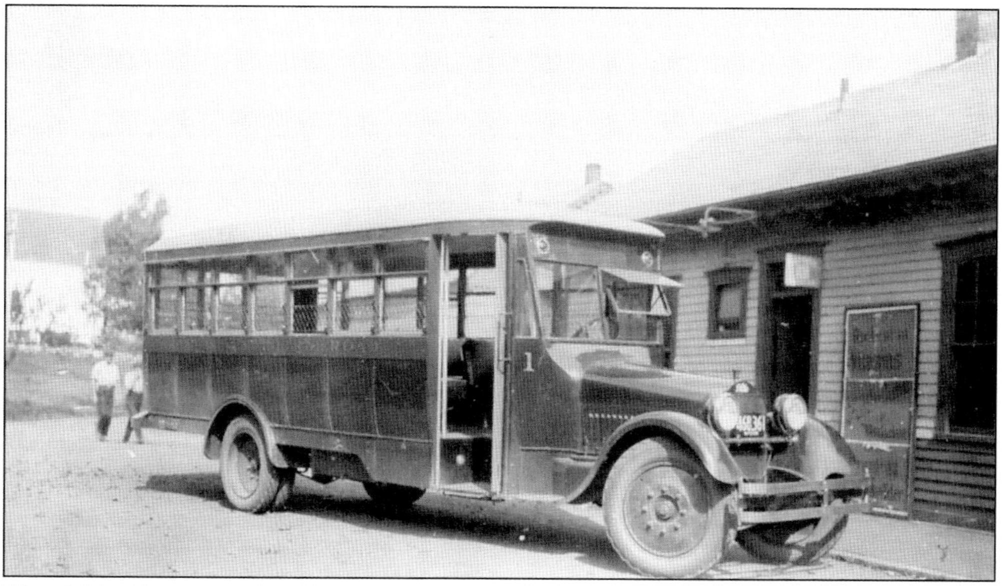

This B&M Transportation Company motor coach, built by the Yellow Coach Company, was used on the Boston–Portland service, which began on July 1, 1925. In June 1925, a second B&M Transportation Company bus operation got under way, again based in Portsmouth. This route ran northward to York Beach, Maine, via York Corner, where connections could be made to Ogunquit, Wells, and Kennebunk.

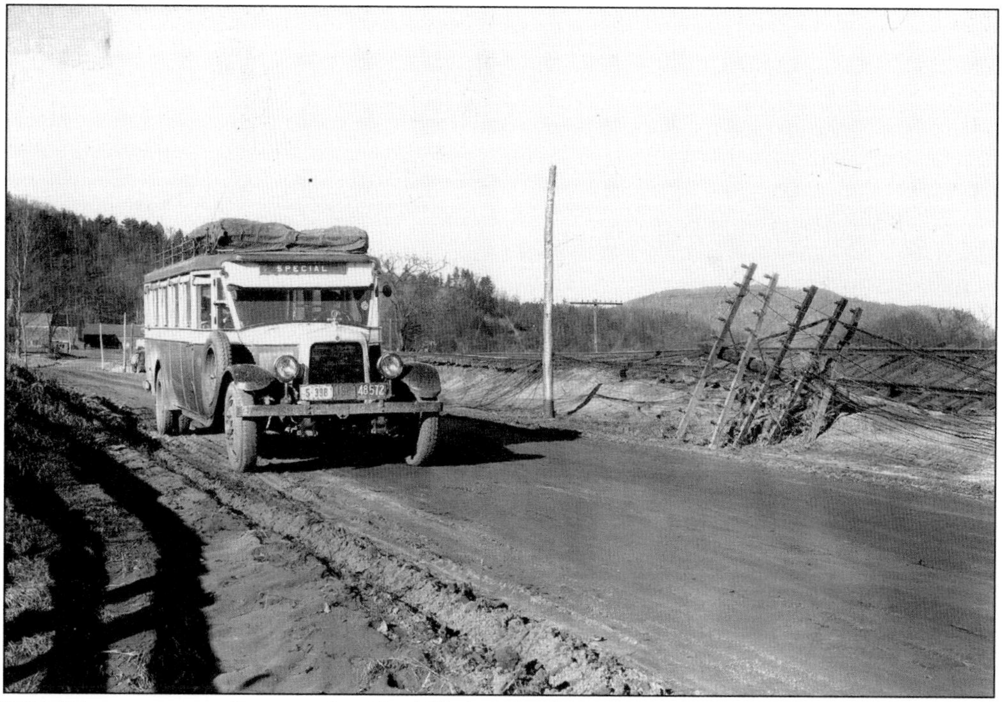

B&M Transportation Company bus No. 115, shown at Westminster, Vermont, provided emergency service after the 1927 floods. In July 20, 1925, a new service began to New Hampshire's White Mountains. The route roughly approximated the *Mountaineer* run from Boston to Bethlehem, New Hampshire, via Portsmouth, Rochester, and Intervale.

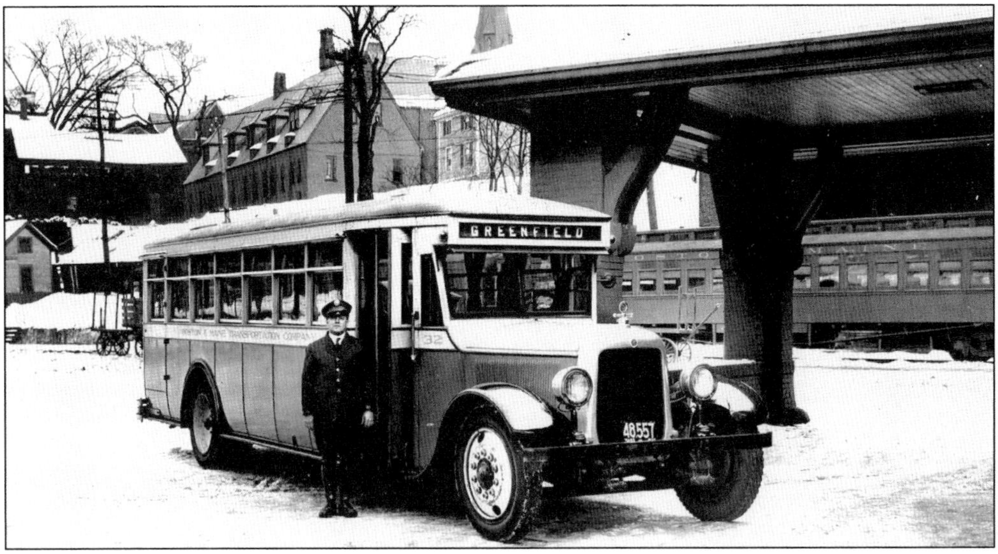

B&M Transportation Company Yellow Coach No. 32 is seen at the Northampton, Massachusetts, railroad station in 1927. The B&M was active in the marketing of intercity bus service, mainly during the 1930s and 1940s. The company operated buses to replace certain lightly used trains and to run along railroad routes, preventing other bus lines from competing with its passenger trains.

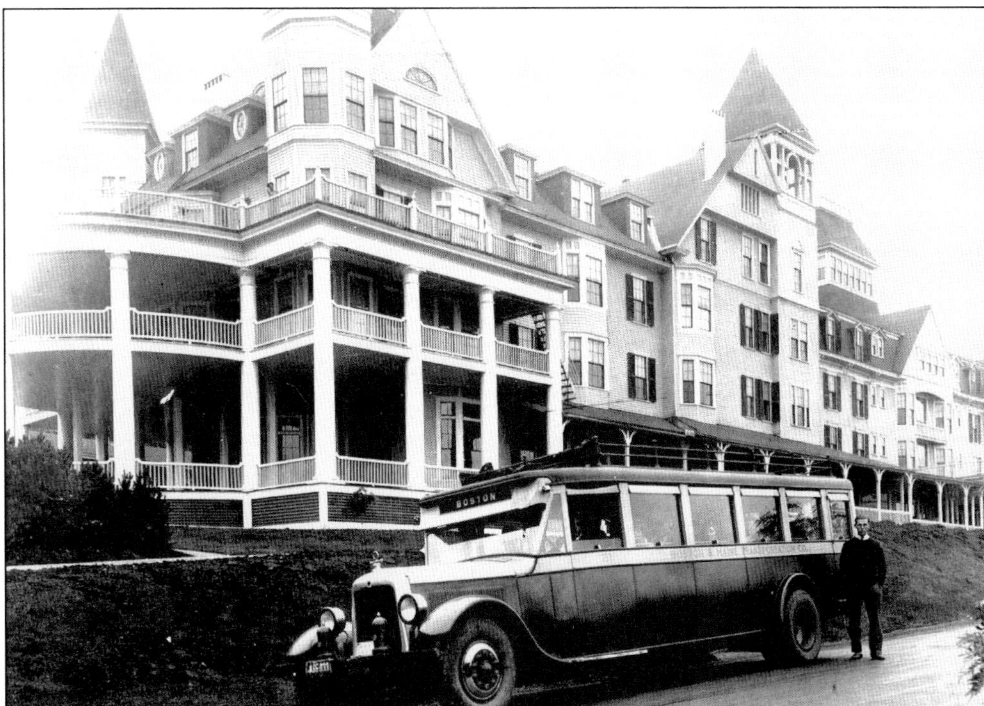

B&M Yellow Coach No. 121 appears at Twin Mountains, New Hampshire, in 1926. Luggage racks were important amenities because there was no storage space underneath the passenger cabin, an early example of "low-floor" transit equipment. The bus would meet the train and take passengers to their favorite resort.

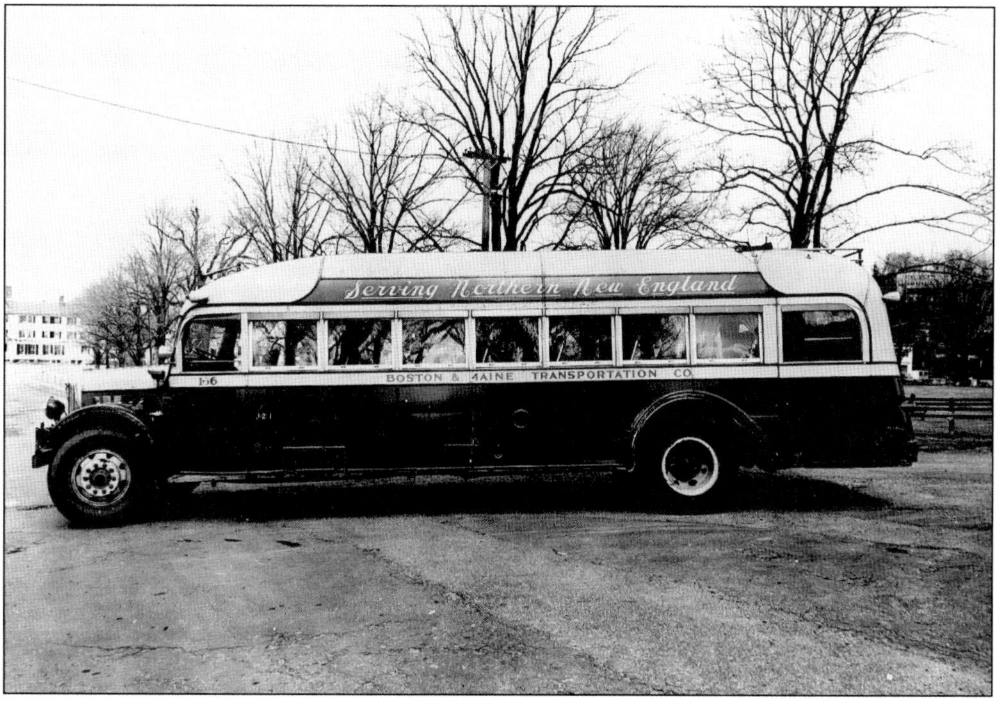

B&M Transportation Company Yellow Coach No. 166 is pictured in Lowell, Massachusetts, in 1941.

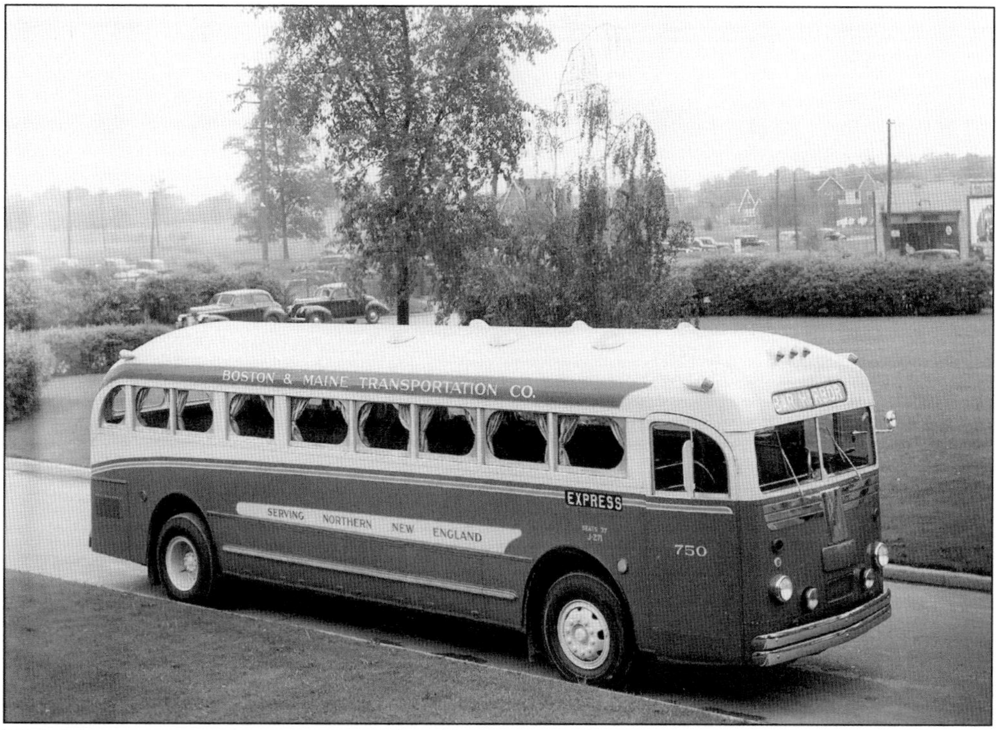

B&M Transportation Company streamlined bus No. 750, shown in East Cambridge, Massachusetts, about 1945, was built by the Yellow Coach Company.

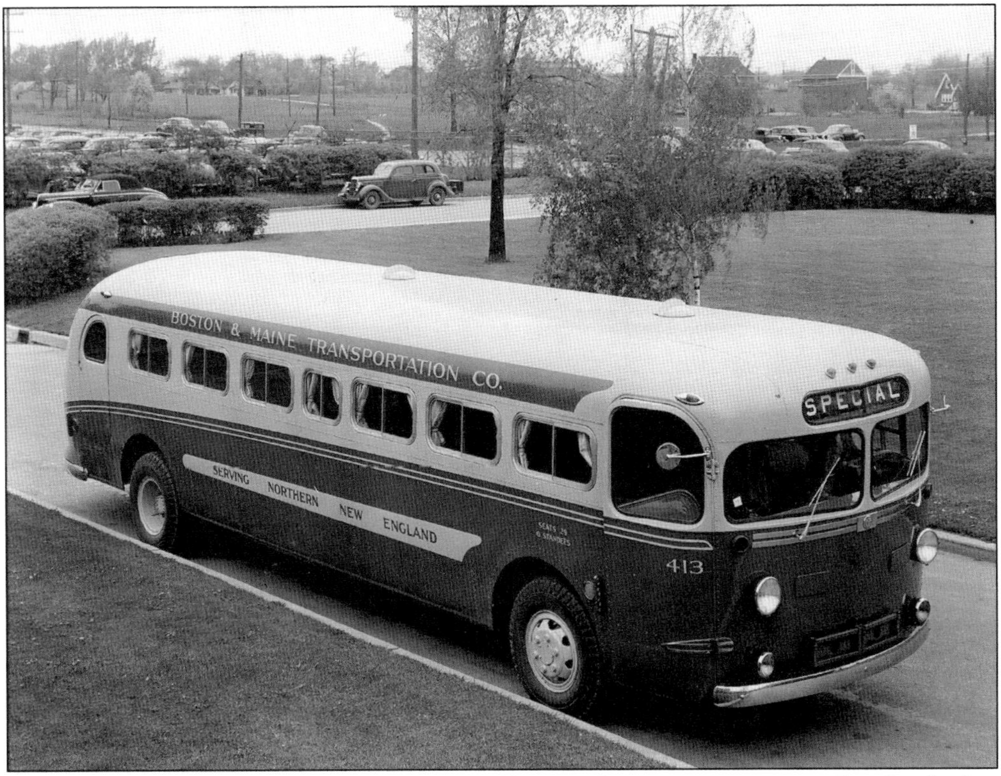

B&M streamlined bus No. 413, also built by the Yellow Coach Company, appears in East Cambridge, Massachusetts, around 1945.

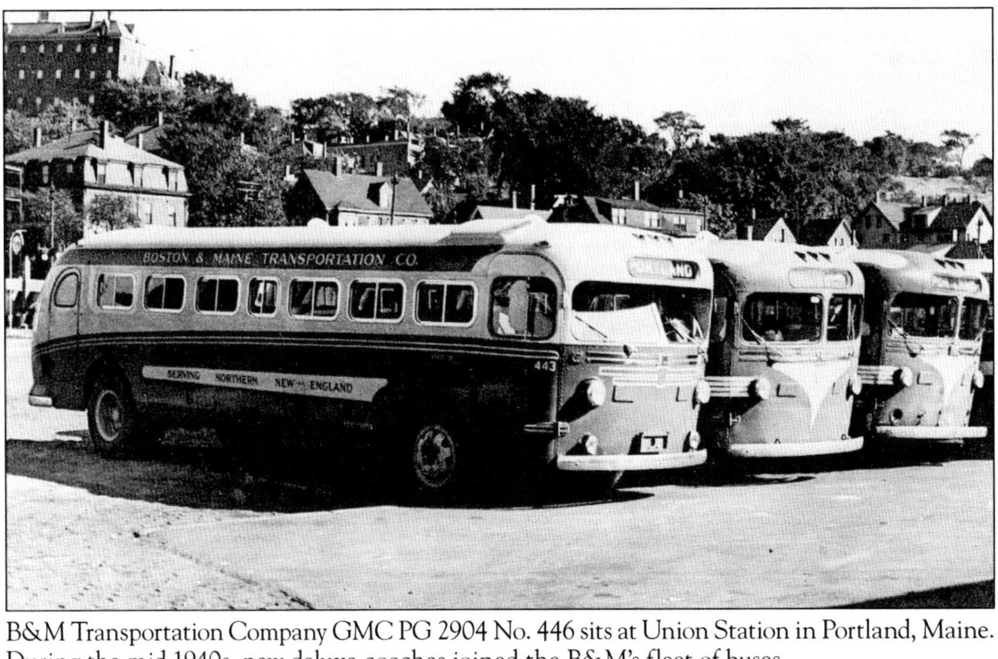

B&M Transportation Company GMC PG 2904 No. 446 sits at Union Station in Portland, Maine. During the mid-1940s, new deluxe coaches joined the B&M's fleet of buses.

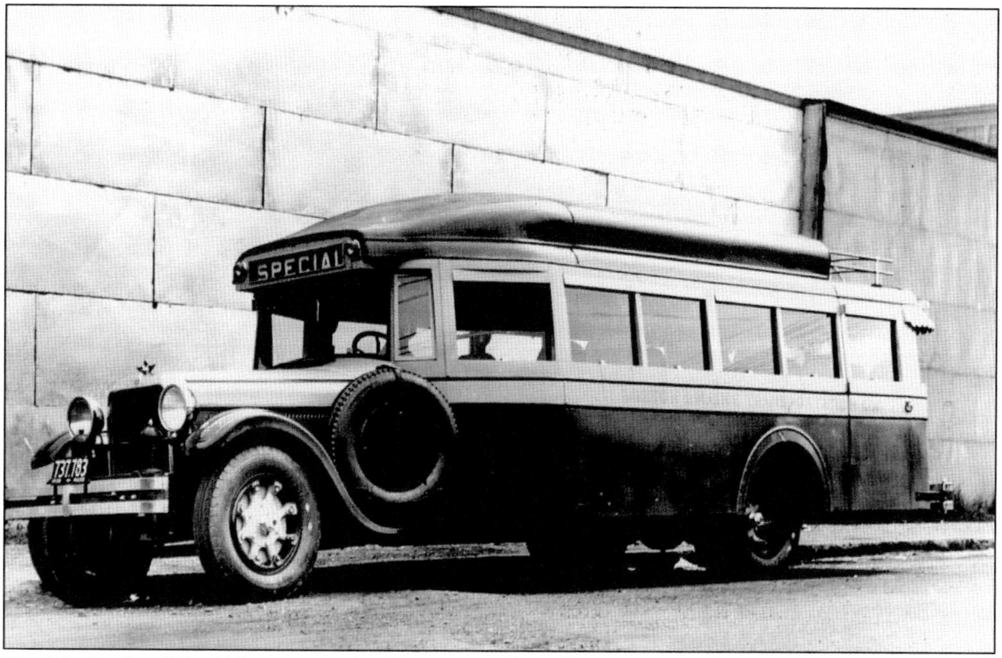

Studebaker bus No. 115 is pictured in Boston in the 1930s. In 1924, the company formed the bus subsidiary Boston and Maine Transportation Company, and by 1957, the B&M had sold it to the Transcontinental Bus System/Continental Trailways.

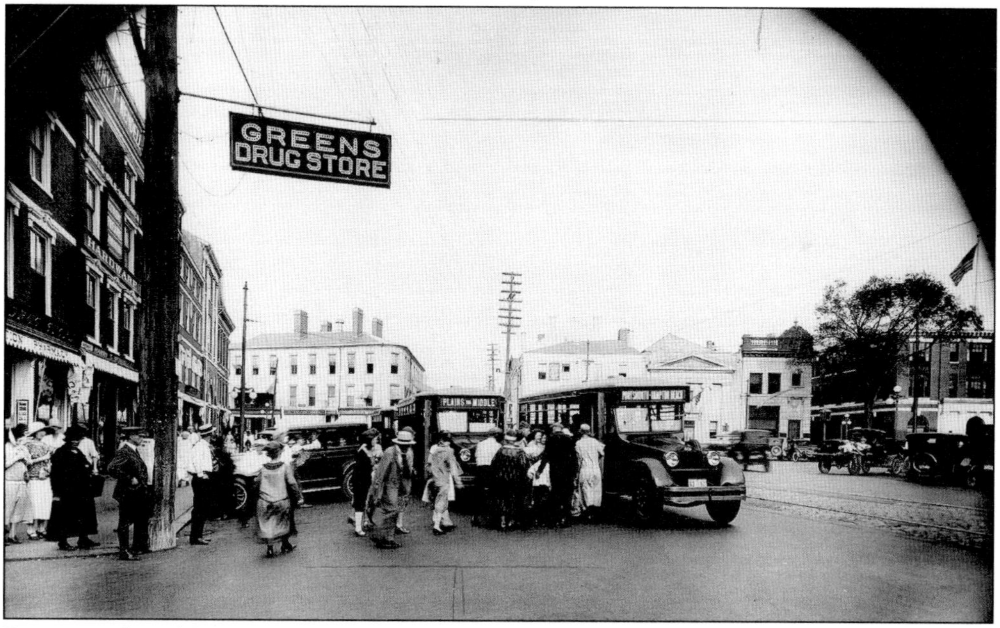

Passengers board B&M Transportation Company buses in Market Square, Portsmouth, New Hampshire, in 1927. The company was known as a "modern, progressive firm" that provided its passengers with economically sustainable and frequent service and first-class bus equipment for comfort and speed. Fans will long remember the sharp, two-toned green buses dashing between towns large and small, and folks in northern New England will recall their ride to visit family, their trip home from a stint in the service, or their journey to see the big city.

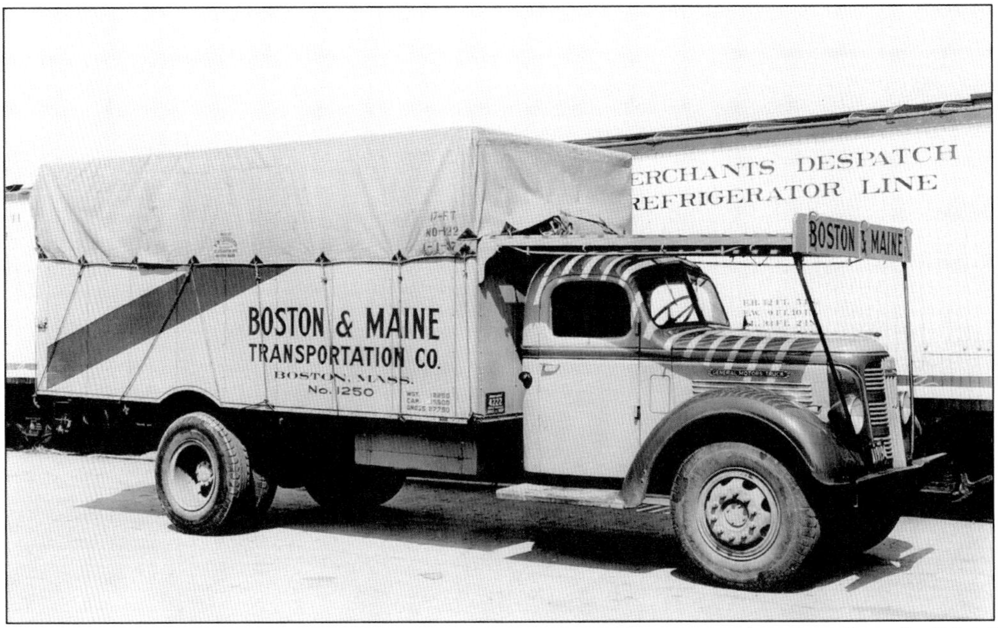

B&M Transportation Company truck No. 1250 is pictured here around 1937. When the B&M formed the transportation company, it also bought a fleet of trucks to transport goods and less-than-carload freight from the stations to the individual businesses. At this time, competition from the motor vehicle was growing.

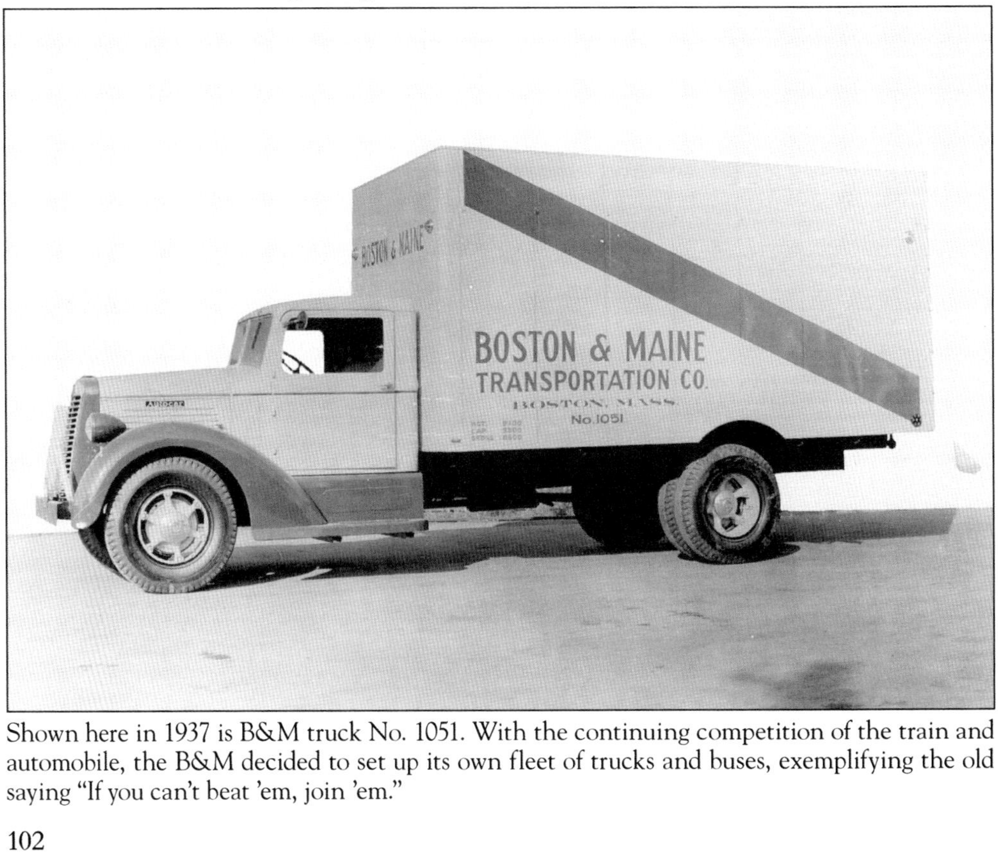

Shown here in 1937 is B&M truck No. 1051. With the continuing competition of the train and automobile, the B&M decided to set up its own fleet of trucks and buses, exemplifying the old saying "If you can't beat 'em, join 'em."

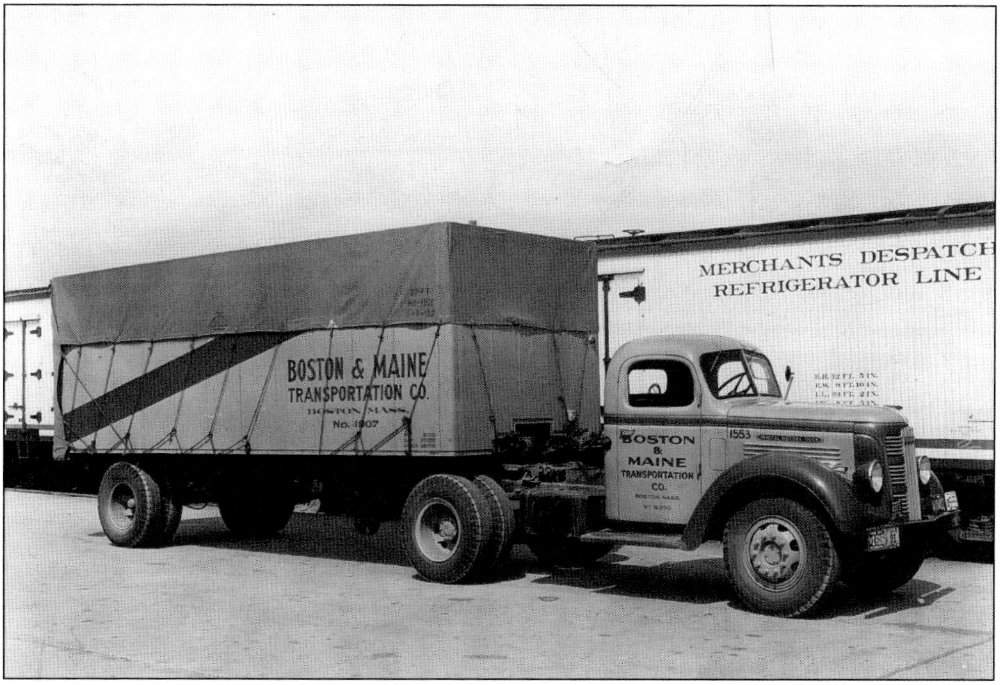

B&M Transportation Company truck No. 1553, with carrier No. 1907, is pictured about 1937. These trucks came in different sizes so as to meet the needs of the growing mobile public.

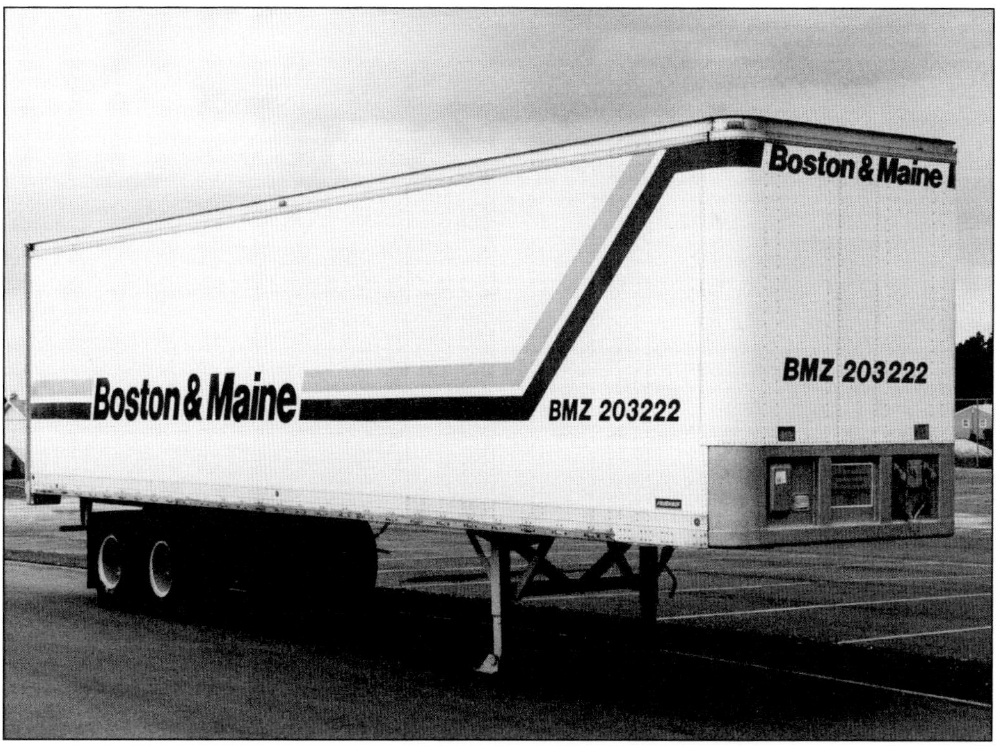

B&M trailer No. BMZ 203222 was one of 250 new trailers leased in 1980.

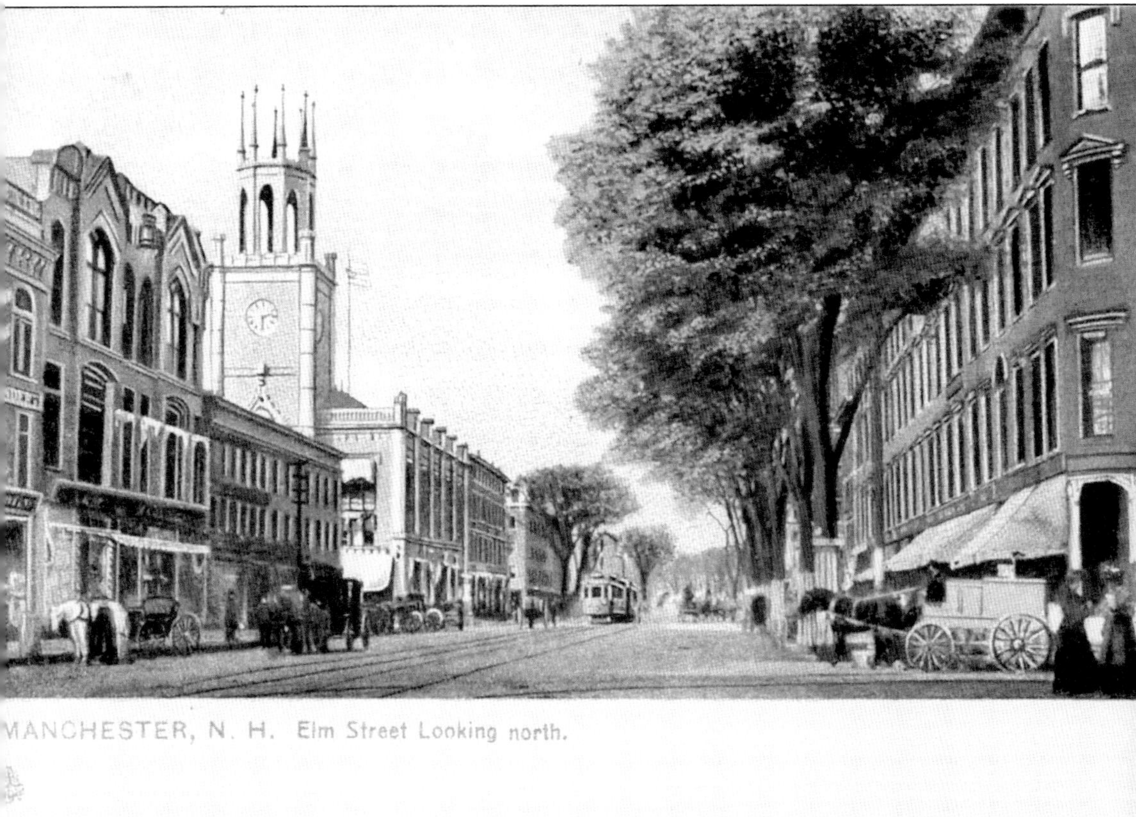

A trolley car travels along Elm Street in Manchester, New Hampshire, the principal street of the city and one of the handsomest thoroughfares in New England. It extends for about three miles, nearly north and south; this view looks north. The street, 100 feet wide with spacious sidewalks, was named for the row of elm trees originally placed in the center of the roadway. In 1901, the Boston and Maine Railroad incorporated the Concord and Manchester Electric branch of the B&M. In time, the Concord and Manchester tracks connected with other interurbans, allowing people to travel by trolley from downtown Concord to Hampton Beach, New Hampshire.

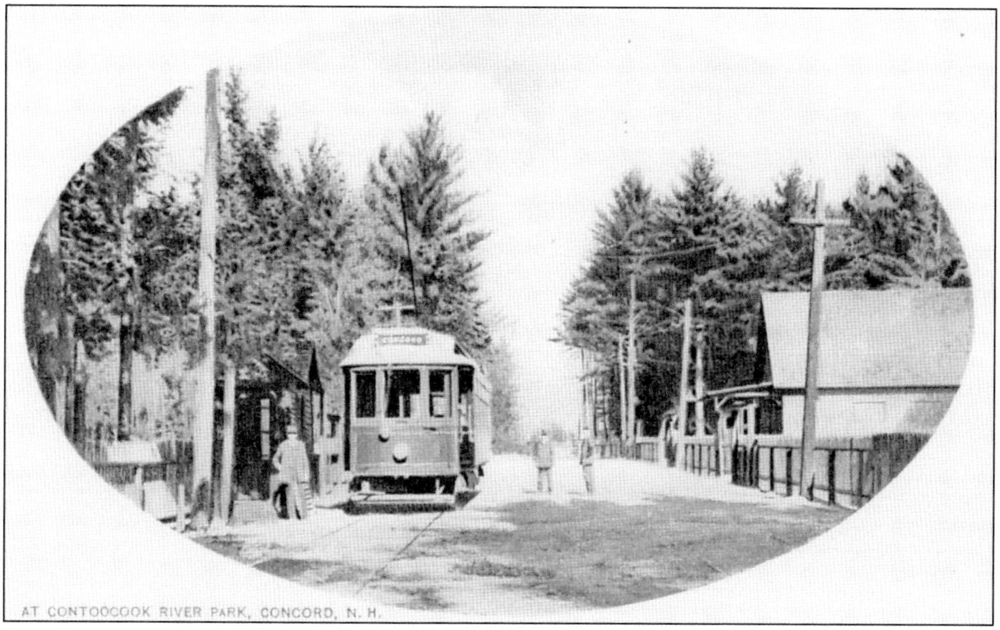

An electric streetcar is shown at Contoocook River Park in Concord, New Hampshire, in the early 1900s. In 1919, about 17 street railways were operating in the state.

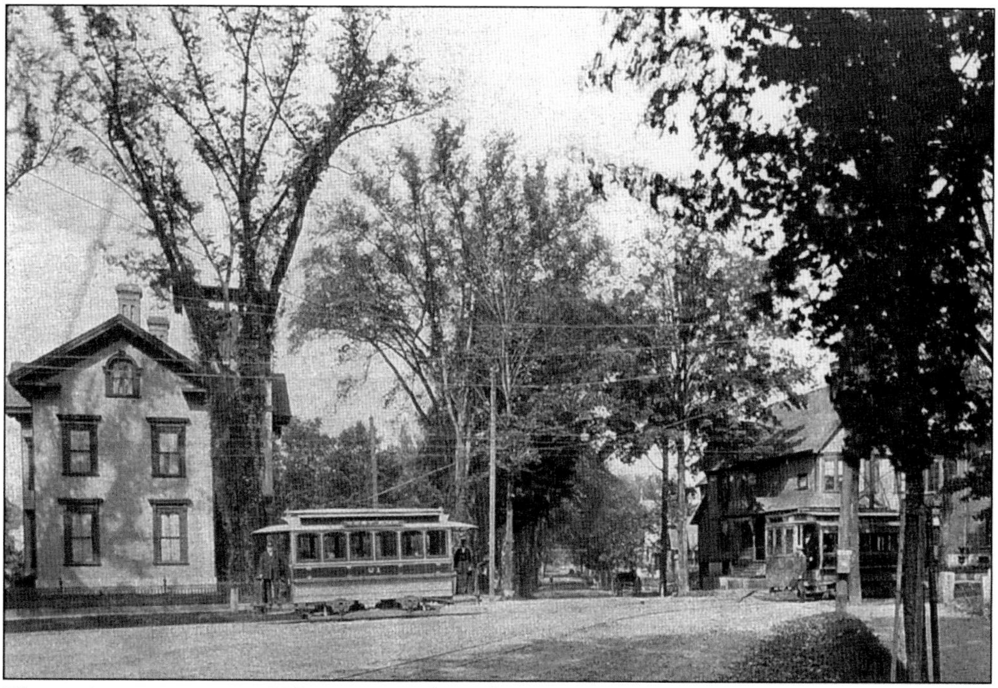

This is the intersection of Pleasant, South, and Green Streets in Concord, New Hampshire, in the early 1900s.

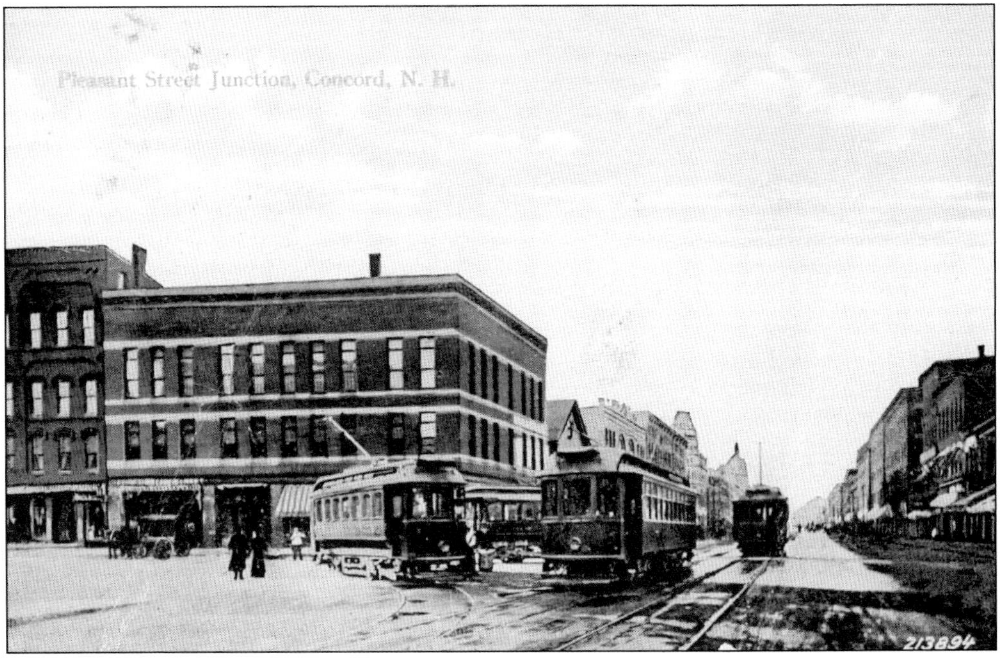

A trolley car sits at the Pleasant Street junction in Concord, New Hampshire, around the 1890s.

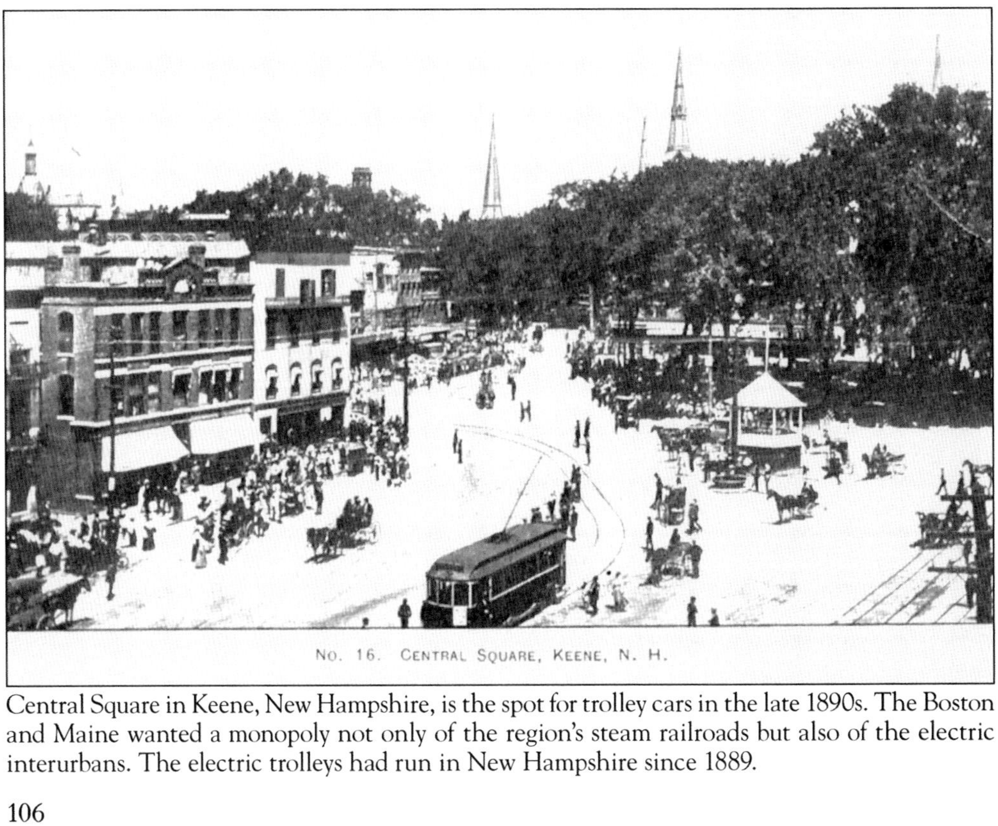

Central Square in Keene, New Hampshire, is the spot for trolley cars in the late 1890s. The Boston and Maine wanted a monopoly not only of the region's steam railroads but also of the electric interurbans. The electric trolleys had run in New Hampshire since 1889.

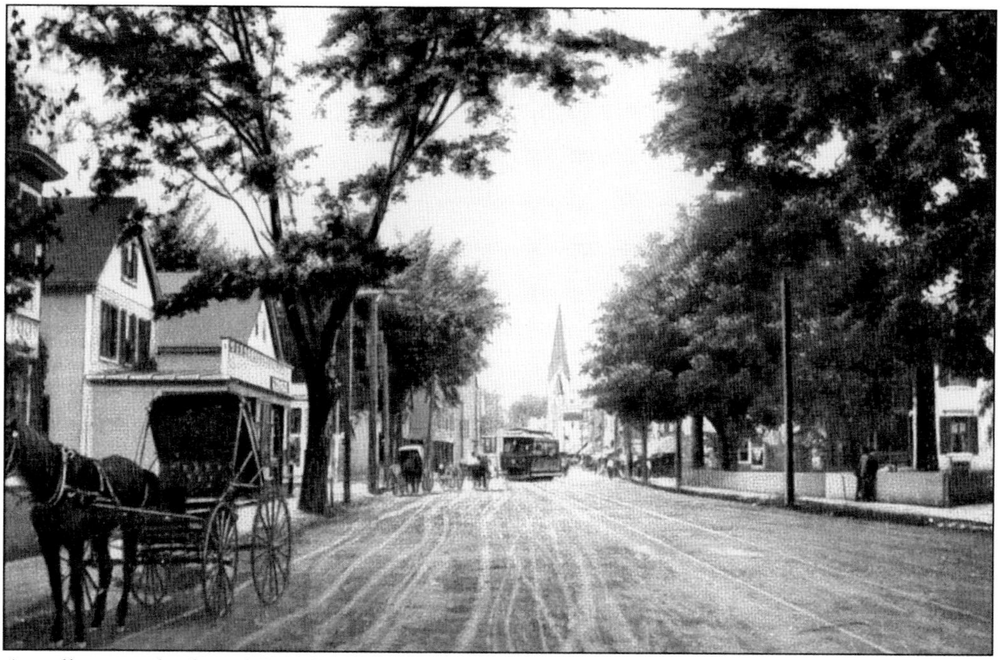

A trolley travels along Main Street in Laconia, New Hampshire, in 1908. This Laconia–Weirs line was very popular for both tourist and locals alike.

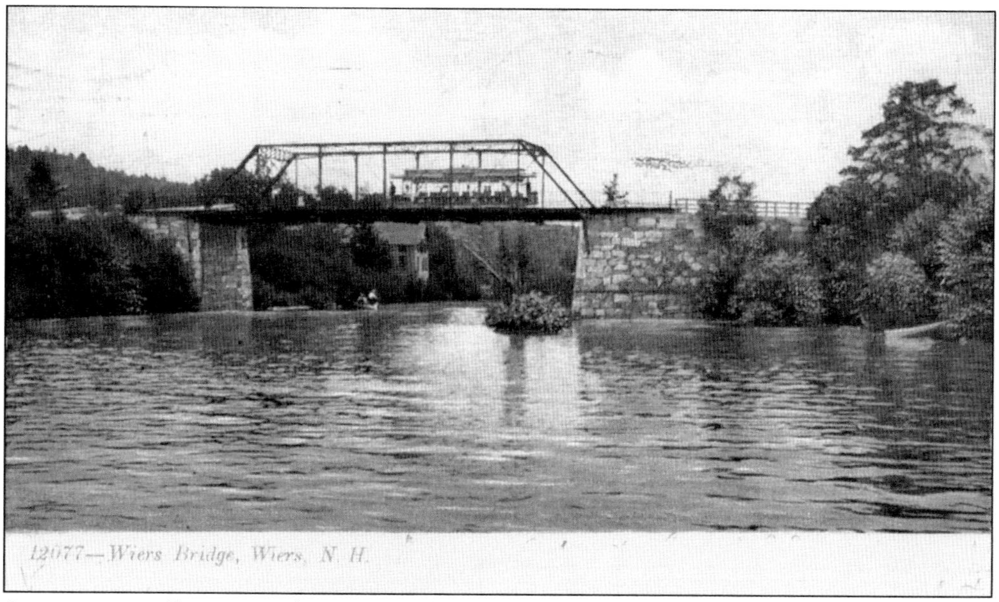

An open-air trolley crosses the Weirs Bridge in Laconia, New Hampshire, in the early 1900s.

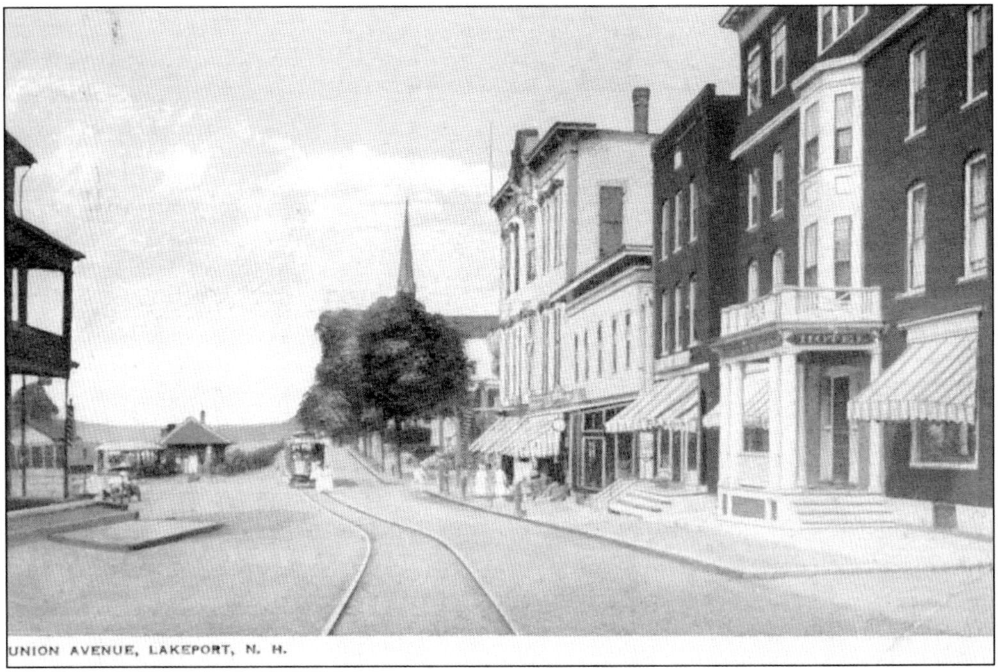

An open-air trolley travels east on Union Avenue, along Paugus Bay to the Weirs, in Lakeport, New Hampshire, in 1923.

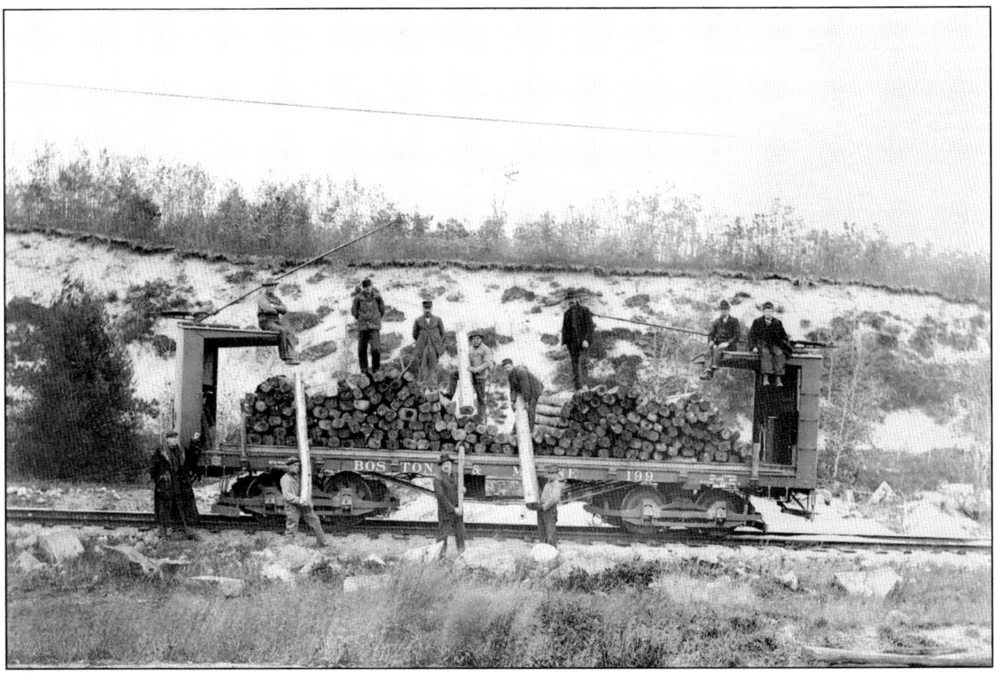

B&M/Concord and Manchester Electric Railway trolley No. 199 is seen near Bow Junction, New Hampshire, around 1903. Most of the trolley lines built in the decade of the 1890s were inner-city lines, like those running up and down Main Street.

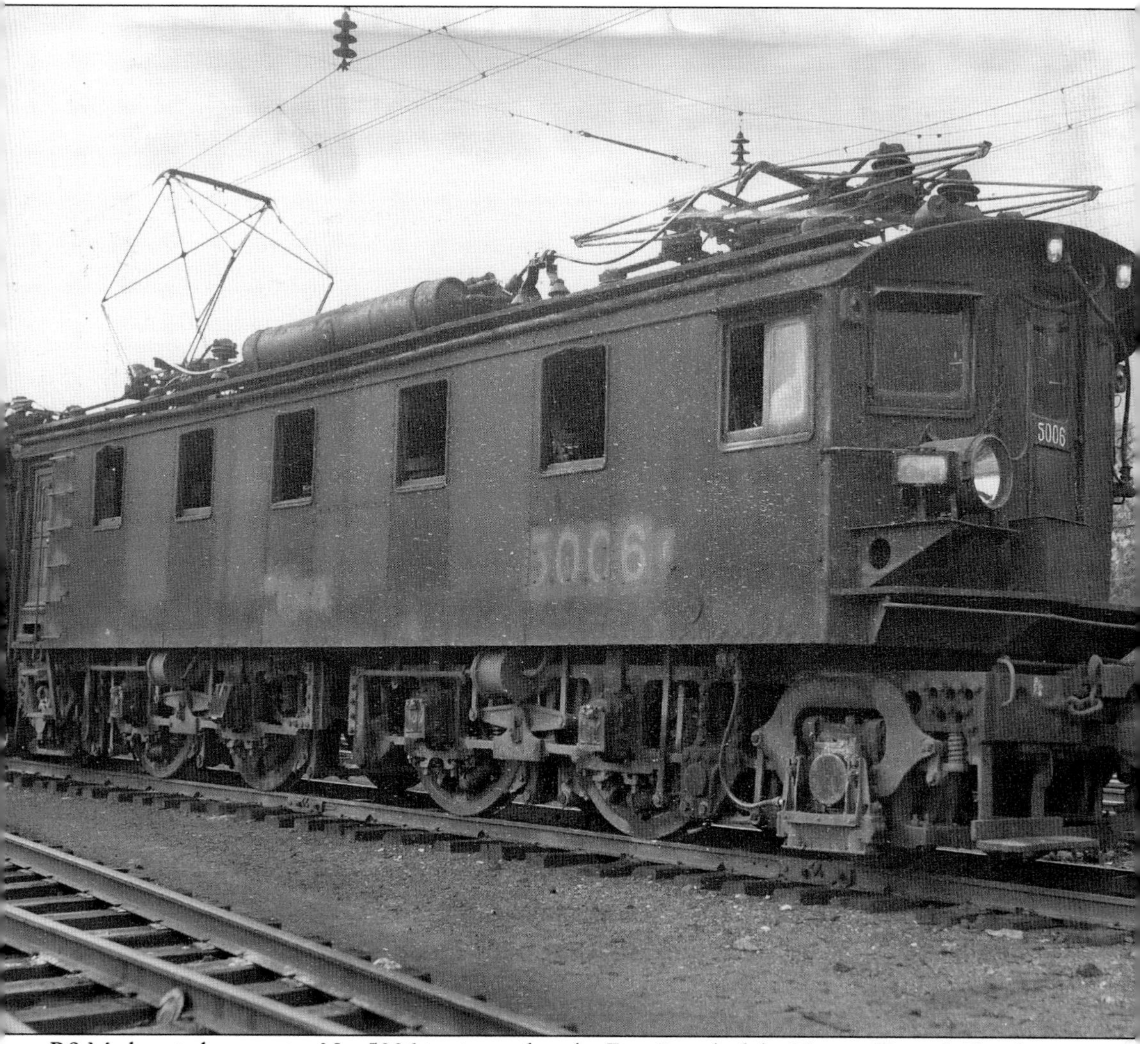

B&M electric locomotive No. 5006 is pictured at the East Portal of the Hoosac Tunnel, Florida, Massachusetts, on September 5, 1945.

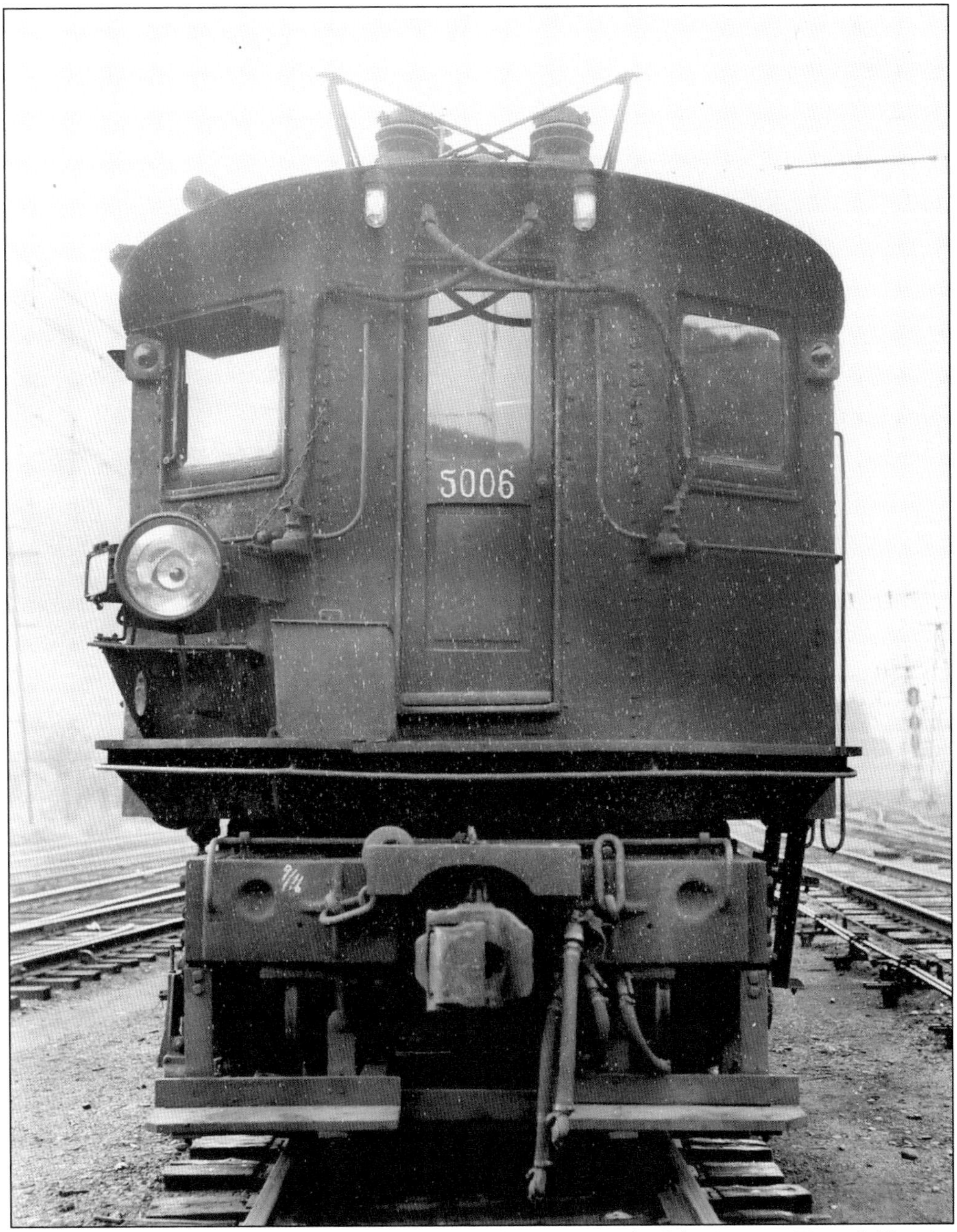

B&M electric locomotive No. 5006 is shown at the East Portal of the Hoosac Tunnel, Florida, Massachusetts, on September 5, 1945.

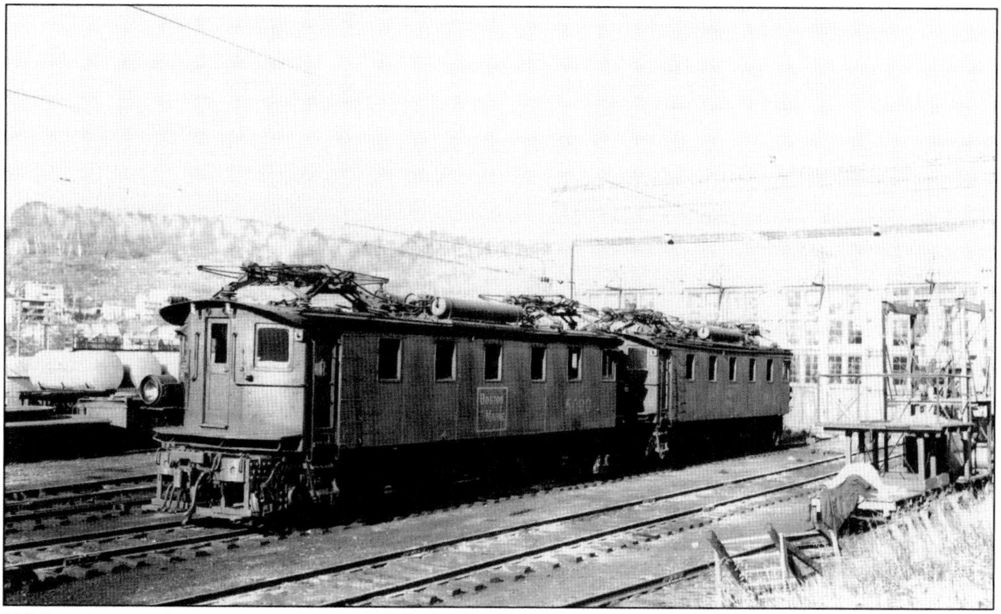

B&M electric locomotive Nos. 5000 and 5002 rest at the North Adams Shop in Florida, Massachusetts, on October 30, 1933.

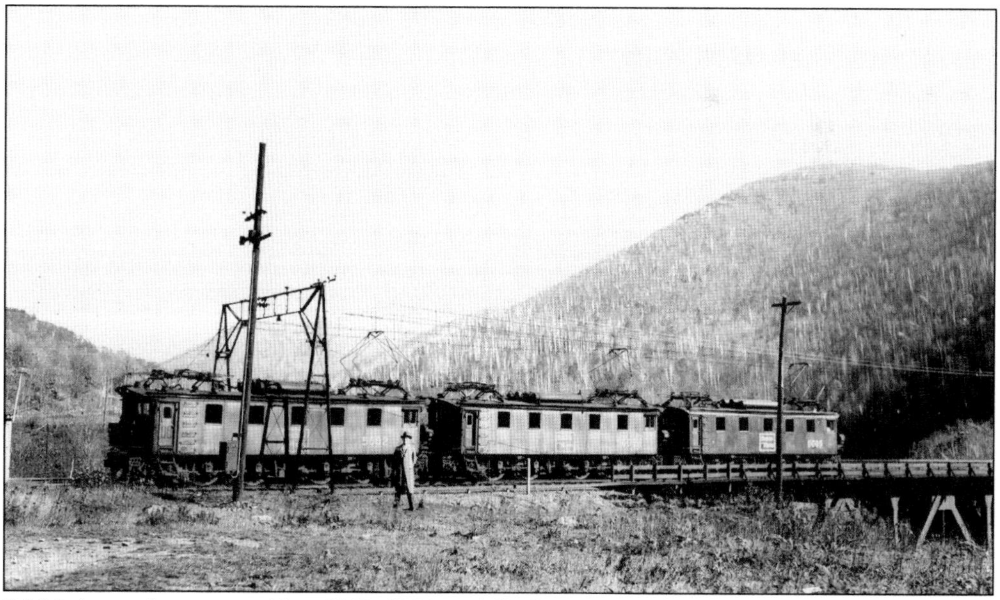

B&M electric locomotive Nos. 5002, 5000, and 5005 are pictured at the East Portal of the Hoosac Tunnel, Florida, Massachusetts, on October 30, 1933.

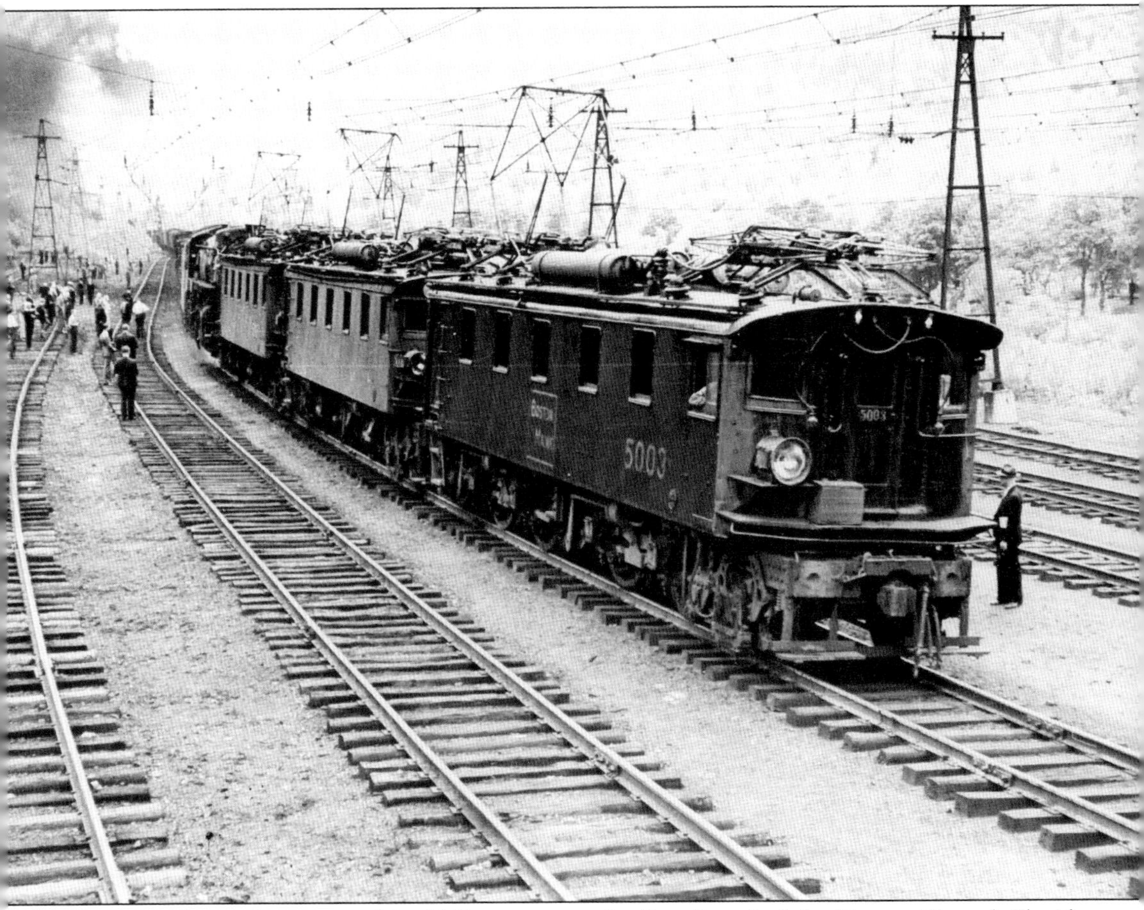

B&M electric locomotive No. 5003 appears at the East Portal of the Hoosac Tunnel, Florida, Massachusetts, in May 1938.

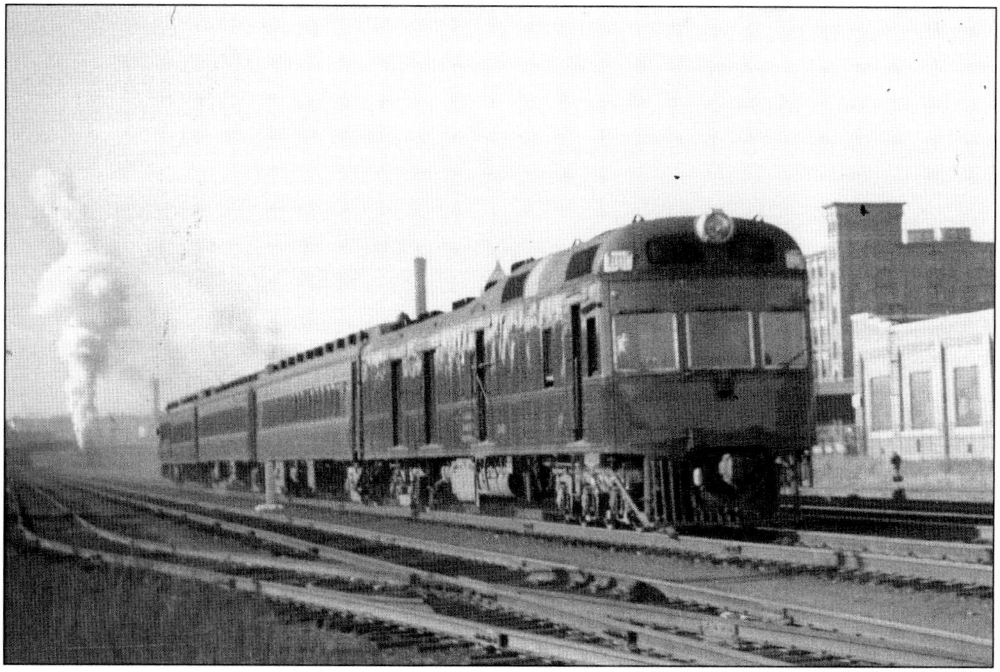

Sometimes called "Mate," B&M diesel-electric motor car No. 1141, rolls a local inboard at Lawrence, Massachusetts, on a snowless December day in 1936.

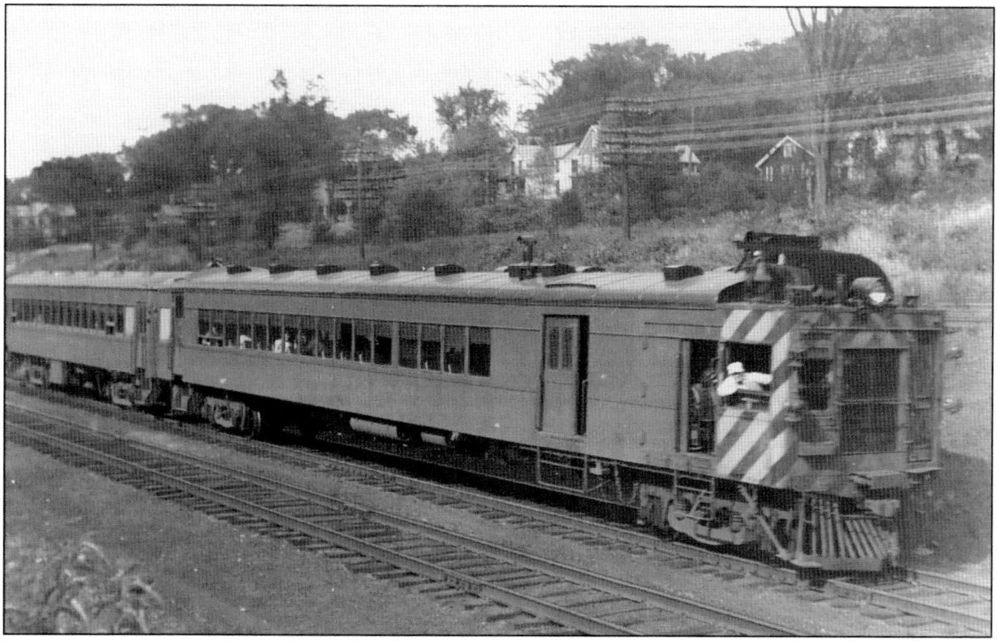

B&M No. 1195, an Osgood Bradley EMC built in 1929, is seen at Greenfield, Massachusetts, on September 21, 1945. Gas railcars were not intended to serve as locomotives, although under certain conditions they hauled more than one trailer. The fleet of gas railcars acquired their striped-end treatment during the late 1930s, but their number shrank until only 11 remained by the end of World War II.

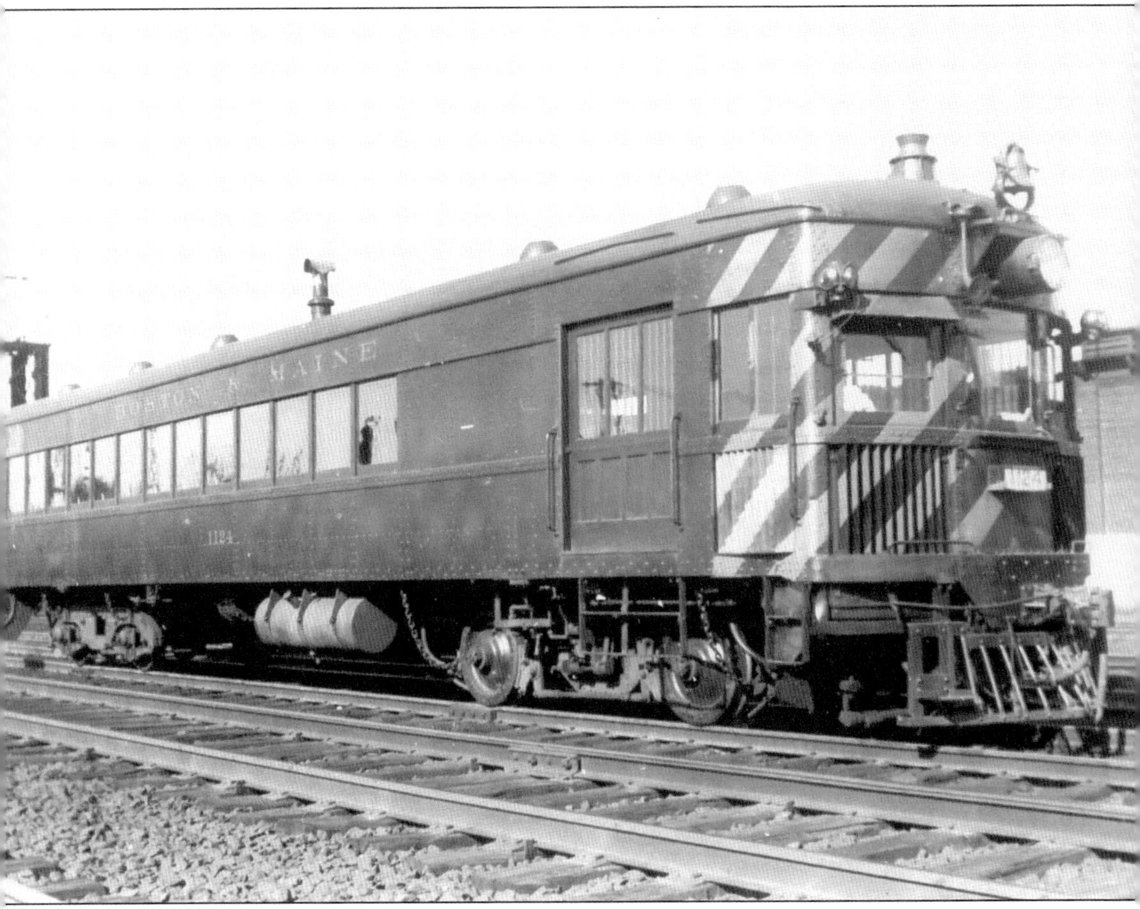

A Brill-built gas mechanical car, B&M No. 1124 is pictured in Lawrence, Massachusetts, on October 12, 1936. Through years of changing assignments, the gas railcars were found all over the system. They spent their lives sputtering through the hills and valleys of New England, where they never received the attention accorded the proud steam locomotives. While it was not necessary on their assigned runs, many maintained that the "gas buggies" could race like the wind. The B&M gas-electric cars made their final runs in 1956 and vanished along with the steam locomotives.

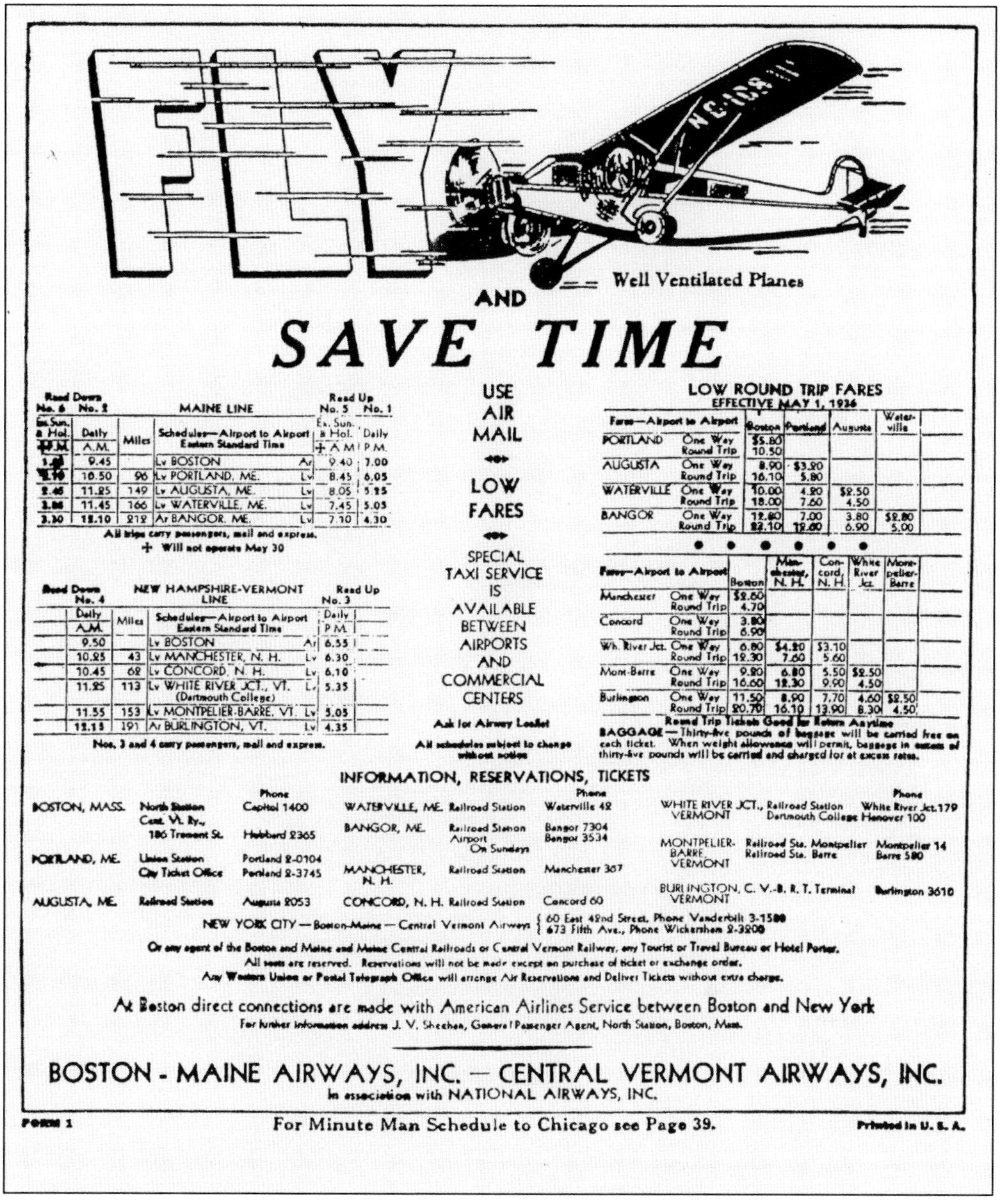

FLY

Well Ventilated Planes

AND

SAVE TIME

USE AIR MAIL

LOW FARES

SPECIAL TAXI SERVICE IS AVAILABLE BETWEEN AIRPORTS AND COMMERCIAL CENTERS

Ask for Airway Leaflet

All schedules subject to change without notice

MAINE LINE

Read Down No. 6 Ex. Sun. & Hol. P.M.	No. 2 Daily A.M.	Miles	Schedules—Airport to Airport Eastern Standard Time		Read Up No. 5 Ex. Sun. & Hol. + A.M.	No. 1 Daily P.M.
[illegible]	9.45		Lv BOSTON	Ar	9.40	7.00
[illegible]	10.50	96	Lv PORTLAND, ME.	Lv	8.45	6.05
2.45	11.25	149	Lv AUGUSTA, ME.	Lv	8.05	5.25
3.05	11.45	166	Lv WATERVILLE, ME.	Lv	7.45	5.05
3.30	12.10	212	Ar BANGOR, ME.	Lv	7.10	4.30

All trips carry passengers, mail and express.

+ Will not operate May 30

NEW HAMPSHIRE-VERMONT LINE

Read Down No. 4 Daily A.M.	Miles	Schedules—Airport to Airport Eastern Standard Time		Read Up No. 3 Daily P.M.
9.50		Lv BOSTON	Ar	6.55
10.25	43	Lv MANCHESTER, N. H.	Lv	6.30
10.45	62	Lv CONCORD, N. H.	Lv	6.10
11.25	113	Lv WHITE RIVER JCT., VT. (Dartmouth College)	Lv	5.35
11.55	153	Lv MONTPELIER-BARRE, VT.	Lv	5.05
12.15	191	Ar BURLINGTON, VT.	Lv	4.35

Nos. 3 and 4 carry passengers, mail and express.

LOW ROUND TRIP FARES
EFFECTIVE MAY 1, 1936

Fares—Airport to Airport		Boston	Portland	Augusta	Waterville
PORTLAND	One Way	$5.80			
	Round Trip	10.50			
AUGUSTA	One Way	8.90	$3.20		
	Round Trip	16.10	5.80		
WATERVILLE	One Way	10.00	4.20	$2.50	
	Round Trip	18.00	7.60	4.50	
BANGOR	One Way	12.80	7.00	3.80	$2.80
	Round Trip	23.10	12.60	6.90	5.00

Fares—Airport to Airport		Boston	Manchester, N. H.	Concord, N. H.	White River Jct.	Montpelier-Barre
Manchester	One Way	$2.60				
	Round Trip	4.70				
Concord	One Way	3.80				
	Round Trip	6.90				
Wh. River Jct.	One Way	6.80	$4.20	$3.10		
	Round Trip	12.30	7.60	5.60		
Mont-Barre	One Way	9.20	6.80	5.50	$2.50	
	Round Trip	16.60	12.30	9.90	4.50	
Burlington	One Way	11.50	8.90	7.70	4.60	$2.50
	Round Trip	20.70	16.10	13.90	8.30	4.50

Round Trip Tickets Good for Return Anytime

BAGGAGE—Thirty-five pounds of baggage will be carried free on each ticket. When weight allowance will permit, baggage in excess of thirty-five pounds will be carried and charged for at excess rates.

INFORMATION, RESERVATIONS, TICKETS

		Phone
BOSTON, MASS.	North Station	Capitol 1400
	Cent. Vt. Ry., 186 Tremont St.	Hubbard 2365
PORTLAND, ME.	Union Station	Portland 2-0104
	City Ticket Office	Portland 2-3745
AUGUSTA, ME.	Railroad Station	Augusta 2053
WATERVILLE, ME.	Railroad Station	Waterville 42
BANGOR, ME.	Railroad Station	Bangor 7304
	Airport On Sundays	Bangor 3534
MANCHESTER, N. H.	Railroad Station	Manchester 367
CONCORD, N. H.	Railroad Station	Concord 60
WHITE RIVER JCT., VERMONT	Railroad Station	White River Jct. 179
	Dartmouth College	Hanover 100
MONTPELIER-BARRE, VERMONT	Railroad Sta. Montpelier	Montpelier 14
	Railroad Sta. Barre	Barre 580
BURLINGTON, VERMONT	C. V.-B. R. T. Terminal	Burlington 3610

NEW YORK CITY—Boston-Maine—Central Vermont Airways { 60 East 42nd Street, Phone Vanderbilt 3-1580; 673 Fifth Ave., Phone Wickersham 2-3200 }

Or any agent of the Boston and Maine and Maine Central Railroads or Central Vermont Railway, any Tourist or Travel Bureau or Hotel Porter.

All seats are reserved. Reservations will not be made except on purchase of ticket or exchange order.

Any Western Union or Postal Telegraph Office will arrange Air Reservations and Deliver Tickets without extra charge.

At Boston direct connections are made with American Airlines Service between Boston and New York

For further information address J. V. Sheehan, General Passenger Agent, North Station, Boston, Mass.

BOSTON - MAINE AIRWAYS, INC. — CENTRAL VERMONT AIRWAYS, INC.

In association with NATIONAL AIRWAYS, INC.

FORM 1 — For Minute Man Schedule to Chicago see Page 39. — Printed in U. S. A.

Pictured here is a 1936 Boston-Maine Airways schedule. These aircrafts were touted as "well-ventilated"—quite an understatement. In 1931, commercial aviation started in northern New England with some experimental flying to Bangor and Halifax by Pan American (sponsored by the Boston and Maine and Maine Central Railroads). Real air service arrived in 1933, when the railroads developed a contract with a group called National Airways. The first official flight of the newly formed line was made on August 11, 1933, using a Stinson trimotor aircraft.

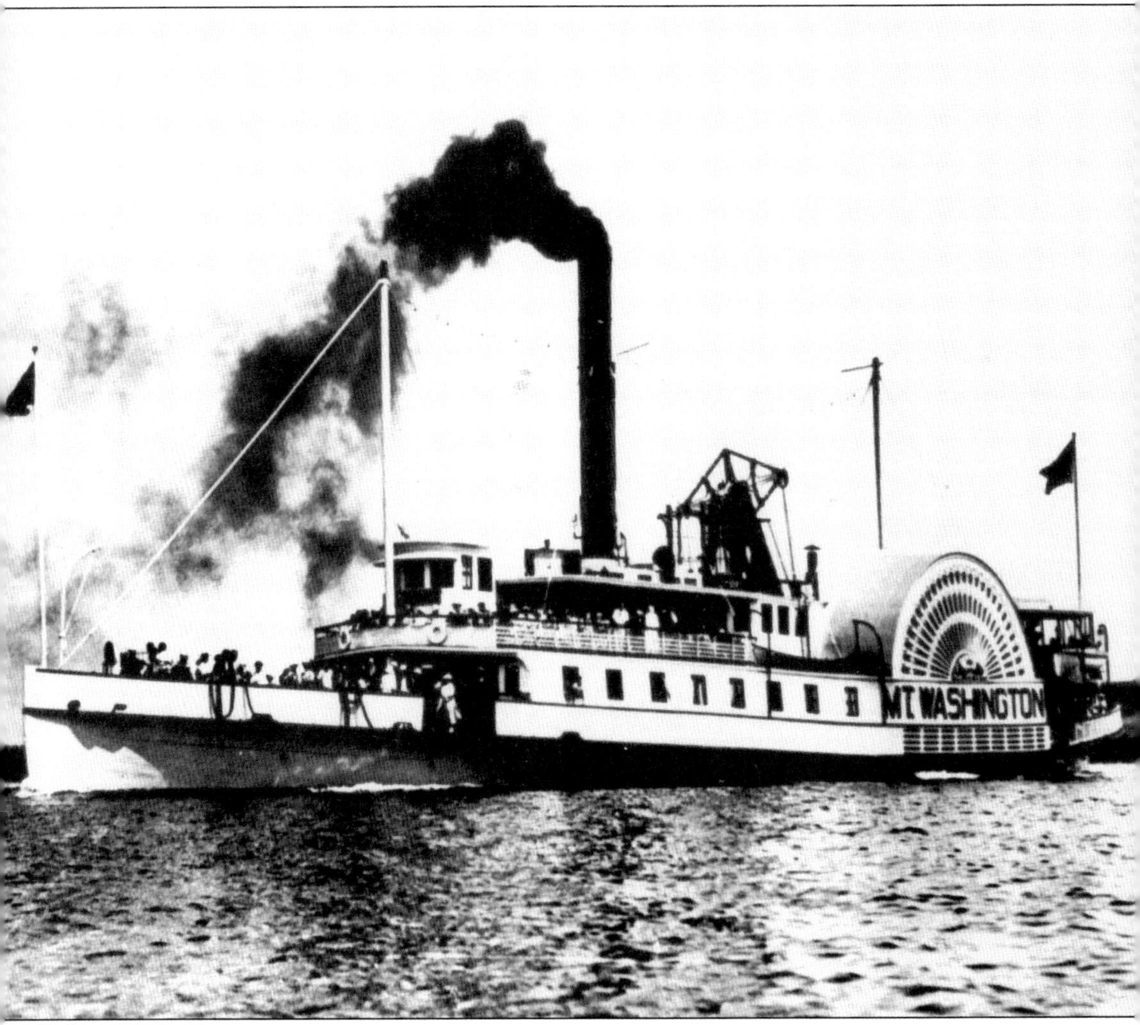

The famous B&M Lake Winnipesaukee steamer *Mount Washington* approaches the Weirs Beach dock in the early 1900s. The *Mount* plied the waters from 1872 until 1939, when it was destroyed by fire at the Weirs Beach dock. Note the tall smokestack belching smoke into the sky, and the walking beam rocking up and down to turn the giant paddle wheels. The horsepower was 450 at full ahead—more than enough to leave any competitor in its wake.

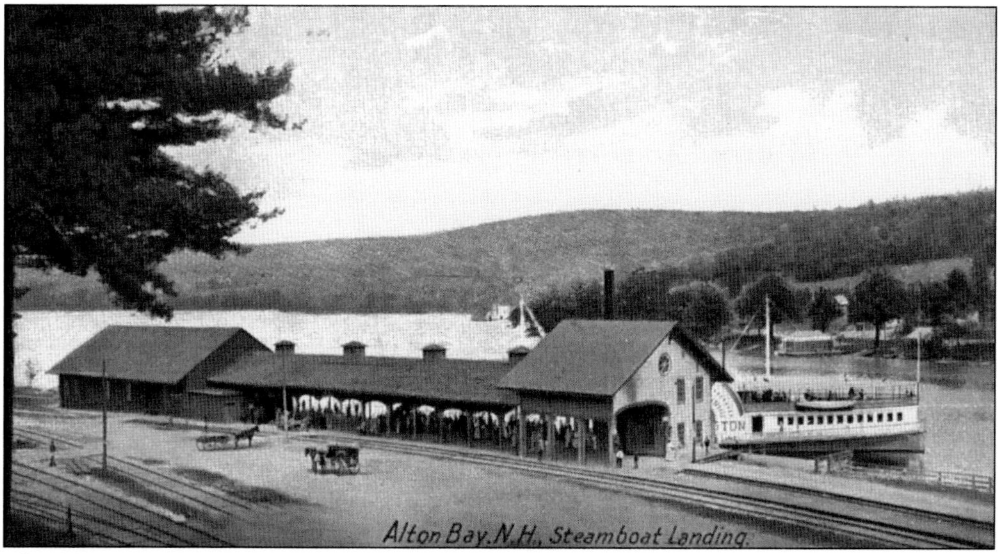

The B&M steamer *Mount Washington* is docked at Alton Bay, New Hampshire, in the late 1800s. In 1872, this new sidewheeler launched at Alton Bay. It was longer, faster, and the most beautiful sidewheeler ever built in the country. A single piston with a diameter of 42 inches and a stroke of 10 feet drove this vessel at better than 20 miles an hour.

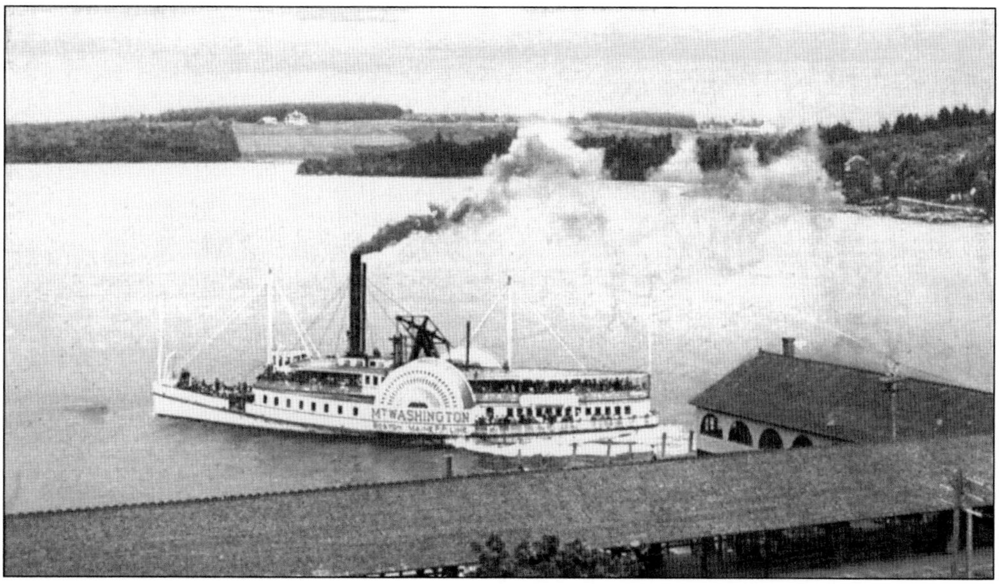

The *Mount Washington* leaves the Weirs Beach dock, Lake Winnipesaukee, New Hampshire, in the late 1800s. In the distance is Governor's Island, a beautiful and exclusive colony.

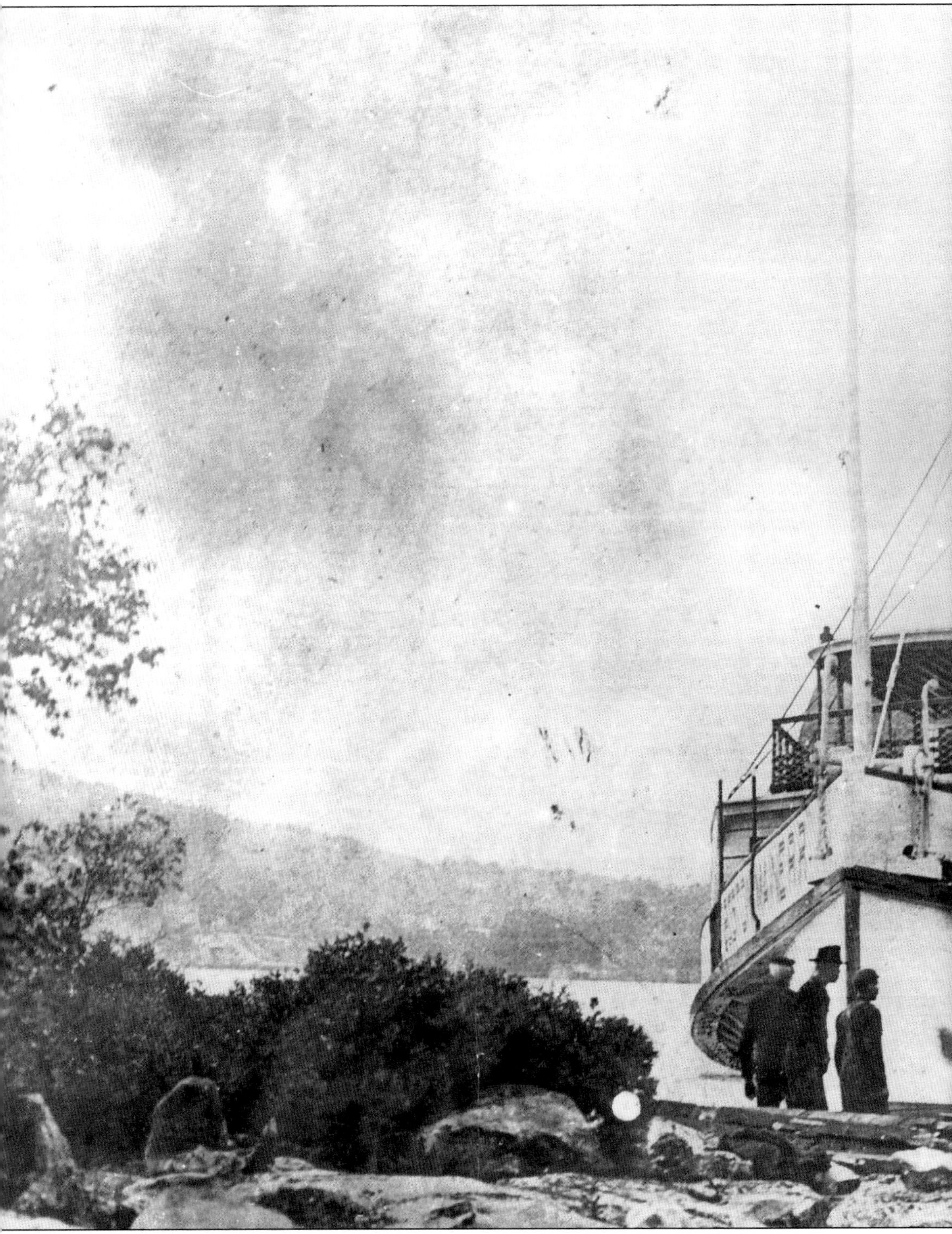

On a foggy Thursday morning early in the season of 1910, the *Mount Washington* ran aground upon the shore of One Mile Island. There was very little damage done, but the *Mount* was laid up for several days. A call was made to the owners of the vessel at that time, the Boston and

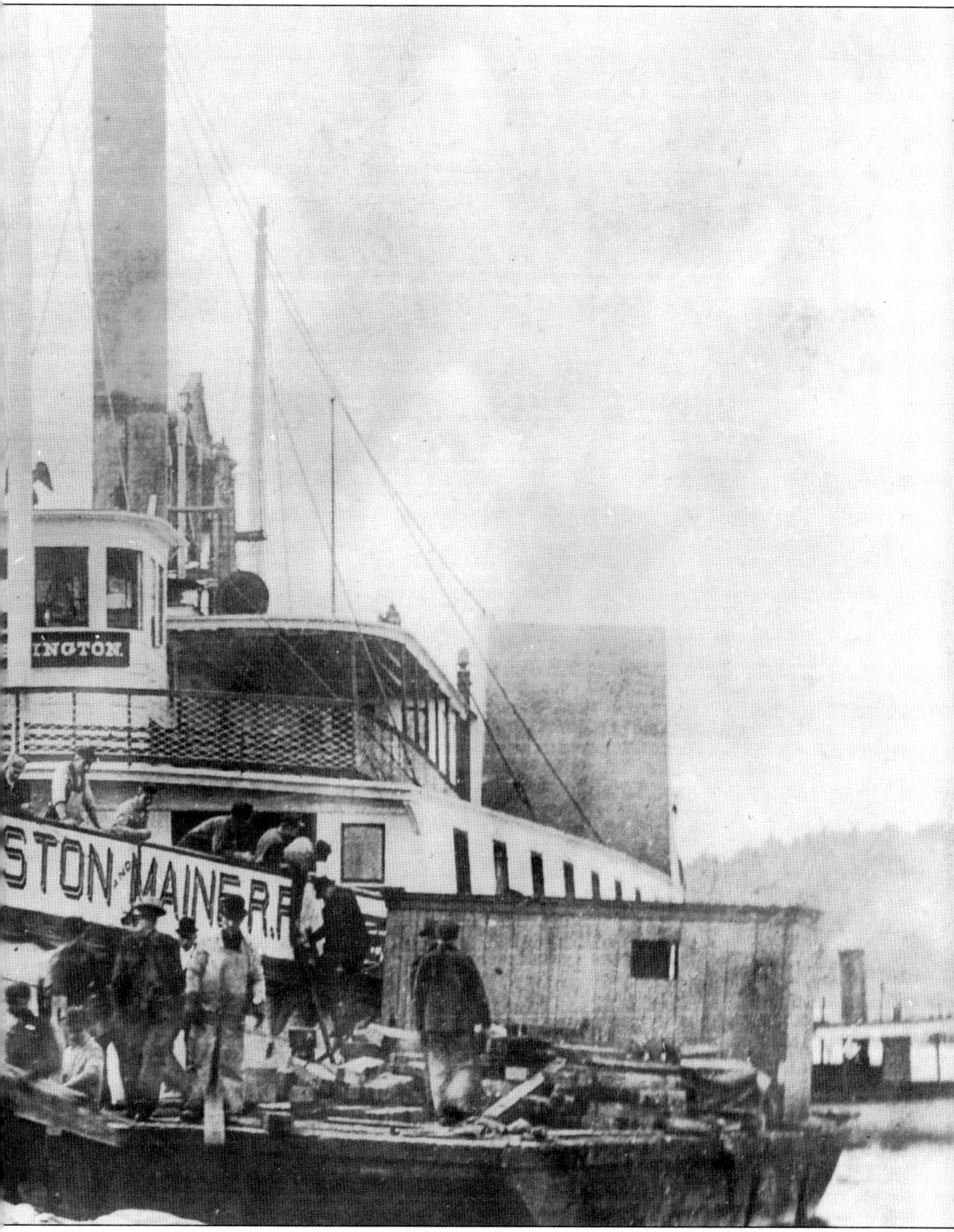

Maine Railroad offices in Boston. That evening, a wrecker and crew were sent out to the *Mount* from the Weirs. The following morning, work began, but it was not until Sunday that the *Mount* was free to resume its schedule.

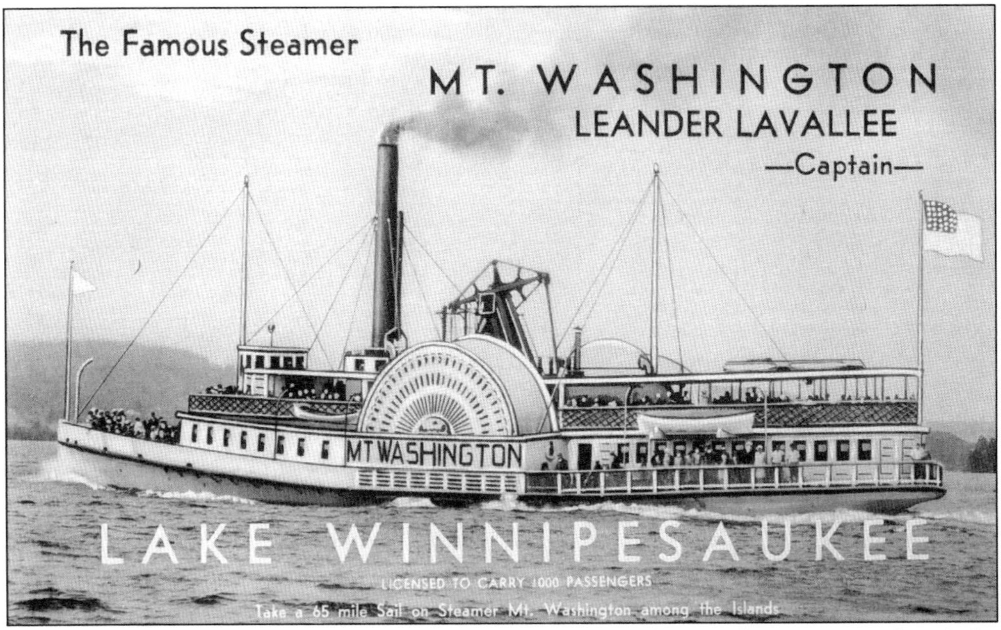

The "Famous Steamer *Mt. Washington*," captained by Leander Lavallee, is pictured on Lake Winnipesaukee in the early 1900s. The advertisement states, "Take a 65 mile Sail on Steamer *Mt. Washington* among the islands of Lake Winnipesaukee. See the most Wonderful Combination of Mountain, Lake and Shore Line Scenery to be found in the world. Take boat from the Weirs—Center Harbor—Wolfeboro or Alton Bay. Inquire at Your Camp or Hotel Office for Complete Information Regarding this Four Hour Sail."

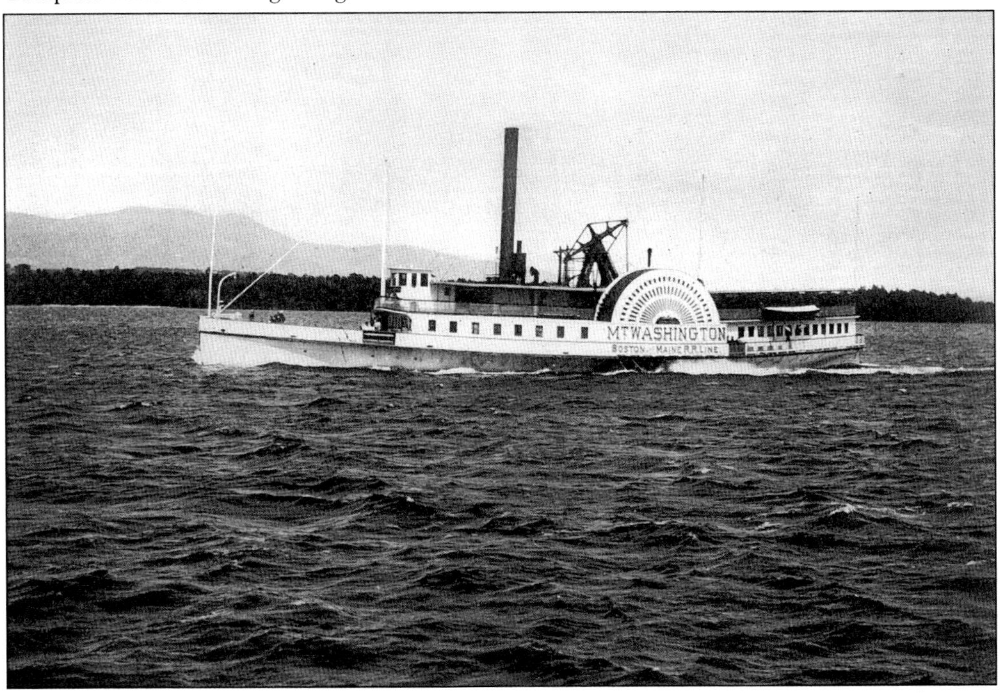

The *Mount Washington* sails on the open waters of Lake Winnipesaukee, New Hampshire, in the early 1900s.

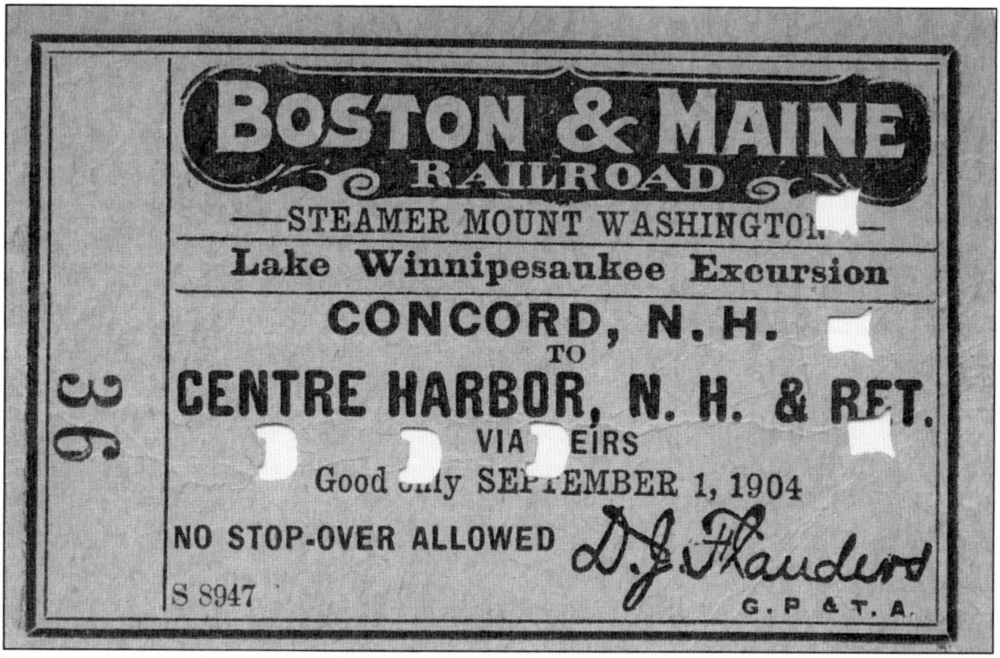

This round-trip B&M Railroad ticket was used by a passenger in order to connect with the steamer *Mount Washington* at the Weirs in 1904. It was good for passage between Concord, New Hampshire, and Center Harbor with "no stop-over allowed."

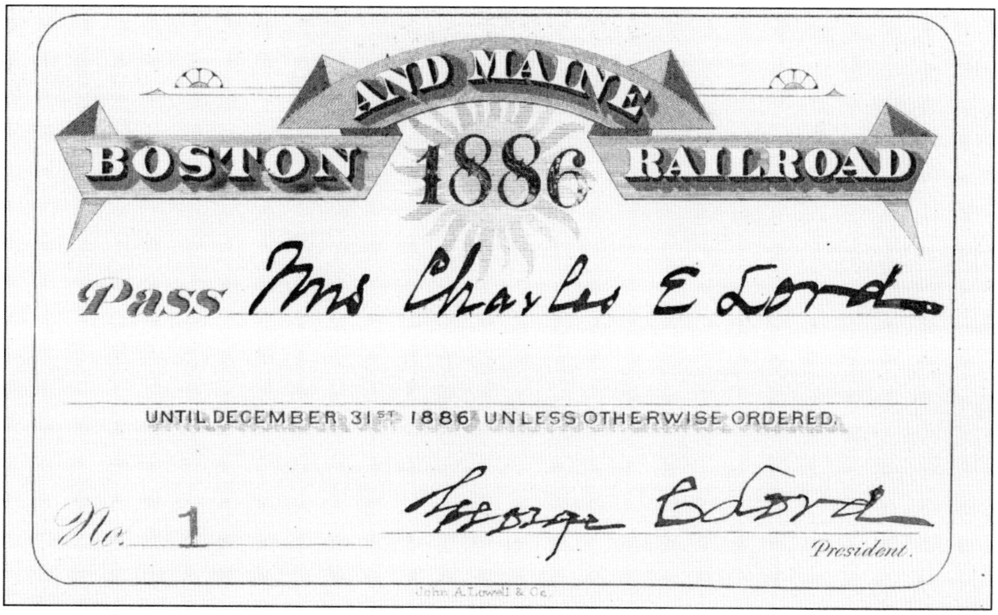

B&M Railroad pass No. 1 was issued to Mrs. Charles E. Lord by president George E. Lord in 1886.

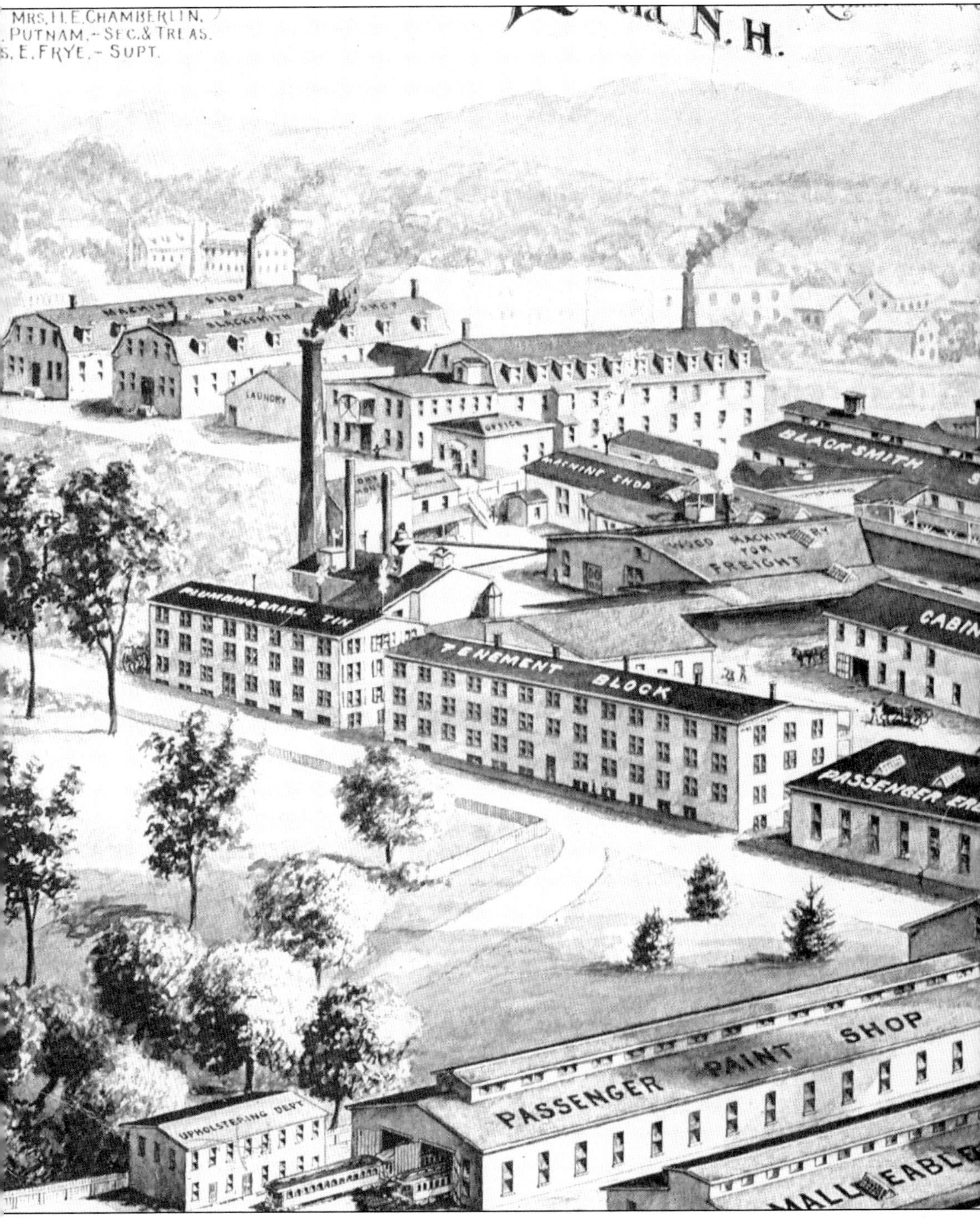

The original Laconia Car Shop was created in 1848 by Charles Ranlet and was known as the Ranlet Manufacturing Company. In 1882, the company was recognized under the corporate name of the Laconia Car Company. In 1897, the property passed into the hands of Hon. Frank Jones and his associates, and the new corporation, chartered under the name of the Laconia Car Company Works, was finally organized on February 25, 1897. The plant covered seven acres of land in the

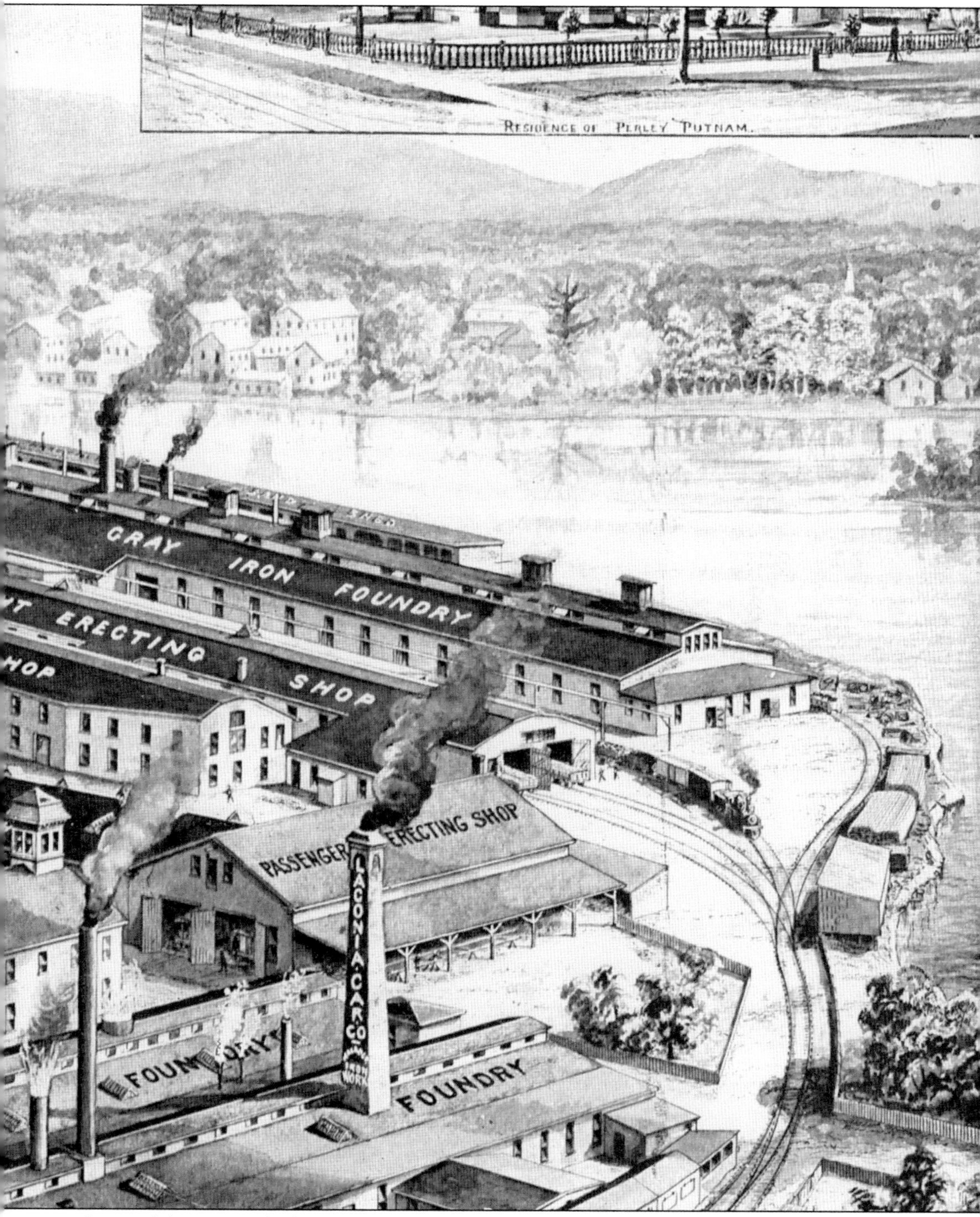

very heart of the city, and a large part of this property was covered with foundries, woodworking and painting shops, and the immense four-story brick building devoted to the malleable iron, which was operated in connection with the car construction business. The Laconia Car Company soon won national reputation for building first-class cars of every description.

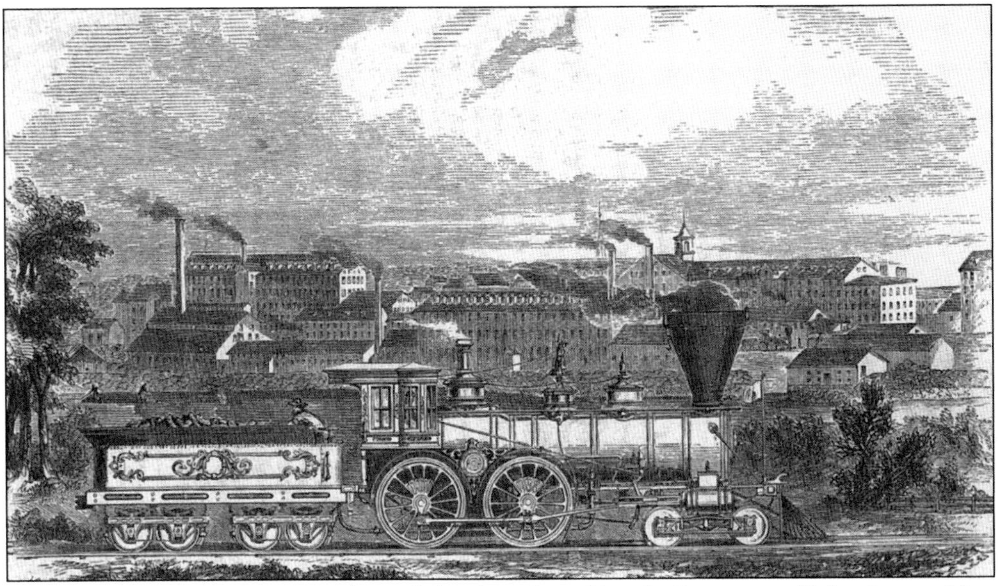

The Amoskeag Locomotive Works and the Amoskeag Textile Company of Manchester, New Hampshire, made up one of the largest and most flourishing corporations in the country. Its character empowered it to manufacture "woolen, cotton, iron, and other goods." The company was divided into five distinct departments: the Land and Water-Power Company, the Amoskeag New Mills, the Amoskeag Machine Shop and Locomotive Works, the Amoskeag Batting Mill, and the Hooksett Company of Hooksett, New Hampshire. The construction of these works dated from about the year 1840.

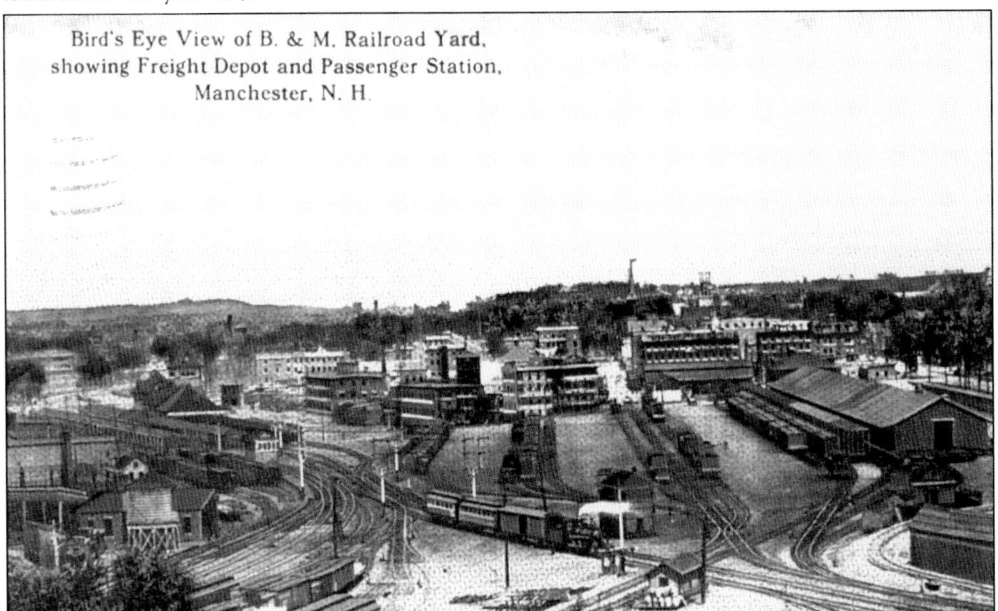

This bird's-eye view of the B&M yard shows the freight depot and Granite Street passenger station on Elm Street in Manchester, New Hampshire, in 1920. Most of the New Hampshire shops and yard facilities were still in full use into the 1950s. However, these facilities would not survive the decade.

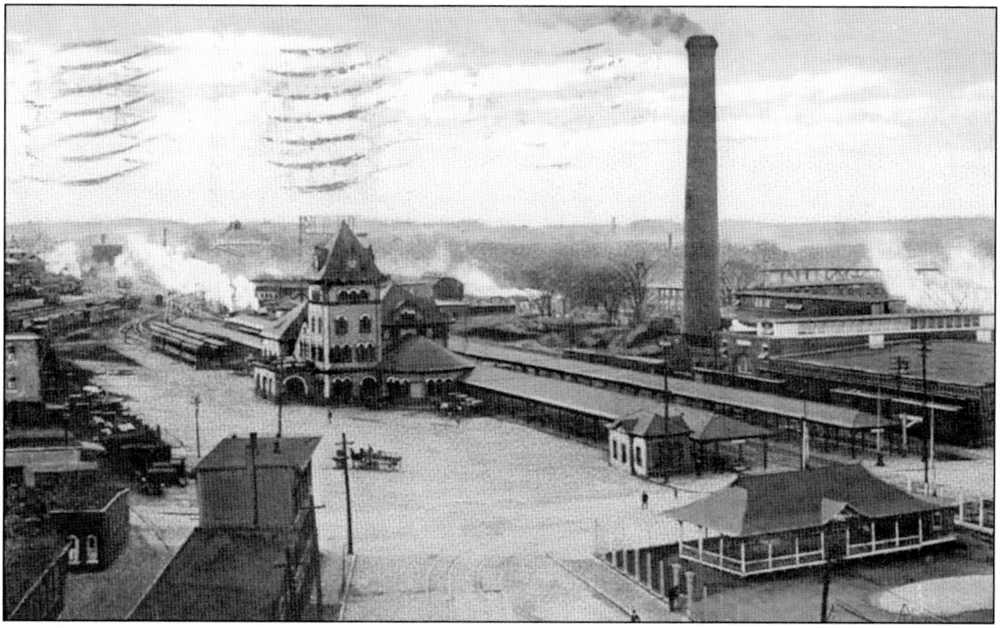

This is a 1915 bird's-eye view of the Manchester Union Station and rail complex.

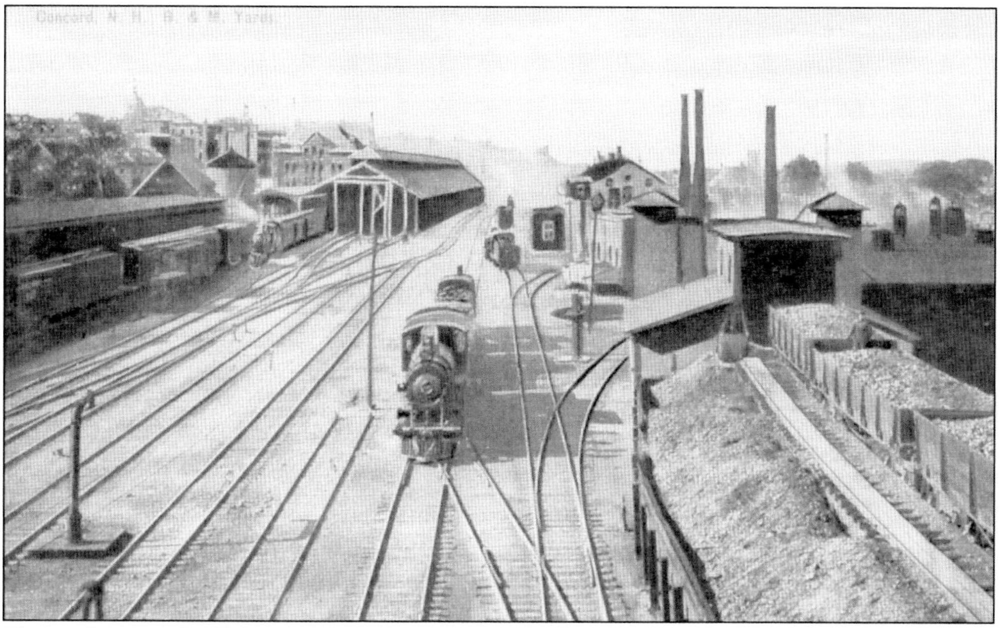

Shown here is the B&M Passenger Street engine house and coaling facility in Concord, New Hampshire. This view gives us some idea as to the complete scope and size of this turn-of-the-century railroad dynasty. The Concord Car Shops were used for a period of approximately 60 years during a time when railroads operated great numbers of revenue equipment. The complex was situated on a level parcel of land 26 acres in size and about a mile south of Concord station, midway between the station and Bow Junction. The carbarns of the Concord Street Railway were located immediately west of the complex. Originally, the shops complex was divided into the motive power and car departments.

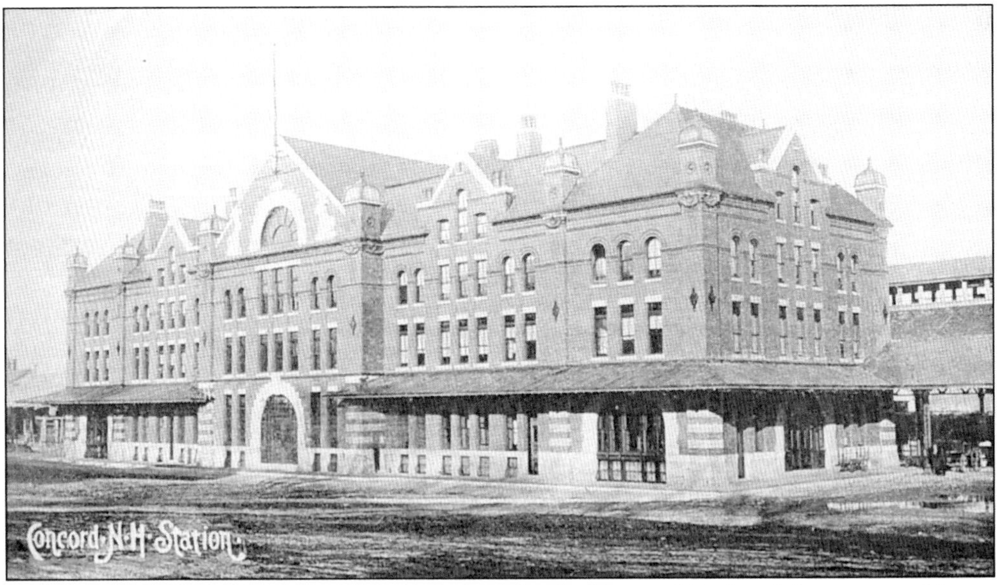

Seen in 1909, this elegant passenger station, built by the Concord Railroad Company and home to its offices, was located at the base of Pleasant Street in Concord, New Hampshire. The railroad era flourished for more than a century. It multiplied the population, paid millions in wages and taxes, and made the community a freight transfer point. The station is now gone from the landscape, along with Railroad Square. During the early 1960s, it was replaced by a shopping center, a retailing town within a city.

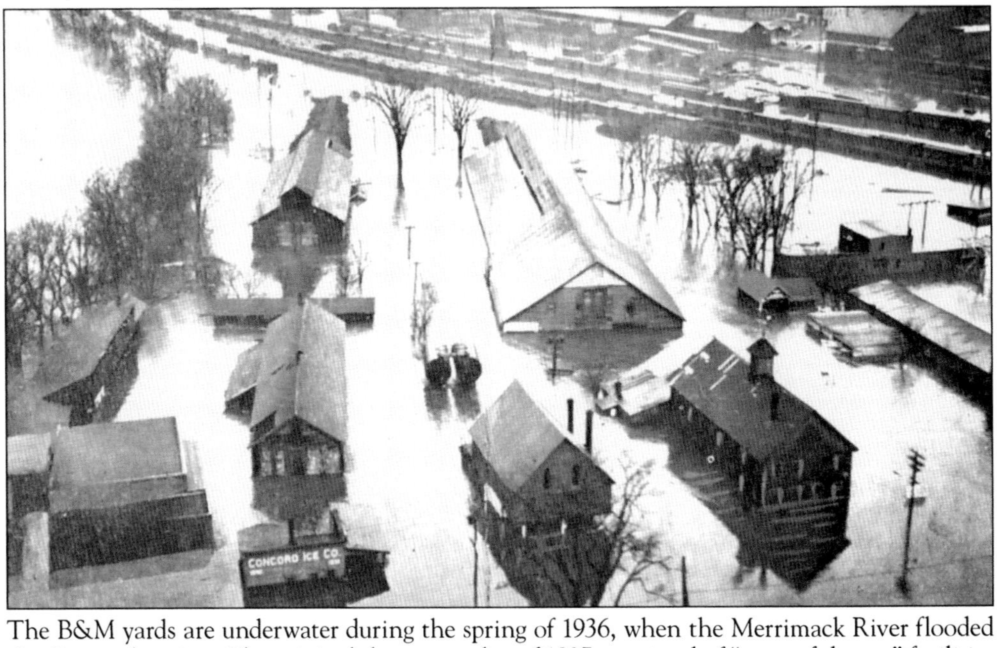

The B&M yards are underwater during the spring of 1936, when the Merrimack River flooded the Concord station. The original shops complex of 1897 consisted of "state-of-the-art" facilities for the repairing, servicing, and painting of railroad equipment. The shop served as a storehouse for the northern New England operating division. The continued growth of the city was fueled by the rapid industrialization and the increase in commerce, which was largely the result of the arrival of the railroad.

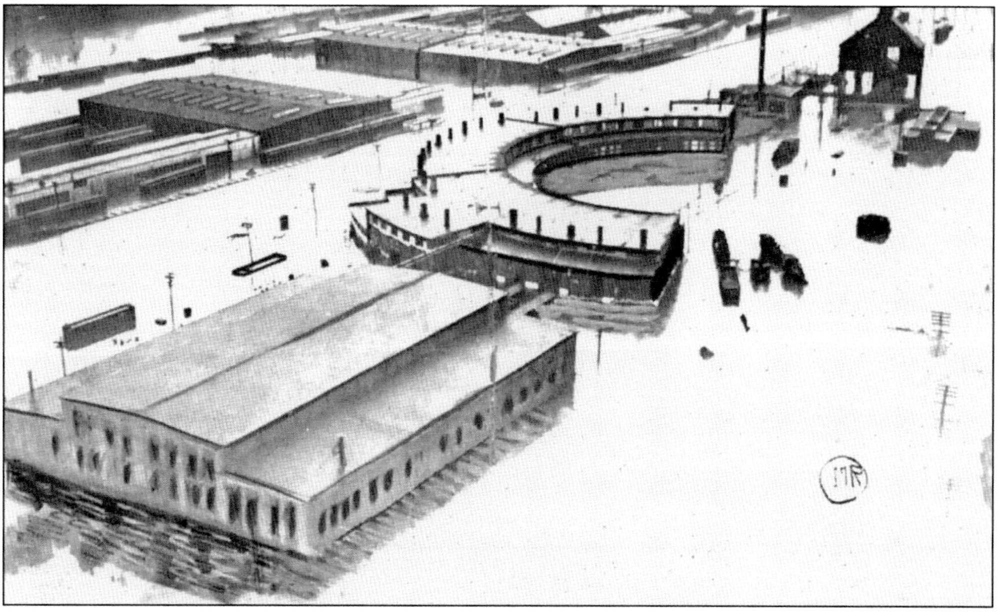

Shown here is the B&M Railroad terminal and roundhouse at Concord, New Hampshire, during the flood of 1936. By the 1900s, Concord's population had reached almost 20,000. Between the years 1840 and 1860, the city had more than doubled in population, from just under 5,000 people to almost 11,000. Much of this growth may be attributed to the trade brought by the Concord Railroad, which arrived in Concord during 1842. The Boston and Maine was for decades the town's largest employer, thanks to the car shops. When opened for use in 1897, the shop complex consisted of six main buildings, occupying over four and a half acres of land.

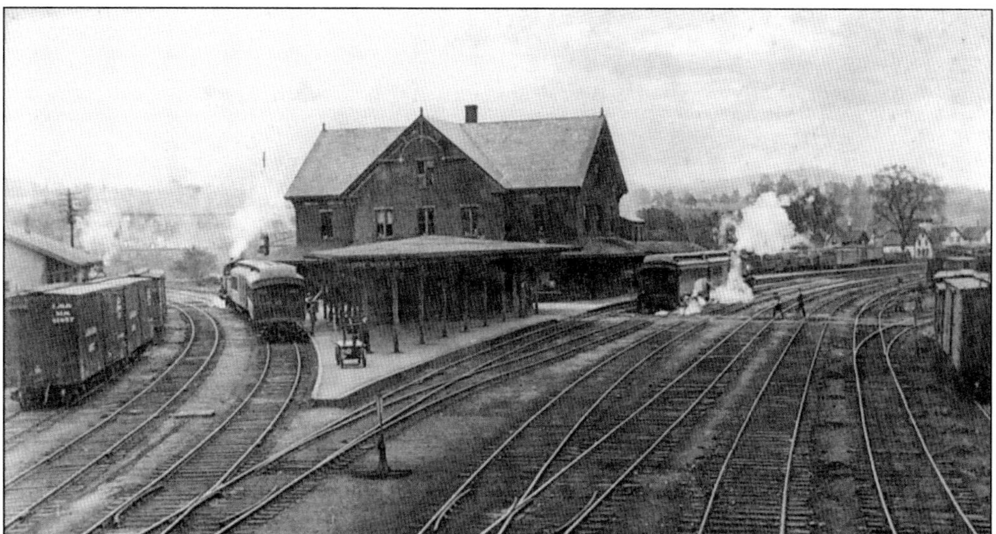

White River Junction, Vermont, was another major terminal and yard for the Boston and Maine Railroad system.

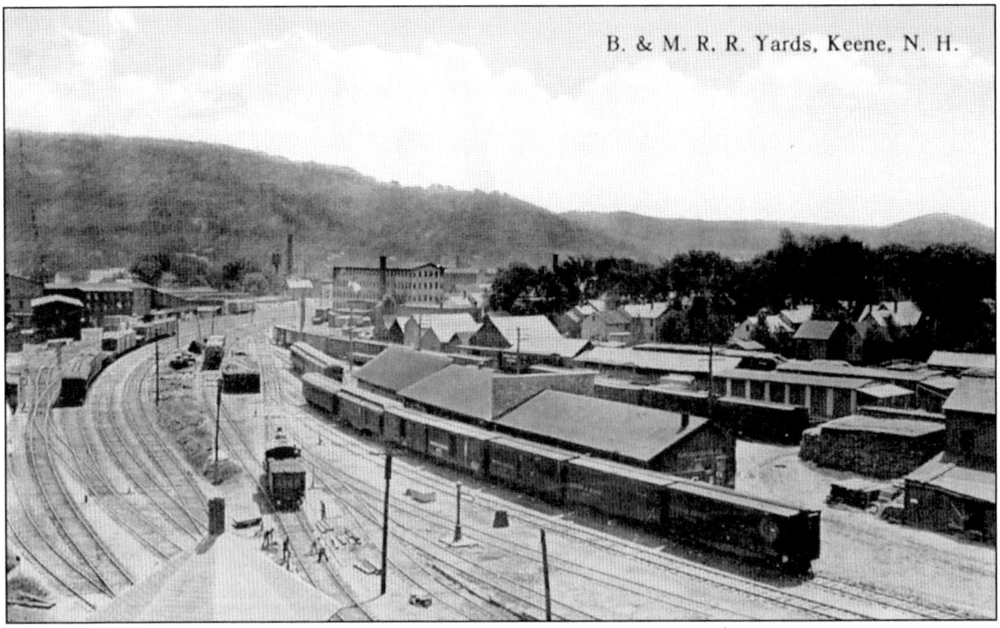

Local railroads developed well-traveled networks of maintenance shops, as evidenced by this 1915 photograph of the B&M yard at Keene, New Hampshire.

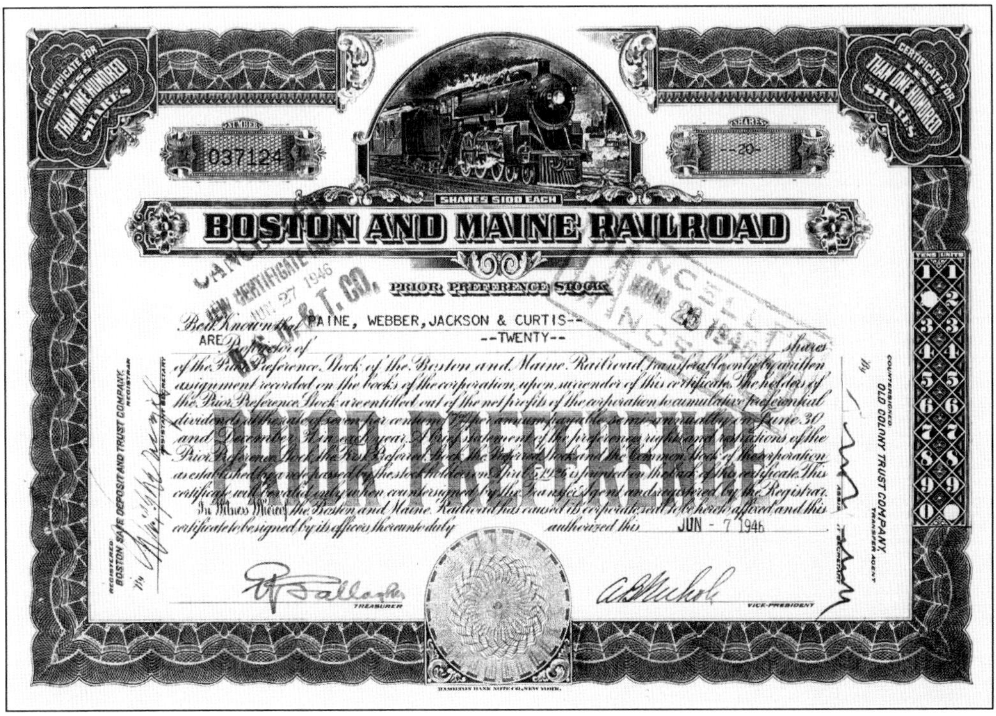

This B&M Railroad stock certificate dates from June 7, 1946.